AFTER BARBARY

A volume in the series

The United States in the World

Edited by Benjamin A. Coates, Emily Conroy-Krutz, Paul A. Kramer, and Judy Tzu-Chun Wu
Founding editors: Mark Philip Bradley and Paul A. Kramer

A list of titles in this series is available at cornellpress.cornell.edu.

AFTER BARBARY

Algeria's Roles in the French and American Empires

Timothy Mason Roberts

Cornell University Press
Ithaca and London

Copyright © 2025 by Timothy Mason Roberts

All rights reserved. Except for brief quotations in a review, this book, or parts thereof, must not be reproduced in any form without permission in writing from the publisher. For information, address Cornell University Press, Sage House, 512 East State Street, Ithaca, New York 14850. Visit our website at cornellpress.cornell.edu.

First published 2025 by Cornell University Press

Librarians: A CIP catalog record for this book is available from the Library of Congress.

ISBN 9781501784729 (hardcover)
ISBN 9781501784736 (paperback)
ISBN 9781501784743 (pdf)
ISBN 9781501784750 (epub)

GPSR EU contact: Sam Thornton, Mare Nostrum Group B.V., Mauritskade 21D, 1091 GC, Amsterdam, NL, gpsr@mare-nostrum.co.uk.

To Sumner and Zoe

Contents

Introduction	1
1. A North African Example for Early US Expansion	11
2. The Civil War as a *Razzia*	33
3. The Limits of Republican Citizenship	51
4. A French Wild West	73
5. Algeria, Puerto Rico, and the Philippines	93
6. Algeria's Ambiguities Among American Pan-Africanists	115
Epilogue: The Politics of Postimperial Nostalgia	142
Acknowledgments	157
Notes	159
Index	207

AFTER BARBARY

Introduction

This book is an exploration of the role of Algeria as a transimperial space in French-American relations from 1830, when France first occupied Algeria, through the early 1970s, in the first years of Algerian independence from French colonial authority. The book shows how French and American politicians, writers, and reformers constructed and imagined Algeria for defining and contesting each country's own imperial regime. Empires, which dominated world history until World War II, were defined by their ability to establish their sovereignty over a specific space, entailing control over territories and the populations that inhabited them as well as over the flows of goods and people that developed in this space. France jealously ruled over Algeria as an overseas French department and the cornerstone of the French Empire, proclaiming it integral to France in 1848. Algeria gradually developed as France's settler frontier until surging as such in the 1880s, and then it became an important defender of France and its empire through two world wars in the twentieth century. The 1945 Sétif independence protest and massacre of Algerian demonstrators by French authorities and European settlers were tragic indicators that World War II also sparked the decolonization movement.[1]

But transimperial history is an approach that relies on the porousness of empires, a central premise of this book. National and federal borders today that allow "illegal" migrants to enter, most controversially in the United States and the European Union, are considered by state authorities—the main but not the only authorities concerned about immigrants—as aberrations, a failure of sovereign authority. In much of the imperial age, in contrast, circulations of people were far less regulated. Governments, for example, if they dealt with passports at all, issued them to migrants or travelers upon arrival, not as a requirement of being able to exit one's domicile.[2]

Using the casual way that passports functioned in the age of empires as an analogy, this book emphasizes that while taking the role of the state structuring imperial space and exercising sovereignty is important, French and American actors outside state authority acted across political and cultural boundaries to produce Algeria as a fissured, dynamic transimperial space.[3] Actually, imperial authorities in Washington, DC, Paris, and Algiers rarely intentionally collaborated, if collaboration implies institutional partnering or alliances. American, French, and Algerian leaders' relationships were more about ad hoc borrowing and repurposing. And state agents were only one kind of several actors in Algeria, France, French colonies, the United States, and US territorial possessions. Algeria thus functioned as an imperial analogy, a lesson, a laboratory, and a remedy for state and nonstate actors alike to appropriate elements of a foreign empire to help realize a domestic political objective. French Algeria, taking on characteristics of both the French and American empires, connected them. The book offers a new methodology for the study of empires from comparative and connected perspectives. The book's evidence, accordingly, is eclectic, drawing on government sources, civilian and military, along with economic treatises, newspapers, popular magazines, ordinary individuals' correspondence, travel literature, novels, museum artifacts, memoirs, and schoolbooks.

This book, moreover, studies American imperialism in a novel way. In its placement of the origins and evolution of American imperialism in conversation with another empire, it continues the trajectory of scholarship away from the premise that American imperialism and, more broadly, American history were exceptional. This is hardly a radical argument at this point. In the last half century historians of the United States have increasingly located its development on a global spectrum, showing the relationship of historical phenomena among Americans to patterns and regimes elsewhere, including assimilation and exclusion, extractive economic practices and income distribution, state welfare, and religious mission-oriented foreign relations and domestic reform movements.[4] Perhaps irresistibly, transnational methodologies have provoked and shaped new transimperial historiography, if only because the transnational turn, besides consolidating scholarly opinion that American imperialism was real, has provoked a reinterpretation of when American imperialism began. Recent scholarship has illuminated how, well before the United States first gained overseas territories at the turn of the twentieth century, American traders, soldiers, missionaries, and reformers, representing various imperialist agendas, interacted with leaders and subjects of European, Asian, African, and Indigenous American empires.[5]

But how actors in those other empires perceived and interacted with their American counterparts has received less attention. This book, particularly in its study of US imperialism in relationship with France, makes a new contribution to studies of connective and comparative imperialisms, which, with a few exceptions, have tended to focus on Anglo-American, German-American, or Anglo-French imperial regimes and exchanges or have emphasized that Americans generally ridiculed French colonialism after the First French Empire.[6]

In some important ways, particularly constructions of racialized identity and legal institutions, French-American imperialism resembled other empires' shared practices. On the other hand, the fact that the United States and France were republics, or at least shared a heritage of republican equality and citizenship originating in revolutions, shaped the nature of their imperial circulations and the meanings of Algeria that those circulations exposed. This was true among both actors who erected and maintained imperial conditions and those who resisted those conditions.[7]

Why focus on Algeria as a basis for studying French-American imperial relations? Besides extending scholarship on transimperial history, as described above, this book fills a gap in the literature on Americans' encounters with Algeria. Extant work appears as a set of temporal bookends, with the few studies between them treating American contacts with North Africa, especially French North Africa, as "almost totally dormant."[8] One end of the scholarship has focused on Algeria's impact on Americans as the notorious Barbary State of Algiers, a regency nominally ruled by the Ottoman Empire.[9] Algerian corsairs in service of the regency's deys, misnamed *pirates* by Westerners, disrupted trade in the Mediterranean Sea and held for ransom captured Christian sailors, Americans among them. Algiers' reputation for treachery shaped negative opinion of Algerians and, to an extent, Islam in the early American republic as well as American "domestic orientals." The US defeat of Algiers in 1815 reduced the scope of Barbary privateering and paved the way for France's capture of the vulnerable city fifteen years later.[10]

On the other end, American historians pick up the thread of North African history only with World War II, when US military forces landed in North Africa in 1942 and then again concerning the great era of decolonization beginning after 1945. Work has focused on the strategies of Operation Torch and other Allied and Axis campaigns without real emphasis on the conflicted status of Algerians.[11] Historians of US foreign relations have shown how the administrations of presidents Dwight Eisenhower and John Kennedy grappled with whether to back or oppose France's attempts to preserve its authority in Algeria in consideration of the Algerian War of Independence and American anti-communist interests and anti-colonial principles, in Africa, the Middle East, and Asia.[12] Historians of Algeria, meanwhile, have illuminated Algerian nationalists' cultivation of foreign support in the years around the War of Independence.[13] Most recently, scholars and military theorists have assessed the US military's development of a doctrine of counterinsurgency warfare during the Global War on Terror by drawing on lessons from French colonial forces' actions to defeat the Algerian nationalist insurgency.[14] Still, historians have not explored various Americans' attitudes toward and interactions with Indigenous Algerians and European settlers and administrators and vice versa, which happened from French occupation and settlement of Algeria in the 1830s through the 1960s.

Likewise, traditional historians of French Algeria, perhaps because of France's republican heritage or the complicated fate of *pieds noirs* ("black feet"), European Algerians whose last generation fled Algeria to southern France during and after the Algerian War of Independence, have not considered how French Algeria resembled other episodes in franchise and settler colonialism.[15] Like traditional scholarship on American imperialism, until the last few decades, French scholarship focused on how administrators in Paris affected people in Algeria and the French colonies and only recently have emphasized imperial legacies of in modern France, particularly attitudes about Muslim immigrants in the metropole as they relate to conflicting memories of colonial Algeria as a pluralistic or a segregated society.[16]

This book is organized into six chapters and an epilogue, proceeding chronologically and thematically. Chapters 1 and 2 show the role of French Algeria during the July Monarchy, the Second Republic, and the Second Empire in Americans' consolidation of national authority in the US West

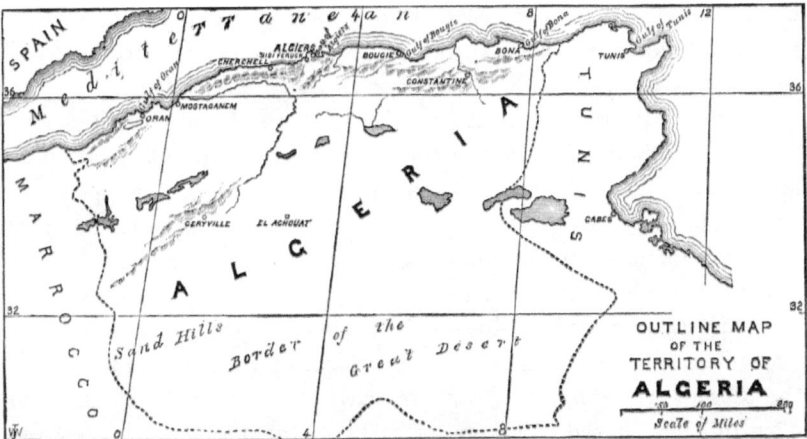

Figure 0.1. A map of French Algeria, 1897. From Thomas Cox, *Decisive Battles Since Waterloo* (G. P. Putnam's Sons, 1897).

and South. Previous scholarship has located the early American republic on a spectrum of Europeans' settler wars in the Americas, Africa, Russia, and Australia, though generally as comparative history.[17] These chapters, instead, show how American writers and policymakers transferred doctrines from French Algeria and embedded them in popular literature and state policies. In this era, Indigenous Americans and Confederate rebels alike became analogous to Algerian forces resisting the French conquest in terms of the US military's use of force and application of new laws of war for treatment of insurgents.

Chapter 1 begins by tracing American interest in the initial French conquest of Algeria for motivation on how to subdue the Seminole Indians in Florida and assesses the image of the Algerian leader Abdelkader in American opinion as a noble but doomed rebel. French struggles to suppress Abdelkader's resistance had multiple resonances in the United States, though the net effect was to inform American expansionists' advocacy of the national government's consolidation of its authority in border areas of insurgency. Some Americans feared the resemblance of expansionist wars in Florida and Mexico to France's inglorious conquest of Algeria and feared a reprisal of the costly North African conflict in the US war with Mexico. Other Americans, particularly Southerners invested in slavery, saluted the French conquest of Algeria as an example of a European empire expanding to secure and extract unfree labor from people of color and foresaw the potential benefits of Americans adapting French strategies to the trans-Mississippi West.

Turning to the years of the American Civil War and its aftermath, chapter 2 casts the sectional conflict as a continuation of Americans' earlier practices of settler colonialism and, like them, a war of territorial incorporation. Union policies and actions reflected both prior and wartime adaptations of the French military's practices of irregular or, in the modern term, counterinsurgency warfare, then known as the *razzia* (derived from the Arabic word for "raid," transliterated as "ghazwah"), meant to surprise and terrify enemy combatants and civilians near them as a form of collective punishment.[18] The Union's appropriation of ways and laws of war from French practices in North Africa shaped its election of harsh treatment of Confederates, like treatment of Indigenous Americans, as uncivilized nonstate insurgents. The wartime Lieber Code, the chapter argues, reflects Americans' adoption of French "harsh" warfare into new laws of "civilized" warfare. The chapter concludes with a demonstration of how, in the 1870s, veteran Civil War commanders William Sherman, Philip Sheridan, and others fought the Plains Wars by renewing the US military's application of the French razzia, a policy ironically first advocated by US Secretary of War Jefferson Davis in the 1850s.

Chapters 3 and 4 then shift the perspective from how Americans viewed and borrowed French practices to how French policymakers adapted American imperial institutions. As a result, the two regimes grew closer in how Algerians, African Americans, and Indigenous Americans experienced laws of citizenship and land rights. The context for chapter 3 were two developments in the 1860s. One was the Union's defeat of the Confederacy and abolition of slavery, which established the principles of race-blind citizenship and legal treatment for the American freedpeople. The other was Emperor Napoleon III's establishment of a path to French citizenship for individual Algerians, via the Sénatus-consulte of 1865. A mix of philanthropy and cynicism, the 1865 decree aligned the French Second Empire officially against the extinction of the "vanishing" Algerians, as had allegedly happened to American Indians. The chapter's description of French colonist Pierre Charles Fournier de Saint-Amant's quixotic plan to resettle American freedpeople in Algeria and equip them with French citizenship suggests the contingencies of this transimperial moment.

Notwithstanding his arabophile reform, however, Napoleon remained an enemy of French liberal republicanism, and his adversaries rejoiced at his downfall via the Franco-Prussian War of 1870–71. The establishment of the French Third Republic in 1870 ended repressive rule in the metropole. As emphasized in recent scholarship on the global liberal impact of American Reconstruction, French republicans saluted the United States: The gift of the statue *Liberty Enlightening the World* was the great expression of French gratitude to Americans for preserving liberal democracy during its eclipse in France.

These studies largely, however, do not consider whether or how Reconstruction affected or reflected European colonialism.[19] In fact, French American acclaim of the Statue of Liberty, particularly Americans' association of it with offering opportunity to European immigrants, obscured the failure of the two race-bound republican empires to equip native-born people of color, both subject to conservative local political authorities, with national civil rights. Symbolized by W. E. B. Du Bois's and Emir Khaled's futile petitions to President Woodrow Wilson after World War I, French Algeria in this way resembled the post–Civil War American South.[20]

Chapter 4 shows how French imperialists in the late nineteenth century more explicitly sought to emulate Americans' "expansionist" policies, considered standard-setting for a settler society of mixed origin, to direct Algeria's economic "recovery" from previous years of government restrictions on territorial land acquisition.[21] Particularly, French policymakers and economists of the Third Republic advocating laissez-faire privatization paradoxically fixed on the US Homestead Act of 1862 as a blueprint for how French Algeria could encourage agricultural development to enable North Africa to become "productive" like the American frontier, implicitly transitioning from franchise to settler colony. Traditionally, the Homestead Act was considered a policy illustrating American exceptionalism in offering the poor city dweller the chance of becoming a self-reliant yeoman farmer. In building on recent studies that locate the American West in a global context of frontier settlement, this chapter traces French imperialists' contorted configuration of that American image.[22] Nominally, Algerian people joined settlers in their eligibility for distribution of land organized into private homesteads and farm lots. Substantively, the period saw a redistribution of land from usage by Algerian tribes to possession by European agricultural and railroad interests, most epically by French Alsatians and Lorrainers who arrived in Algeria as refugees after the Franco-Prussian War. French Algeria first became romanticized as a nostalgic home for these French and other European settlers at this time, similar to how American families moved into the Great American Plains after the Civil War, enduring isolation but becoming part of the national folklore.

Chapter 5 shifts attention back across the Atlantic, its setting the US acquisition of overseas territories for the first time. Just as French imperialists had studied various regimes to find techniques for development of Algeria in the late nineteenth century and found US frontier policy attractive for this purpose, Americans faced with the challenge of legitimizing possession of de facto colonies found French Algeria a propitious legal analogue. Prompted by the legal case of a Puerto Rican woman, Isabel González, seeking entry into the United States as a US citizen, American newspapers and the US judiciary, in the Insular Cases, took account of the status of Algerian people in the French Empire for guidance on the question of how to treat Puerto Rico and the Philippines, former colonies of the Spanish Empire annexed by the United States via the 1898 Treaty of Paris. While US rule of the Philippines as a basis for creation of the US imperial state has been studied lately from comparative imperial and transimperial perspectives, including the context of French Indochina, French Algeria's role has not been recognized.[23]

American angst over the status of Puerto Ricans and Filipinos was exacerbated by the Philippine-American War of 1899–1902, which erupted when the Filipino people rejected US annexation. The US military's subjugation of nationalist resistance led by Emilio Aguinaldo devolved into an irregular war, its atrocities shocking American civilians, though in that regard not unlike Americans' wars of incorporation over the previous century. Again, as they had in the Indian Wars and the Civil War, US military commanders urged their troops to act brutally against both armed rebels and civilians who might provide them aid. And again, as they had in the past, US strategists called on counterinsurgency "lessons" migrated from French Algeria to deploy in the US's new East Asian frontier. French Algeria, in other words, helped align the US empire with its European counterparts, providing examples of both how to conquer "uncivilized" peoples and how to establish a legal regime for Puerto Rico and the Philippines as unincorporated territories, contrary to the previous US practice of acquisition of territories with a framework for their eventual grant of US statehood. Algeria as an integral part of France foregrounded and provided a legal precedent for the emergent overseas US empire.

Chapter 6 shifts the focus from US overseas empire-building to the pan-Africanism of American Black nationalists and civil rights advocates. In *Wretched of the Earth*, Frantz Fanon, the Martinican and ideologue of Algerian revolutionary nationalism, posited that revolutionary violence could restore the dignity of and unify colonized people. Using Fanon's argument as a premise, the chapter traces the diverse images and functions of French

Algeria from the Paris Exposition of 1900 through the exodus of the international section of the Black Panther Party from Algeria in the early 1970s. The chapter shows that the history of African American writers' and activists' engagement with Algeria was complicated. It confirms that Algeria's uprising against the French Empire inspired African American writers and activists, providing them a sense of transimperial solidarity and an anti-colonial vocabulary with which to critique US civil rights deprivations. But the chapter shows that this solidarity lasted only momentarily—ironically, but not surprisingly, curtailed by Algeria's state-building steps as a republic in the decade after achievement of independence in 1962.

Before that, Algeria played several functions for a range of African Americans across the century, helping form their cosmopolitan identities. Algeria in 1900 was constructed as an "Oriental" resort and an African stub of Europe. It then functioned as a powerful example in arguments that "Negroes'" military valor in World War I and endurance of racist treatment amid World War II's vindication of democracy attested to their merit for full civil rights. In the post-1945 era, Algeria first inspired African American writers in Paris, who, rubbing shoulders with France's imperial subjects there, gained perspective about not only the global nature of racial discrimination but also the contours of American privilege in post–World War II Europe. During and shortly after the Algerian War of Independence, Algeria became an ephemeral center of pan-Africanism and an actual refuge for notable American Black nationalists. The chapter emphasizes that it was French Algeria's liminal status and the ambiguous racialized identities of Algerian people that sustained its relationships with African American observers; its postindependence development triggered its disappearance as a pan-African transimperial space.

The book's epilogue comments on French Algeria's somewhat surprising recent reemergence in French-American relations. In the 2010s, the United States and France, among other countries responding to impacts of global trade, immigration, and identity politics, saw the emergence of nostalgia for settler colonial imperialism as a powerful political force, with particular appeal to disaffected, conservative communities. Nostalgic imperialism portrays the past as a time and place of greater economic stability than the present and preservative of a social hierarchy in which racialized communities knew and accepted their places, collaboratively solved problems, and protected one another from outside threats.[24] In the recent United States and France, the epilogue argues, narratives of nostalgia fueled the popularity of far right political parties that reflected both particular aspects of the countries' respective histories and attributes common to nationalist movements ascendant across the Atlantic world.

While nostalgic imperialism was a phenomenon noticeable on both sides of the Atlantic Ocean, particular to recent nostalgic national movements in the United States and France was the evocation of cultural memory of wars in which heroic defenders of local government were overwhelmed—the American Civil War, lost by the Confederacy; and the Algerian War of Independence, lost by European settlers turned refugees, the pieds noirs.[25] Cast as a symptom of a larger drift away from traditional patriotic values, politicized memory of each war emerged as a central issue in its country's cultural fracturing, the ascent to power by right-wing parties, and embrace of nativism. Expressed in defense of monuments and historic sites commemorating white hegemonic rule and attempts to develop school curricula in which history lessons would mitigate the fabled wars' causes and help cast their losers as ancestors of modern-day beleaguered patriots, resurrection of war memories was an important plank of nostalgic politics poised to dominate the American and French political landscapes in the 2020s. These memories' resonance in the United States and France as a potent political force was a persistent, volatile legacy of French Algeria's connective role between the two postimperial republics.

Chapter 1

A North African Example for Early US Expansion

Ten years after visiting the United States in 1831–1832, an experience that became the basis of his famous *Democracy in America*, the French aristocrat Alexis de Tocqueville arrived in Algiers. A notable supporter of the French conquest of the Ottoman province, Tocqueville remarked on the city's redevelopment newly under French possession: "On all sides one sees nothing but recent ruins, buildings going up; one hears nothing but the noise of the hammer. It is Cincinnati transported onto the soil of Africa."[1] A few historians of French–American relations have recognized Tocqueville's commentaries on Algeria and the US interior as analogous zones of frontier democracy.[2] However, similarities in French–American relations soon after France's arrival in Algeria, suggested by Tocqueville, have remained obscure. This inattention is especially true concerning their shared ambition for "territorial empire," even though US congressmen used this phrase as early as 1827 in development of policy towards Chickasaw and Choctaw peoples, and French legal scholars adopted it in surveying the imperial jurisdiction of the Napoleonic Code by 1844.[3] In the period before the US Civil War, France and the United States targeted Algeria and the Gulf Coast, respectively, for development for white settlers. This chapter traces comparisons made by French and American commentators in the shaping of policy about these frontier territories. In particular, the exploits of Emir Abdelkader El Djezairi, a Sufi sheik and the religious and military leader of Algerian resistance to French occupation, elicited broad expressions of sympathy in the United States, but also helped Americans become aware of the unromantic aspects of imperial warfare against Indigenous peoples.

In the revolutionary year 1848, ironically, the new French Second Republic declared the annexation of Algeria as an overseas French department. This duality of France, the only European colonial power that experienced significant popular upheaval in the "springtime of the peoples," was not lost on American observers. This was especially true given the context of the recently victorious outcome of the US war with Mexico. The Second Republic's paradoxical display of both democracy and conquest, liberation and nation-state building, produced an equally paradoxical reaction in the United States—like France, a burgeoning empire reliant on migrants who were encouraged to go into frontier spaces that had been conquered from alien peoples in order to fulfill national destiny and develop economically profitable settler societies through agricultural colonization.

Thus, the land, climate, and people of Algeria, the means of irregular warfare by which French forces accomplished Abdelkader's defeat, and the outcome in a declaration of Algeria's annexation, shaped Americans' perceptions of their own conduct and challenges in early territorial expansion. The fledgling French empire in North Africa encouraged American expansionists to justify territorial conquest and settlement as a variant of conservative European state-building.

The Emergence of French–American Transimperialism

The year 1830, familiar to US historians for the passage of the Indian Removal Act, was important for a distant but analogous event, the bombardment by French forces of the Barbary State, Algiers. France decreed that its mission, similar to what Napoleon Bonaparte had proclaimed earlier in Egypt, was to liberate the Algerian people from the tyranny of the Ottoman governor of Algiers, Hussein Dey.[4] In substance the intervention signaled relocation and renewal of French colonial interest after the losses of Canada and Haiti. Over time, French expansionists would seek to populate Algeria with settlers, similar to Americans' settlement in areas formerly occupied by Indigenous peoples.

France also attacked Algiers to eliminate its commerce raiding and the tribute that Hussein Dey demanded to allow Mediterranean trade. This reason for war was quite familiar to US citizens. During the early American republic, North Africa was notorious as the Barbary Coast. Barbary captivity narratives, describing the treatment of Christian sailors held for ransom by the regencies of Algiers, Tunis, and Tripoli had circulated in the Atlantic world since the sixteenth century. A muted impact of the literature in the United States was to raise doubts among readers who recoiled at North African "white slavery" about justifications for the enslavement of African Americans.[5] More prominently, the Barbary Wars, 1801–1805 and 1815–1816, were occasions for the United States to forcefully differentiate US policy from European precedent. Europeans traditionally paid the Barbary States tribute, as did the administrations of presidents George Washington and John Adams, to ensure their commercial ships could sail in the Mediterranean without risk of capture of ships and crew. But presidents Thomas Jefferson and James Madison chose to deploy the fledgling US naval fleet and Marines, which expanded during the War of 1812, to force the Barbary States to give up their "piracy" and to ensure American commercial independence. In 1818, however, the Barbary States resumed raids in the Mediterranean, lasting until the French intervention in Algiers in 1830, although they did not capture any more American ships.[6]

After the Barbary Wars, the United States quickly evacuated its military forces from North Africa, whereas the intervention of King Charles X in 1830 began a French military occupation that would last well over a century. Yet French Algeria continued to connect France and the United States in more ways than simply its inspiration for artists' portrayal of Oriental allure and savagery, as postcolonial scholars have emphasized.[7]

The French conquest of Algeria would utterly change the former Barbary State's image for Americans. This was true even though Americans initially received little news about the French occupation of North Africa. A few weeks after the arrival of French forces, the US consul general in Algiers, Henry Lee, described a surprise attack by Algerians on a French force eating breakfast. French troops avoided complete annihilation only because their "superiority of discipline" exceeded the Algerians' "natural courage." Yet Lee also predicted that French rule in North Africa would never be secure. His dispatch anticipated how the early French occupation of North Africa would challenge assumptions many US citizens had about French discipline and Algerian indiscipline.[8]

Henry Lee's ambivalence echoed in American newspapers, whose editors were skeptical of French motives and keen to contrast the French trans-

Mediterranean investment with Anglo-American settler development. In 1835, the *Richmond Enquirer* noted that Marshal Bertrand Clauzel, the second French governor general in Algiers, had proclaimed "the prospect that the French colony there may one day be as flourishing and as populous as those planted by the English in the United States."[9] While Clauzel's reported reference was slightly dubious—perhaps suggesting that the source for this story in an American newspaper was a British newspaper report—French advocates of Algeria's colonization over the next century would intermittently cite the success of the British North American colonies, and especially the US development of the frontier, as motivation for their plans for Algeria.[10]

A more detailed American account of the French arrival had been provided earlier by David Porter, a somewhat controversial US naval officer. Porter saw service in the First Barbary War and the War of 1812, and he coined the memorable phrase "Free Trade and Sailors' Rights" before being court-martialed in 1826 for exceeding his orders in an expedition to stop piracy in the West Indies. He then resigned from the US Navy and was appointed commander in chief of the Mexican Navy before resigning that post upon appointment as US Minister to the Barbary States. Porter arrived in Algiers in August 1830 after the French capture of the town in July. To remove Porter's position from jeopardy, President Andrew Jackson then prevailed upon Congress to establish the office of *chargé d'affaires* to the Ottoman Empire, and appointed Porter to that position.[11]

Before sailing for Constantinople in April 1831, Porter wrote a letter to a colleague in the Department of the Navy describing Algiers during the first days of the French occupation. Less enthusiastic than Tocqueville, Porter had little sympathy for rapacious French soldiers or obstinate Muslims, though his criticism of the former was mitigated by evidence that France intended to install European institutions in North Africa. "The French appear somewhat at a loss what to do with Algiers," he began, but noted that the new regime planned to create an "agricultural society" by awarding land grants. Porter assumed that it was to be Swiss, not French settlers, who would "interpose a barrier of armed peasantry" between French troops and Arabs in the interior. Likewise, French engineers were widening the streets of Algiers and numbering the town's dwellings. But because Hussein Dey allegedly had taken most of the Algerian treasury when he fled to the Italian port city of Livorno, Porter claimed, French occupiers were compelled to "resort to every means" of remuneration, already compelling the Bey of Tunis to submit to a treaty and outright extorting money from the Karamanli dynasty that ruled Tripoli.[12] Porter predicted that should French troops attempt to occupy Tripoli and Tunis, they would be subjected to "a war of extermination carried on by bigoted Arabs."[13] Writing from Menorca, Spain, in route to Constantinople, he did not foresee that within a decade it would be French forces that would resort to a military strategy of extermination.[14]

Thus, again, Americans had a mixed reaction to scant news of France's initial takeover of Algeria. The French presence in North Africa seemed a sort of follow-up to the earlier US rebuke of the Barbary States' piracy, which Westerners considered outside the laws of civilized nations. But French ambitions to "civilize" North Africa appeared far-fetched. In 1837, a New York newspaper reported without comment that a petition with two thousand signatures had been presented to the French Chamber of Deputies "praying for a vote that Algeria is an integral and indivisible part of French territory."[15] French visions to transform the Ottoman regency into a *France transméditerranéenne*—a phrase coined in 1832 by the *Société Colonial de l'Etat d'Alger*—sounded grandiose.[16]

This initial American perception of French Algeria as an illusion shaped Americans' understanding of the challenges of territorial conquest, an awareness further informed by stories of French measures to capture Abdelkader, who emerged as a formidable anticolonial adversary in 1832, using surprise mounted attacks, persuading or strong-arming rival tribes to join his alliance, and enforcing Arab boycotts of French commerce. Perhaps aware of French–American animosity over the lingering controversy of spoliation claims dating from the Napoleonic Era, in 1836, Abdelkader audaciously contacted a US consul in Morocco to offer the United States possession of any Algerian port it might choose, on condition of a US alliance with his regime.[17] The spoliation controversy, dating from the United States' Quasi-War with France, 1797–1801, had recently been resolved, thus the United States abstained from direct involvement in the surging French–Algerian conflict. James Leib, the US consul in Tangier who declined Abdelkader's offer, wrote that "any . . . encouragement [by the United States] to the Barbary Powers for hostile action against Europeans would be adverse . . . to the progress of civilization."[18]

As Leib's comment suggests, US policymakers were hardly drawn to Abdelkader's invitation to help defend North Africa. At the time they still associated him with the notorious Barbary States. But French actions gave Abdelkader the opportunity to disabuse Americans of that image, and, in so doing, created ideological space for the Algerian leader, as an anti-colonialist, to disrupt, if not overcome, many Americans' prejudices against Muslims, or at least Arabs, in North Africa.[19] In 1837, French General Thomas

Robert Bugeaud agreed by the Treaty of Tafna to concede most of Algeria, other than its port cities, to Abdelkader's rule. Abdelkader's short-lived regime brought uniform taxation and representative tribal government to North Africa for the first time. However, when a French expedition violated the treaty in 1839, Abdelkader renewed resistance, proclaiming a *jihad*. In December of that year, King Louis-Philippe retaliated by declaring that Algeria was "a land forever French," and ordered its complete conquest.[20] Initially, the French strategy was defensive. But the plan of the commander of French forces, Sylvain Valée, to construct a wall around the French occupied zone was ridiculed. Bugeaud, Valée's replacement, favored more aggressive, irregular tactics that became known as the *razzia*, under which French troops plundered Algerians' fields, crops, and livestock, and episodically massacred civilians.[21] From that time until and even beyond his capture in 1847, Abdelkader's prowess in defying French imperial forces gained broad popular support in the United States.[22]

Examples of reports about Abelkader suggest that his status as an anticolonial freedom fighter resonated with Americans who still saw themselves in that way and overcame prejudice against his race and religion. One Virginia newspaper hailed his command of twenty thousand troops and artillery attack on Algiers, initially thwarting the French campaign for the Algerian interior and demonstrating his capacity to wage conventional as well as unconventional warfare.[23] A Virginia literary magazine, meanwhile, published a poem. Its first and last stanzas read,

> Well done, my gallant Arab chief!/ Lord of a steed and lance,/ Lead on your desert-born, and brief/ Must be the sway of France;/ Teach her, that Afric's burning sands/ Are ruled alone by flashing brands! . . . What though ye bend at Mecca's shrine,/ Though call'd an Infidel;/ What though your God's no god of mine,/ Fight on, and fight ye well!/ For he who breaks a tyrant's rod,/ Need never fear the Christian's God![24]

Praise was even more widespread in the northern US states, similarly focused on Abdelkader's sobriety. The fact that his troops were Arabs made his leadership impressive (see fig. 1). He had "single handedly" kept "in check the very flower of the French army," in 1840 inflicting five thousand casualties on a French force of some sixty thousand troops deployed on the plains around Algiers. Abdelkader's father had educated him "as well as an Arab can be," and he even carried a small library with him during campaigns, the theological works from which he drew to preach a daily sermon "to

A North African Example for Early US Expansion 17

Figure 1.1. Regular infantryman in the Algerian resistance army of Emir Abdelkader. From Jean-François-Nicolas Loumyer, *Moeurs, usages et costumes de tous les peuples du monde: d'après des documents authentiques et les voyages les plus récents* (Librairie historique-artistique, 1844). Album Archivo Fotográfico, S.L.

propagate upon war and politics." He was "no fanatic," and readily discussed religious matters with Christians, presumably French officials with whom he had conducted negotiations before the former broke the peace."[25]

American newspapers, not surprisingly, were not above reporting on war atrocities, given their titillating appeal. One such incident, concerning a French force's capture, killing, and beheading of an Algerian chief, Sidi Embarek, second in command to Abdelkader, explicitly showed "the moral condition of the French army of Africa." Embarek's severed head, the report revealed, was covered with honey, salted, and carried to Algiers to be "served up at a *soirée* of Marshal Bugeaud." Bugeaud was reported to have declined to eat "the head of the brave chief of the desert," and instead to have organized a military funeral.[26] Beheadings were an aspect of warfare practiced sporadically by both sides in Algeria, but American observers at the time tended to focus on the French practice.[27] The story concluded sarcastically, "Marshal Bugeaud and his African heroes are getting a little in advance of the rest of Europe, and vindicating French claims to superior civilization in the art of war, as in the art of cookery."[28]

An even more sensational outrage occurred in 1845, several years into General Bugeaud's resort to harsh tactics of the razzia. The nadir was reached when a French officer, Colonel Amable Pélissier, having cornered the resistant Ouled Riah tribe in a cave, ordered his men to build a fire at its mouth to asphyxiate its occupants. The incident became internationally controversial, partly because Bugeaud defended Pélissier's action, and the American press focused on the story.[29] Perhaps revealingly, 1845 was the first time that an American newspaper used the term "French Algeria."[30]

Abdelkader's resistance, in short, momentarily transformed France's ambition to "civilize" Algeria as a settler colony into the debasement of Western civilization. France had justified the invasion of Algeria partly because the Ottoman governor of Algiers was a tyrant. But with the rise of a new face of Algiers, Abdelkader, the tyrant became Gallic, not Ottoman. By 1845, declared the *New York Herald*, the most widely read American newspaper, Algeria's cost to France had "no parallel . . . in the whole history of civilization."[31] Abdelkader's mini-epic of resistance, which inspired an Iowa town to name itself Elkader in 1846, shows the multilayered, anti-imperial role Indigenous peoples could play in the first part of the nineteenth century.[32]

American Territorial Wars

To be sure, however, French colonial warfare merely caused many Americans to emphasize the hubris and costs of French claims to the enlargement of "civilization," rather than to renounce the principle or objectives of such claims. Reports about French political debates and military efforts in Algeria helped Americans shape and rationalize their own, nearer wars of expansion, and to glean lessons to avoid, or to emulate, first in the so-called Second Seminole War, 1835–1842, and later the Mexican War, 1846–1848.

The often forgotten Second Seminole War has been termed the "sole exception to the successful execution of the [US] policy of Indian removal," and perhaps the longest and most costly war the United States ever waged against a particular Indigenous people.[33] Resistance to the Indian Removal Act by the Seminole Indians of Florida was the contemporaneous US analogue to Abdelkader's war against France. Both Seminole Indians and the forces of Abdelkader sometimes tortured prisoners of war, murdered Indigenous people who cooperated with imperial forces and white civilians who had no official duties, and mutilated enemy corpses. Killings for revenge and inhumane treatment of prisoners and dead bodies, to be sure, have been common practices in world history; ironically, Europeans with a background in the brutal Thirty Years' War (1618–48) had misinterpreted traditional, limited Indigenous American wars as games.[34] But beginning in the colonial era, Indigenous peoples' recourse to "savage" tactics reflected their dwindling resources and recognition that limited or honor-seeking warfare—for example, "counting coup" among Indigenous Americans and traditional "ghazwa" among Bedouins—was becoming ineffective or irrelevant. Ruthlessness, on the other hand, amplified the psychological impact of attacks on imperial forces and civilians.[35]

American and French newspapers' reporting on native peoples' guerrilla warfare had a dual effect on white audiences. Sometimes reports of atrocities in the United States helped dissuade white Americans from coming to or remaining in native areas. For example, General Duncan Clinch, commander of US Army forces in Florida, confessed that his troops were afraid to attack Seminole Chief Osceola. After he was captured, Osceola confirmed that he had killed US prisoners of war but rejected accusations that he had targeted women and children. When asked about his tactics, Osceola mimicked soldiers struggling to fire and load, then demonstrated how Seminoles skirmished before fleeing.[36]

More often, newspapers and military officials interpreted Indigenous fighters' behavior as a justification for retaliatory, "uncivilized" measures. General Thomas Jesup, Clinch's replacement, issued the unprecedented order that US troops could enslave any Blacks they might capture in Florida.[37] While US military leaders and reporters cast acts of reprisal by "insurgents" as a sign of racial or cultural degradation, the atrocities committed by imperial forces, because they were done on behalf of a recognized belligerent, were construed as at once legitimate and tactical choices, not reflective of "real" American or French national values.[38]

It was in fact during the Second Seminole War that American writers first linked the behaviors of the erstwhile anticolonial United States and European colonial powers. The war broke out when many of the approximately five thousand Seminole Indians of Florida rejected an 1832 treaty obligating them to relocate to the Arkansas Territory. In calling for removal westward of the Seminoles and other remaining eastern tribes, President

Andrew Jackson had ridiculed them as "a few savage hunters."[39] An essay in an American magazine, *Littell's Living Age*, comparing the circumstances of the United States, France, Russia, and Britain, echoed this sentiment. The writer observed that these powers, together, "represent[ed] the side of civilization as against barbarism." All four powers espoused an ideology of a "'mission' to civilize," had armies, and together held a near monopoly on gunpowder, "which multiplies the power of the disciplined body as against the undisciplined nation." Against these powers were arrayed, respectively, the pitiful Seminole "painted savage," "the marauding [Algerian] African," the "Caucasian [Circassian] bandit," and the "effeminate Asiatic" tribes of Central Asia.[40]

The essay's point, in fact, was that the various "representatives of barbarism" were offering stubborn resistance to conquest, defying the science and progress allegedly behind the Western powers' mission to civilize. Regarding the Second Seminole War, the essay acknowledged that the United States had "triumphed" over the Seminoles by 1844, but still emphasized the war's embarrassing aspects. It attributed US success in the war to a disparity of population—"fourteen millions of men on one side, and eight thousand on the other." Despite Americans' statistical advantage, "the war against the miserable Indians and . . . a few runaway negroes . . . has been ingloriously conducted": "There is not in the history of wars among the civilized nations a parallel for the wantonness, imbecility, and corruption which distinguish this humiliating, dishonorable, infamous crusade." By 1842 the Second Seminole War had cost half as much as the War of 1812 with Britain, an epic conflict that, in contrast, had covered the US Army and Navy "with glory" and "achieved an honorable peace." Meanwhile "of Indian warfare we have not seen the end." Unconventional war, waged against Indigenous peoples whose ways of war bogged US forces down and provoked them to adopt "barbarous" tactics of their own, was ambiguous, expensive, and protracted, in contrast to how Americans in the 1840s liked to remember their earlier anticolonial triumphs.[41] Americans' knowledge of foreign imperial wars challenged their belief in their own anticolonial identity.

If the Second Seminole War was not a heroic war, it was not as embarrassing, the *Littell's* writer continued, as France's "indiscreet" and "graver" situation in the Mediterranean. In this context, French Algeria appeared as a warning. In North Africa, the theater of war was "hardly limited to [an area like] the peninsula of Florida," and instead threatened to encompass the entire area of the Sahara Desert. In Algeria, after fourteen years of occupation, France had "only secured military fortresses and some lines of military communication," and the tools of "civilization" with which France initially hoped to subdue Algeria—technology, advanced military weaponry, and troops disciplined to fight according to rules and orders—had proven ineffective. In addition, France appeared poised to continue to balloon the supply of soldiers in Algeria. *Littell's* estimated that there would be three hundred thousand French troops in North Africa in 1850, seven times the size of the US military at the time.[42] The first decades of the French war in Algeria alerted Americans to the challenges of resorting to irregular warfare to extend state power, and, not for the last time, the limits of superior technology and weaponry in such a conflict.

Proslavery Inspiration

Of course, there were differences between warfare conducted amid the lakes and swamps of Florida and across North Africa's desert plains and mountains. This difference was not lost on US statesmen committed to rapid territorial expansion, for whom the most attractive horizon in the 1840s for the United States was west, not south.[43]

Partly because proslavery Americans inhabited many positions of authority concerning US foreign relations before the Civil War, American expansion into the trans-Mississippi River Western territories necessarily involved the expansion of slavery.[44] To the extent that such a policy required cultivation of alliances with sympathetic European powers, France played a prominent role in proslavery expansionists' calculus, as a counterweight to Britain. British efforts to ban the international slave trade and abolish colonial slavery made it unlikely that Britons would support a robust US defense of slavery in the Western hemisphere, facilitated by territorial expansion. In contrast, until 1848, France showed less interest in abolitionism. Independent of American pressure, and reflecting concerns about French African trade, for example, in 1845 the French legislature rejected a multinational treaty negotiated by Foreign Minister François Guizot (which also excluded the United States) that would have declared the African slave trade to be piracy and granted British ships a right to search signatory ships and seize slave cargo.[45]

Algeria's Arab slave trade also positioned France as a possible proslavery American ally. In 1840, the July Monarchy approved a plan to open Algeria to caravans of slaves from the Sahara, and an 1845 law called for the gradual emancipation of slaves in French colonies, but not Algeria.[46] French expansion in Algeria actually brought more slaves into declared French territory, and, as governor-general, Bugeaud opposed interfering with the Arab slave trade, which he believed was crucial to developing trade with sub-Saharan Africa.⁴⁷ Echoing Bugeaud, officials of both the July Monarchy and Second Republic emphasized that Arab slavery was "Oriental," not colonial, and therefore, like Indigenous unfree labor in British India, should be left alone.⁴⁸

These various factors boded well for French support of analogous US practices in land west of the Mississippi River, even though the land was claimed at the time by Mexico as Alta California, a remnant of the Spanish empire. Additionally, many Americans, like French officials who castigated the Barbary States, considered the government of Mexico perennially weak, in a South Carolina congressman's words, "our [the Americas'] sick man."⁴⁹ After achieving independence from Mexico in 1836, Texas was the first southwestern region to draw American expansionists' attention. After annexation debates began in earnest in 1844, US statesmen considered international reaction. In instructing the US minister to the July Monarchy that President John Tyler expected France not to oppose the annexation of Texas, Secretary of State John Calhoun described the former Mexican province's attractiveness for American settlement in terms similar to those with which French imperial apologists described plans for Algeria. Texas was currently "a wilderness with a sparse population, consisting for the most part of wandering . . . tribes."⁵⁰ Thus, it was Americans' "destiny to occupy that vast region; to intersect it with roads and canals; to fill it with cities, towns, villages, and farms" and to make it "a peaceful and splendid addition to the domains of commerce and civilization."⁵¹ Texas's alleged topographical and cultural emptiness paralleled Algeria's alleged emptiness prior to the French arrival.⁵²

Calhoun emphasized that Texas could be assimilated peacefully by the United States. He and others were dismayed, therefore, when the United States declared war on Mexico in May 1846 after the Mexican government refused to either relinquish its claim on Texas or sell Alta California to the United States. The war, lasting only twenty-one months, proved far shorter than the recent conflict with the Seminoles. Still, its prospect of becoming a war of attrition provoked criticism, based on the French North African experience. Early in 1847, for example, American newspapers reported a massacre by US troops of twenty-five Mexican civilians in a cave. The account stirred images of the international controversy two years earlier, when French Colonel Pélissier ordered the asphyxiation of a resistant Algerian community hiding in a cave.⁵³ Meanwhile, the essayist Ralph Waldo Emerson drew a more explicit parallel between the two wars of conquest. In an Independence Day address Emerson mused that the Mexican War's strongest advocates were a part of a transimperial movement to engage in colonial and territorial war, a "war-party . . . which every nation holds within it."[54] Similar to the earlier portrayal of the Second Seminole War as an episode in inglorious colonial war, Emerson observed that while "England, France, [and] America are forbidden war with each other, they spend their ferocity on Sikhs, Algerines, & Mexicans and so find a vent for their piratical population."[55]

The main criticism of a war with Mexico, however, was that it created the possibility that the United States might attempt to annex parts of Mexico that were heavily populated, not only the less populated northern regions. This possibility provoked Americans to consider how Mexico resembled Algeria on account of its millions of unassimilable native people who would obstruct its settler democratization, as the trans-Atlantic commentator Alexis de Tocqueville prophesied for French North Africa. To illustrate, in the Senate in February 1847 John C. Calhoun spoke against a congressional appropriation for the Mexican War. Like periodicals that earlier had compared the costs of the war against the Seminole Indians to those that Europeans incurred in Africa and Asia, Calhoun warned against going to war to gain land south of the Rio Grande River because it would require a "guerilla war, such as now exists between France and the Arabs in Africa," requiring untold financial investment and mobilization of soldiers. To Calhoun, conquest of Mexico would be doubly disastrous, since Americans would then need to choose between either assimilating "8,000,000 of [sic] people all professing one religion, and all concentrated under a powerful and wealthy priesthood" or holding Mexico as a "subject province," which, history showed, would cause the US government to become despotic.[56]

Other statesmen and journalists, reflecting both US Northern and Southern opinions, echoed Calhoun. Former US Secretary of War Joel Poinsett, drawing on his experience in the Second Seminole War, wrote that the United States should avoid entrapment in "another Algeria" in Mexico. Poinsett predicted that the "Guerilla warfare" and "fanaticism" of Mexican people was "formidable" and could thus visit on Americans burdens similar to "the waste of French blood and treasure in Algeria."[57] Congressman Richard Brodhead, a Pennsylvania Democrat who helped organize the Wilmot Proviso, a bill that would have banned slavery from any territory gained from Mexico, asked how US forces could win in Mexico without resorting to the sixteen campaigns he estimated had already been mounted by France in Algeria. Likewise, a Washington, DC newspaper predicted sarcastically that the administration of President James Polk, which had declared war on Mexico, wished to "civilize" the country by bringing it "under our Military Dominion; to convert her into an Algeria for the United States; to garrison her territories with whatever force, say a hundred thousand soldiers at least," no matter the expense and for an indefinite period of time.[58]

Supporters of the war against Mexico, again both statesmen and journalists, invoked Algeria in different ways. Some portrayed the French colonial war as an immoral conflict, costly to France's treasury and reputation, but did so in order to justify a different sort of US action against the Mexican republic. War advocates emphasized that the war had begun in April 1846 when Mexican forces had killed four US soldiers on the north shore of the Rio Grande River, violating US "sacred soil."[59] This Mexican provocation, war hawks claimed, obviously differentiated the US war's origin from the alleged triviality of a personal insult, the so-called Fly Whisk Incident, which had precipitated the French invasion of North Africa.

Other defenses of the war illustrated how French Algeria had versatile meanings. Suggesting Americans' lasting memory of the Barbary Wars, an Indiana newspaper argued that the Mexican "acts of depredation" resembled hostile acts once committed by Algiers, Tripoli, and Tunis. As Barbary attacks had justified President George Washington asking Congress to authorize a force to protect American maritime commerce, "President Polk and the Congress of 1846 are right in regard to Mexico."[60] Meanwhile, during a debate in Congress over the war's costs and goals, Georgia Senator John Berrien called on Congress to refuse any US acquisition of Mexican territory by conquest.[61] Berrien, although a critic of Polk's "usurpation of power" in conducting the war, indeed what historians consider an unprecedented display of executive power in US history, actually defended US war-making against any European critic. While "senseless rulers" controlled Mexico, Algerian resistance to France was led, Berrien reminded Congress, by the "Arab chief" Abdelkader, whose "proud spirit" merited a US salute.[62] Berrien's invocation of Abdelkader as a heroic symbol, as a means of justifying American aggression against less worthy leaders of the Mexican republic, was perhaps the most ironic American invocation of Abdelkader during the nineteenth century.

The Mexican capitulation in February 1848 seemed to vindicate arguments that Mexico was not the US's Algeria—although possibly because Algeria's lesson served as a warning. In the war's negotiated settlement the United States annexed only Alta California, not the Mexican heartland, contrary to what President Polk had contemplated in late 1847 as punishment of Mexican forces' failure to surrender more quickly.[63] Various factors contributed to US restraint in this instance, including racial and religious skepticism about absorbing the Mexican population as well as arguments about American Manifest Destiny emphasizing the distinctiveness of American expansion from more avaricious European practices. Americans' concern about foreign examples of wars of annexation also played an important role. Although their contiguous border made Texas and Mexico different from Algeria's separation from France by the Mediterranean Sea, they were dual analogies to French Algeria, one the fulfillment of national destiny, which Americans generally supported, the other the lesson of imperial warfare against people of a different creed, leading to the problem of those alien people's assimilation, which Americans nearly uniformly rejected. As a skeptical Washington, DC, newspaper put it, "to bring all Mexico under our Military Dominion" meant "to convert her into an Algeria for the United States," and the paper mocked the war's advocates' claim that the conflict would bring "civilization" to Mexico.[64]

An Irony of the Revolution of 1848

Americans' mixed attitudes toward the 1848 revolution in France, which erupted a mere three weeks after the treaty that ended the Mexican War was signed, have been documented. Americans spontaneously celebrated the overthrow of King Louis Philippe on the premise that US-style republicanism was taking hold in the heart of Europe. American newspapers reported the happy coincidence of the toppling of the July Monarchy and the birthday of George Washington; American towns renamed themselves after the poet, historian, and leader of the provisional government, Alphonse de Lamartine; and Americans of different ethnicities and genders could be seen wearing revolutionary cockades and flying the tricolor. Important American reformers celebrated the Second Republic's dramatic reforms. Abolitionists, especially the celebrated former slave Frederick Douglass, hailed the emancipation of slaves in the French Caribbean colonies of Guadeloupe, Martinique, and Guiana. In a speech to working men in Rochester, New York, Douglass drew attention to the greeting by Adolphe Cremieux, as the Second Republic's provisional government's minister of justice, to a delegation of Black and mixed-race Parisians who called on him to express gratitude for the abolition of colonial slavery. Douglass praised Cremieux's language of "Citizens, friends, brothers!"[65] Other abolitionists invoked the French emancipation to emphasize US hypocrisy in its claims of exceptional democracy and maintenance of slavery.[66] Meanwhile, the Second Republic's abolition of colonial slavery was unpopular in the South, stirring the specter of the great and terrible Haitian revolution, even though the French emancipation of 1848 was far less violent, and the French government compensated the *colon* sugar planters for the loss of their West Indian slave property.[67] Northerners were generally more sympathetic toward French emancipation, but most Americans, North and South, recoiled at bloodshed associated with the June Days uprising of laborers and socialists and considered it a reminder of French people's incapability for stable republican government.[68]

Given the attention Americans had given France's costly investment in Algeria over the previous two decades, it is no surprise that they interpreted the French upheavals of 1848 partly in light of their trans-Mediterranean, imperial consequences. That is, surprisingly, the revolutionary Second Republic's incorporation of Algeria and recommitment to transform the region into a settler society struck many Americans as a sober measure of law and order. Many proslavery Americans particularly, although not exclusively, saw Algerian annexation as a foreign parallel to the prospects of the post–Mexican War West—an act by a powerful, modernizing nation, reflecting an imperial ambition analogous to their own to develop frontier territory for migration and agriculture. Suggestive of the paradoxes of the moment, American reports revealed that it was the same Adolphe Cremieux, hailed by the abolitionist Frederick Douglass for his egalitarian welcome to French *gens de colour*, who pronounced the assimilation of Algeria in 1848.[69]

Algeria's pivotal role in republican France was revealed at a critical moment in the turbulent days of 1848. After popular elections, the National Assembly convened in May, determined to cut government costs. On May 15, a socialist-inspired mob, provoked by the assembly's refusal to render assistance to Polish people seeking to overthrow the country's occupation by Russian and Austrian forces, briefly occupied the National Assembly, proclaiming a socialist provisional government. Republican military units, the National Guard, dispersed the socialists, but the event made the government determined to clear Paris of the unemployed and abolish the public labor workshops. On June 23, some fifty thousand angry insurgents barricaded the city and laid siege to the government. Again, government troops rallied, this time retaliating ferociously, blowing up barricades and chasing the insurgents from house to house—the latter measure adapted from tactics developed in Algeria over the previous decade.

Both insurgents and government forces committed atrocities during the June Days, during which some ten thousand people were killed. A few American reporters actually were on hand to witness the conflict. The novelist Donald Mitchell, for one, arrived in Paris shortly before the June Days as a reporter for the *New York Courier and Enquirer*. Likewise, George Kendall covered events in Europe for the *New Orleans Picayune*.[70] Mitchell and Kendall represented the Paris events as macabre and sinister. Mitchell, writing about June 25, emphasized that the insurgents' "violence is equaled by their cruelty; in defiance of all civil usage, they have murdered their prisoners either beheaded them . . . or hanging them to their window bars. Such is the action of the advocates of what they call a Social Republic!" Kendall, meanwhile, seeking to get as close as possible to barricade fighting, at one point observed a charge of the National Guard while huddled in a nearby doorway. His vantage point did not warm his view of the workers. He concluded, "The most important element at work in bringing about the revolution was socialism."[71]

Both Mitchell and Kendall, relying on their own observations as well as French government statements in the Paris press, tended to emphasize the brutality of the insurgents, similar to how conservative French newspapers and other opponents of the labor uprising characterized it.[72] They described a *cuirassier* being impaled and disemboweled and soldiers having their hands or feet cut off. Both emphasized the savagery of women. "Two fiends in female form even cut up the bodies of some of the younger lads . . . of the Guard Mobile . . . and taking the flesh to a pork butcher . . . told him to make it up into pies!" "Several women were arrested who had sold poisoned brandy to the soldiers."[73] Mitchell reiterated, "Socialism . . . that shameless doctrine which instructs us that all the systems of Public Liberty now current throughout the civilized world are spurious . . . this is the doctrine which has set on the workmen of Paris to their revolt."[74] Mitchell's and Kendall's shocking accounts registered with American readers and shaped American public opinion about the French revolution as calamitous.

However, the fact that veterans of the Algerian war, especially Louis-Eugène Cavaignac, named governor-general by the provisional government after sixteen years' service in North Africa, played a prominent role in suppressing the June insurgency further influenced Americans to see it as a clash between forces of order and chaos. Mitchell, for example, in a memoir, contrasted the resolute Cavaignac and his prevaricating civilian colleagues who devised the government's plan to take Paris's streets back from *les blouses* in the summer of 1848:

> Poor [Alphonse de] Lamartine in distress goes from General to General, asking advices; he draws street plans of defence; and [François] Arago lays the measure of his great mind to palace angles, and range of batteries. A long-headed officer who has seen service in Algeria, is of the conclave; he smiles at the fervor of Lamartine, and the mathematical arrangements of the Astronomer; he says very little, but he thinks a great deal;-he is just the man to bring this brewing storm to quick, and fearful issue! It is Cavaignac, the Minister of War.[75]

Perhaps even more revealing, Mitchell labeled the workers peopling the barricades a "tribe," thus evoking an image of not only American Indians but also Algerian Bedouin.[76] "They are fierce and hot, and angered with hunger and thirst." In earlier years, American popular opinion tended to sympathize with Algerian resistance to the French occupation, especially in reaction to the heroic deeds of Abdelkader. Fascination with the Algerian leader, however, hardly represented support for the Algerian cause, and suggestions of Paris workers as savage rebels signaled a shift of sympathy toward the forces of "law and order," not only in Paris but in the French Empire.[77]

Thus, while American observers deemed both General Cavaignac and the workers of Paris ruthless, Americans supported the conqueror of Algeria as an agent of restoring republican stability in France. The *New York Herald* published a three-column biography of Cavaignac in late 1848, concluding, "France owes a deep debt of gratitude to him." The story traced Cavaignac's career in Algeria, where his "master spirit" had brought "life, fertility, and animation" to North Africa. Echoing Tocqueville, the *Herald* observed, "Among the vestiges of Roman edifices and constructions" were now rising houses, farms, cultivated fields, aqueducts, schoolhouses, "and all the lively and animated exhibitions of European life and civilization." All of this had been accomplished "on the individual [sic] system of individual enterprise"—not by Fourierists, the followers, some of them American, of the French utopian socialist Charles Fourier or by "any of the [other] socialists," such as the Saint-Simonians.[78] Based on his reputation for civilizing Algeria, Cavaignac was elected to the National Assembly. Thus, he resigned as governor-general of Algeria to become a humble public servant, "little dreaming," the *Herald* continued, "what a tragical [sic] necessity would soon arise for his military skill and command in the streets of Paris."[79] In effect, the *Herald* explained that Cavaignac's arrival in Paris at a critical moment for the Second Republic was due to his success in putting Algeria on a path to economic prosperity by shunning socialist remedies.

Likewise, Americans praised the French solution to Paris's volatility by expelling its malcontents. In a further response to the June Days uprising, the French Second Republic, under the direction of Cavaignac and a fellow Algerian veteran, Louis Juchault de Lamoricière, deported some thirteen thousand rebels to Algeria. After his coup d'etat in 1851, Napoleon III likewise banished another ten thousand republican dissidents to France's North Africa departments.[80] American observers applauded the Algerian deportations as a reasonable solution to a concentrated, disenfranchised labor force. One periodical rendered the comment,

> Twenty thousand workmen of Paris have joined in a petition to the Assembly for aid to emigrate to Algeria in a body. Well, if scores of thousands more could be despatched [sic]. The two hundred thousand *prolétaires* in the capital are more dangerous to it and to France, than the millions of American negro slaves to their masters and states.[81]

In other words, France's dispersion of dissidents to the frontier was praiseworthy because such measures would create conditions more similar to American society, where the restive American slave class was already dispersed across the agricultural South. In 1820 Thomas Jefferson had encouraged the dispersion of people held as slaves into the Far West to facilitate abolition, and in 1845 John L. O'Sullivan had echoed Jefferson in explaining why the United States should acquire Texas as a safety valve for slavery. The French government's usage of Algeria as a solution to the problem of urban unemployment, an imperial fail-safe, echoed these Americans' earlier ideas for how the West could slowly rid the United States of the peculiar institution. The French Second Republic's attempt to legitimize its precarious rule of France by display of military power beyond but not within Europe was thus proven successful, at least in terms of American opinion.[82]

The perspective of Richard Rush, US Minister to France, provided a sort of official testimony to Americans' receptivity of, if not uniform support for, French conquest of Algeria, offsetting the shock of the turbulence of revolution in Paris. Rush was conspicuous for his determination, over British objections, to ensure that the United States was the first country to offer diplomatic recognition to the Second Republic in February 1848 by scurrying through barricaded streets to the Hôtel de Ville, the provisional government's headquarters, within days of the initial sacking of the Tuileries.[83] But Rush also spoke for his countrymen that summer when he observed that France had figuratively created Algeria by bringing it into the community of law-abiding nations: "Happily," Rush wrote, "for commerce and civilization, France, by converting Algiers into Algeria, has broken up that nest of [Barbary] pirates."[84] Americans' perceptions of the French Second Republic's policy to make Algeria more of a settler colony offset their revulsion at the turn of the French revolution in May and June 1848.

By late 1850, American newspapers, even ones suspicious of the first popularly elected French president, Louis Napoléon Bonaparte, who handily defeated Cavaignac, were reporting the "progress" of Algeria's colonization, represented by an array of statistics, without mention of the conquest's human or financial costs. A European population of 115,000 now was developing 133 towns and villages, established across 42 colonies, connected by 64 telegraph stations, and meanwhile digging 250,000 meters of irrigation canals.[85] The "business-like" aspect of French reports on such statistics of civilization "was not what one expects from France," the *National Era*, an antislavery newspaper based in Washington, DC, remarked with grudging approval.[86] French antislavery groups, although they could not organize the abolition of the Arab slave trade, had been successful in committing France not to bring slaves into Algeria, an important step toward North Africa's repopulation and agricultural development by European settlers.[87] Occasionally, American writers emphasized that the persistent Arab slave trade, especially of women, made French claims of civilizing Algeria hypocritical, but generally the vision of North Africa as a settler frontier resonated with American observers, North and South.[88] A *New York Times* story reported that although French developers were using Algerian war prisoners to build roads in newly vanquished areas, the projects were exerting pressure to reform on Arabs, who were "gradually losing that rapacious, roving, and inconstant nature," always a "barrier to their advancement." Wealthy Arabs, at least, were building houses and taking up animal husbandry.[89] While American opponents of slavery monitored news that Napoleon III wished to open Algeria to imports of unfree labor from West Africa, India, and China, for most American observers, the French spread of civilizing institutions in North Africa justified the use of non-European forced labor.[90]

Proslavery Americans' inspiration by Algeria hardly diminished in the wake of France's 1848 emancipation proclamation. *The Southern Press* newspaper printed the same year-end story of Algeria's post-1848 development that the antislavery *National Era* did, but concluded with the additional news that since abolition, sugar production in the French West Indies, "following the fortunes of the British [abolition of Caribbean colonial slavery]," had declined.[91] Plans to bring bound labor to Algeria, therefore, showed that

French imperialists were realizing the error of abolition or at least limiting its effects. France, in the spring of 1848 appearing as a "hotbed" of "pseudo-philanthrop[ic]" abolitionism, was reemerging within a beacon of a race-based empire. "Experience [has] proved that the interests of mankind, of civilization, and of Christianity, required that . . . savage and semi-civilized peoples . . . should be subjected, enslaved, or in some way *compelled*, to adopt and follow civilized ways," observed a Louisiana periodical.[92] Indeed, in light of French treatment of Algeria, the United States could hardly be condemned if it were to reopen the African slave trade, a momentous reversal of US policy since 1808, but a vital means to propel Southern expansion, itself a development certainly in keeping with a global "law of expansion" among powerful countries, according to a South Carolina secessionist in 1859.[93]

Yet, despite the encouragement that French Algeria provided proslavery Americans on the eve of the Civil War, their situation in the United States was becoming more precarious. Even if empires of unfree labor abroad seemed healthy, slavery was under threat in the United States itself. The Republican Party, committed to prohibiting slavery's westward expansion, gained federal power in 1860, precipitating war over the two sides' visions of the American West. As a New Orleans newspaper warned in 1857, if the Kansas territory were to become off-limits to slavery, it would have a domino effect: first Missouri, then Kentucky, Maryland, and Virginia were likely to abandon the institution. At that point, "the cotton States, having been shorn of a great proportion of their strength, will be as completely at the mercy of the fanatical North, as Algeria is at the mercy of France."[94] Likewise, Stephen Douglas, a US senator opposed to slavery's restriction, analogized Republicans' threat to the South to asphyxiation, as "the French did Algeria, when the Arabs took to the caverns . . . smoke them out, and keep them burning until they die."[95] On the eve of the Civil War, proslavery Americans saw the South as both a burgeoning slave empire and a casualty of the North's expanding free labor empire. French Algeria provided a territorial model for the first perspective and frightening imagery for the second.

In *Democracy in America*, Alexis de Tocqueville had famously studied the status of Indigenous Americans during his tour of the United States. After European settlement had, over two centuries, caused the Indigenous population in eastern North America to decline drastically to a minority, Tocqueville concluded that their domination by would-be American democrats was a natural phenomenon. Concerning Algeria, Tocqueville was impatient for US-style conditions to emerge, though over far less time than it had taken in the Western hemisphere. This prospect justified, if necessary,

Algeria's destruction.[96] Likewise, American observers of the early republic era, witness to the French conquest of Algeria, emphasized the domestic and military problems attending French imperial construction, not as developments to be scoffed at but as an example that they should study. France's enormous investment to conquer Algeria encouraged Americans about the prospect of territorial conquest in North America, helping jar them from illusions that territorial conquest could somehow resemble earlier heroic ways of war.[97] Thus, in the first decades of France's desert war in Algeria, Americans became less convinced than the foreigner Tocqueville that they possessed any unique ability to establish a territorial empire—but, because of the Algerian lesson, they were more prepared to accomplish it.

Chapter 2

The Civil War as a *Razzia*

In the summer of 1860, Americans' attention was riveted by two heroic images rooted in the French war in Algeria. In August, American newspapers reported Abdelkader's rescue of more than a thousand Maronite Christians to protect them from massacre by Druze and Sunni Muslim forces during a civil war in Mount Lebanon. Abdelkader, who had been paroled by Napoleon III and exiled in Damascus, Syria, also gave shelter to numerous Western Christians living in Damascus including the US vice consul Mikhayil Mishaqa, a Lebanese man who had converted to Protestantism after contact with a mission of the American Board of Commissioners for Foreign Missions.[1] Abdelkader's humanitarian intervention sparked a revival of praise that he had first received over his stalwart resistance to French invasion forces during the 1840s. This time European and US leaders bestowed official honors on him. Reversing France's treatment of Abdelkader, Napoleon III awarded him the Grand-croix de Légion d'honneur, the country's highest order of merit. American newspapers, North and South, predicted the fall of the Ottoman Empire, whose local officials were complicit in the Christian massacres. The American press, with unintended foreshadowing, reported the grisly details of Syria's civil war.[2]

That summer also saw the emergence of the American Zouaves, military units, in the North and South, that, particularly at the outset of the Civil War, became the most theatrical expression of American soldiers' adoption of French colonial practices. The original Zouaves were light-infantry corps in the French army, formed of Berber, Arab, and European volunteers in Algeria, who served under French officers.[3] By 1854, there were four French Zouave regiments, composed principally of Europeans with a small number of North African interpreters. While even in 1855 some American newspapers still saluted the Zouaves for "saving" Paris during the June Days of 1848, the Zouaves' service in the Crimean War more conspicuously brought them to Americans' attention.[4] Lew Wallace, future US Minister to the Ottoman Empire and author of the novel *Ben Hur: A Tale of the Christ*, recalled that an 1856 magazine article on the "Algerian Zouaves of France" alerted him to the Zouaves' special training and inspired his formation of an Indiana Zouave regiment.[5] In 1859, Elmer Ellsworth, an Illinois law clerk and militia trainer, learned of Zouave troops from a veteran of a French Zouave unit in the Crimean War, Charles De Villiers, and used a Zouave military manual to train the National Guard Cadets of Chicago, which he renamed the United States Zouave Cadets. In July 1860 Ellsworth's Zouaves performed exhibition drills in a railroad tour of twenty cities, including a performance for President James Buchanan.[6] The tour aided Americans' popular impression of the French Algerian war as heroic, not distasteful. A poet in New York depicted the "dauntless" French Zouaves' triumph over the "sallow Arab troop." While previously "many a voice was heard to scoff / At Algiers and at Malakoff," now "we're very sure what they / Have done can here be done to-day/. . . . American Zouaves!"[7]

Ellsworth demanded that his troops abstain from tobacco, alcohol, gambling, and even billiards, a puritanical regimen that was contradicted by the exotic oriental uniforms that they and the other Zouave units they spawned wore. Ellsworth's unit's uniform consisted of a bright red cap with gold braid, a light blue shirt with rippled silk facings, a dark blue jacket with orange and red trimmings and closely placed brass buttons, a red sash and loose red trousers, russet leather leggings reaching from the ankle to the knee, and a white waist belt. Wallace claimed, "There was nothing of the flashy, Algerian colors in the uniform of the Eleventh Indiana," but his Hoosiers' Zouave uniform was hardly homespun.[8] Their outfit "[was] a visor cap, French in pattern, its top of red cloth not larger than the palm of one's hand; a blue flannel shirt with open neck; a jacket Greekish in form, edged with narrow binding, the red scarcely noticeable; breeches baggy, but not petticoated; button gaiters connecting below the knees with the breeches, and strapped over the shoe."[9]

Lew Wallace admitted that the effect of the 11th Indiana Zouave Regiment's fancy uniform "was to magnify the men in battle," a false attraction to military service among the young men who responded to Ellsworth's tour by forming some seventy Zouave regiments in the North and twenty-five in the South near the outset of the Civil War, across nearly thirty US states.[10] American Zouaves capitalized on their French counterparts' reputation for extreme physical fitness, unorthodox fighting methods, and recruitment of outcasts. In an Independence Day demonstration, Ellsworth's Chicago cadets, instead of shouldering muskets and marching in lines, leapt and yelled, loaded their weapons while prone on the ground, jumped up to fire, then lay down again. An Iowa Zouave unit trained by "jumping ditches and climbing fences," and its members were required to be able to swim across the Mississippi River.[11] A South Carolina journalist described a Louisiana French American Zouave unit as a "splendid set of animals; medium sized, sunburnt; muscular and wiry as Arabs . . . and some of them would vie, for cunning villainy, with the features of the prettiest Turcos that Algeria could produce."[12] A focus of Zouave training was showmanship and fighting with a bayonet, although in the era of rifled musketry such a skill was already outliving its usefulness. Elmer Ellsworth died famously as the Civil War's first officer casualty after having daringly broken into an Alexandria, Virginia, hotel to cut down its Confederate flag. He was the victim not of a bayonet stab but of a shotgun blast.[13]

Few Civil War regiments actually underwent Zouave training, however, and distinct Zouave units grew scarce during the war for various reasons, including in the South a general shortage of uniforms as the war dragged on and, in both North and South, the association of Zouaves with various kinds of scandal.[14] These factors eventually overcame their exotic appeal. A Rhode Island nurse serving in the Peninsular Campaign, Katherine Wormley, was shocked that a Zouave regiment was also serving as nurses. Reacting to the Zouaves' alternative, flowing garb, she muttered, "For an American citizen to rig himself as an Arab is demoralizing." Whether for their clothing or their "gentleness," Wormley determined that the Zouaves did not possess "the usual manners and ways of men."[15] Meanwhile, resorting to Zouave attire herself for self-preservation, a Mississippi woman, Cordelia Scales, who feared assault by Union soldiers, predicted that a friend would "take [her] for a Guerrilla" on account of her dress in "a black velvet zouave" and brandishing of a pistol while horse-riding.[16] At the other extreme, a Louisiana Zouave unit, perhaps seeking to emulate French African troops' notoriety, gained a reputation for committing atrocities against wounded Union soldiers.[17] Parallel to their alien personal encounters with Zouaves and their accouterments, Americans who read accounts of the French invasion of Mexico in 1862 and gradual advance toward Mexico City learned of French Zouave units accompanying the pretender Maximilian on his entry into the capital on June 12, 1864. Such images discredited the Zouave figure as a worthy symbol of the republican soldier.[18]

Reflecting their enduring popular interest but also their marginalization as actual military units, Zouaves gained various roles in wartime theater productions. In Baton Rouge, a Zouave troop advertised as "men [who] have seen service in Algeria, the Crimea, and the plains of Italy" were "well-worth seeing" because of not only their military "spectacles" but "their little vaudevilles and farces which are replete with humor." Perhaps anticipating audiences' concern for the performers' immorality—and just as Elmer Ellsworth would have had it—an advertisement assured readers, "They are all gentlemen and nothing is said or done in their performances to offend the most fastidious. Let every lady go and see them."[19] In Cincinnati, a female Zouave drill team shared the stage with a panorama of James Fenimore Cooper's novel *Last of the Mohicans*.[20] In Cleveland, actors named The Arabs performed a Zouave musket drill, offering a martial interlude to, or perhaps culminating, a stage performance of "capital farces." "Go see the Arabs tonight, by all means," urged a reviewer before their departure for a next performance in Pittsburgh.[21] A North Carolina observer opined that American Zouaves were on the whole "eccentric," whiskey-drinking, "slightly exaggerated volunteer[s]" who did not "suit the taste of our people." "We have tried," the writer observed, to imagine "[Confederate General P. G. T.] Beauregard *en Zouave*, but without success." The conclusion was that while "there are a great many clever fellows in the Zouave costume . . . they would be quite as clever out of it, and look a little more like constitutional Southern soldiers."[22]

Americans' paeans to Abdelkader on the eve of the Civil War, and various reenactments of Zouave forces during the conflict, however, hardly encompassed how the great national crisis from 1860 to 1865 reflected influences of the French-Algerian colonial war. More substantively, US war policymakers interested in innovation in offensive and irregular warfare and its legal justification enacted strategies reminiscent of French actions in North Africa.[23]

Under the Shadow of Bugeaud

Such borrowing and adaptation happened within the context of the influence of French military thought on the US military over much of the nineteenth century. A prominent figure in this discourse was Antoine-Henri Jomini, a Swiss officer who served as a French general from 1807 to 1814. Jomini's *Summary of the Art of War* appeared in English in 1854. Maxims from his other works, also derived from writings about the Napoleonic Wars, were taught at the US Military Academy beginning in 1817, principally by Dennis Mahan, a student of the French Military School and a West Point instructor for nearly fifty years. Jomini emphasized a few key principles. One was the capture of the enemy's territory. A second was the massing of force into interior lines, facilitating communication and identification of a key point on the enemy's line or fortifications that infantry should attack, which could offset an opponent's numerical advantage. A third was fighting to achieve decisive or war-ending results, not partial victory. Jomini cautioned against attacks against an enemy behind fortified lines, a qualification to his general endorsement of offensive warfare, on which Mahan taught and on which he and his student, future Union general-in-chief Henry Halleck, published their own work.[24] Americans were able to rely largely on Napoleonic military practices to win the Mexican War of 1846–48, despite warnings before the war by critics that the conflict would degrade into irregular or even guerrilla warfare.[25]

Of course, some of Jomini's principles, especially his emphasis on offensive warfare, overlapped with irregular, counterinsurgency strategy and tactics proven effective in French colonial warfare.[26] On the other hand, based on the experience of guerrillas' and partisans' effective harassment of Napoleon's troops in invasions of Spain and Russia, Jomini had warned against unconventional wars such as developed in French Algeria and in US conflicts with Indigenous Americans and during the Civil War. In "national wars" and "civil wars," as Jomini termed them, where a whole people were called to fight, his principle that armies should mass their forces against a specific point in the opponent's force would be moot. Guerrilla and even irregular warfare, for Jomini, besides presenting different challenges from conventional combat between armies, tested soldiers' commitment to behave chivalrously; civilians, in any case, he maintained, should be treated with courtesy and justice.[27]

Jomini's attitude towards *petite guerre* contrasted with that of Thomas Bugeaud, the influence of whose development of counterinsurgent strategy on the nineteenth-century American military has gone unappreciated. With a background in the Napoleonic Wars and urban riot control for the July Monarchy, Bugeaud, as France's fifth governor-general in the new colony of Algeria, abandoned a predecessor's approach merely to maintain various small garrisons against assaults by the leader of Algerian forces, Abdelkader. Bugeaud realized that various aspects of war in Europe had no place in North Africa. As Thomas Rid puts it, "There were no enemy positions that could be attacked, no fortifications, no operationally relevant locations, no strategic deployments, no classical lines of communication, no adversarial army, [and] no decisive battles."[28] Bugeaud thus adopted tactics of the *razzia*, marrying the lethality of European war technology and the unpredictability and the moral ambiguity of colonial conflict.[29]

Various US soldiers worked to bring Bugeaud's way of war to the United States; the informality of this conveyance helps explain its historical obscurity. In 1845, Lieutenant Miner Knowlton, a West Point instructor of cavalry and artillery tactics, served as an aide-de-camp to Bugeaud in Algeria. The next year, he participated in the US occupation of Texas that precipitated the Mexican-American War.[30] Stationed at Corpus Christi, Knowlton applied knowledge from North Africa in combating Mexican guerrillas who preyed on American supply lines. As in Algeria, Americans held whole villages and towns responsible for insurgent attacks. Six additional American officers, including future Civil War generals Philip Kearny and John Wool, studied at the French military school at Saumur between 1832 and 1840 and brought similar lessons back to the United States. French veterans of the Algerian campaigns were teaching new tactics based on their experiences fighting desert Bedouins and mountain tribesmen.[31] Kearny negotiated a position for himself with the Chasseurs d'Afrique, with whom he participated in several combat engagements. He then returned to the United States with a report that praised strategies that offset Abdelkader's penchant to attack French troops "with the suddenness of our own Indians." Kearny delivered a translated copy of the French cavalry manual, which the War Department issued in 1841 as *Applied Cavalry Tactics as Illustrated in the French Campaign*.[32] Meanwhile, in the Mexican-American War, Wool, like Knowlton, drew upon his exposure to counterinsurgency warfare with the French military. In charge of suppressing guerrilla attacks, Wool enforced collective responsibility for nearby depredations, organized protected hamlets for Mexicans pledging neutrality, hanged Mexicans who killed discharged US soldiers, and enforced levies of money and livestock on villages near US forces.[33]

Kearny's was not the only antebellum US military manual that drew on lessons from French Algeria. There was also *The Prairie Traveler*, published in 1859 by Captain Randolph Marcy, a book based on his decade of service in Texas and the Indian Territory. *The Prairie Traveler*, despite its innocuous name, was the most important work on frontier warfare published by the War Department.[34] In it, Marcy highlighted the influence on his thinking of French General Eugène Daumas's *Le Grand Desert*, an 1848 memoir that mixed exotic tales of life in the Sahara with analyses of French ways of war developed there.[35] Daumas served in Algeria from 1835 to 1850 and from 1841 onward headed the Arab Bureau, established to collect data on Algeria's Indigenous population. Marcy wrote that the "manner of making war" practiced by North African Arabs and "the wandering tribes that inhabit our Western prairies" were "almost precisely the same."[36] Marcy drew on Daumas's description of French counterinsurgency to prescribe how US forces should travel through Indian-inhabited regions, use advance and rear guards, forge relationships with tribes, and track elusive enemies.

It was not only US military officers who acknowledged French Algeria as a model for counterinsurgency strategy. In a report to President Franklin Pierce in 1856, US Secretary of War Jefferson Davis emphasized how French experience on its African frontier shaped his interest in preparing the US cavalry for territorial duty. Davis recommended a system to administer the American frontier that had, he felt, "much parallelism" to Algeria. Beyond the fact that the trans-Mississippi West and North Africa shared desert and mountainous terrain, other factors "afford[ed] us the opportunity of profiting by [French] experience." The Indigenous Americans of the Southwest, Davis anticipated, would prove susceptible to counterinsurgency strategy that the French had developed: deployment of troops near settled areas in sizable garrisons capable of projecting force "wherever it is deserved." Such a strategy had instilled in "the [Algerian] native tribes," Davis erroneously noted, "such respect for [French] power that it has seldom been found necessary to chastise any tribe a second time."[37] Davis's anticipation of Americans' reliance on garrisons to house frontier soldiers, from which they would launch razzias on Indians, reflected how US officials seeking to build a territorial empire were adapting French colonial, not Napoleonic, military practices. After the Civil War, the US conquerors of Davis's Confederacy deployed his counterinsurgency strategy in the Great Plains. It is not ironic that in the antebellum era, Davis, representative as an ambitious American imperialist, was eager to apply Algeria's lesson to US southwestern expansion.[38]

The Flying Column

To be sure, Union generals early in the war adhered closely to Napoleonic methods. Most conspicuously, George McClellan, commander of the Army of the Potomac, particularly focused on the capture of key places and, as in the 1862 Peninsula Campaign, sought to avoid costly battles—important emphases of Jomini.[39] In July 1862 even General William Sherman, commanding the Army of the Tennessee, ordered that it would be a "lasting disgrace" for any officer to be found ignorant of "the principles of the Art of War (Mahan and Jomini)."[40]

But novelties of the war eventually led innovative, perhaps desperate Union forces to eschew Jominian principles and widen the scope of the war, creating a logistical and moral context for display of evidence that Union military and political officials adapted means of warfare honed by French forces in Algeria. In 1863 the Civil War, especially once Britain and France did not intervene on behalf of the Confederacy, intensified as a "national" struggle, heightening the role of civilians and civilian morale in the war's outcome. The nature and severity of Confederate guerrilla and partisan warfare in border areas of Missouri, Kentucky, Tennessee, and Virginia blurred the distinction between soldiers and civilians and helped excuse US forces' plunder of Southerners' private property and destruction of the Southern landscape far from the battlefield. And the Confederacy's response to the US military's recruitment of men formerly enslaved, pursuant to the Emancipation Proclamation, that such troops, if captured, would be treated as fugitive slaves provided Union officials a basis for declaring the war a conflict between forces of "civilization" and "savages."

A first step in the Union military's movement away from Jominian warfare was its turn in 1862 toward a more rapidly deployable force: the flying column. Flying columns were military units with ancient origins, but by the early nineteenth century they were a formation commonly deployed by armies against unconventional enemies, a relevant context in which to understand the Union military's eventual treatment of the South.[41] In Algeria, through experimental, harsh, and ultimately successful combat against Abdelkader's insurgent forces in the 1840s, General Bugeaud embraced the Algerian razzia tactic—"the ruse, the raid, and the ambush"—and adapted it for usage by flying columns, which included a few battalions of infantry and squadrons of cavalry, one or two howitzers, and a small transport train by mules or camels.[42] Bugeaud's goal was to increase the frequency of French contact with Algerian troops and to destroy Algerian people's sustenance, enabling superior French firepower to become more intimidating and decisive.

Figure 2.1. Une razzia en Crimée la Veille Du Réveillon: Sauve qui peut, malheu-reux qui est pris [A Razzia in Crimea on New Year's Eve: Run for Your Life, He Who Is Caught Is Unfortunate]. From *Affaires d'Orient* (Wild, 1855). Collection De Vinck (Histoire de France, 1770–1871), Bibliothèque Nationale de France.

The US military, of course, had previous experience with swift-moving irregular forces, even as recently as the Crimean War, when razzias entered Europeans' lexicon (see fig. 2).[43] A *New York Times* reporter there attributed French troops' superior performance to their experience in Algeria.[44] But the development of flying columns, and eventually resorting to brutal tactics of the French razzia, can be found in such evidence as a plan provided to the Union armies by Alexis Godillot, a French man better known as an innovative tanner who first changed footwear from being identical on both feet to having a right foot and left foot. Since at least 1848 Godillot had supplied uniforms to the French army, including its forces in Algeria, and in 1860 wrote a study that documented General Bugeaud's logistical innovations there.[45] Godillot sought to devise the means for French soldiers in the field to carry all necessary equipment on themselves, thus dispensing with supply trains entirely.⁴⁶

The Civil War afforded Godillot the occasion to help Bugeaud's way of war cross the Atlantic. Frequently a visitor to the United States in the 1850s to buy machinery for his textile factories in Saint-Ouen-sur-Seine, in October 1861 Godillot supplied US military equipment and uniforms modeled on the French light-infantry *chasseur* for ten thousand soldiers.⁴⁷ He also provided a sketch of the organization of a French colonial flying column. US Quartermaster General Montgomery Meigs received Godillot's paper and, on January 2, 1862, distributed it as a circular, conceptualizing columns of two thousand infantry, four hundred cavalry, two artillery pieces, and fifty horses. Troops were to be organized into squads of eight, each man carrying compressed rations and specific camp or medical supplies. Initially, wagons were replaced by mules, except for resupply after each march. As Meigs's translation of Godillot read, "Go on thus, advancing always. Alarm the enemy, break up his camps, and keep always advancing. These are the tactics which the French army employs with success."⁴⁸ On March 7, 1863, the Army of the Potomac distributed Special Order No. 85, calling for implementation of Godillot's plan, with the goal to create lighter, more agile forces that were less dependent on supply depots and wagons. A year later that doctrine was foundational to Ulysses Grant's adoption of "hard war" against the South. In giving Grant overall command of Union forces, President Abraham Lincoln ominously assured Grant he should prosecute the war without "any restraints."⁴⁹ To the extent that Union strategists adopted French military practices, Grant's orders culminated a pivot from the Napoleonic doctrine of Jomini to the counterinsurgency doctrine of Bugeaud.

While several Union commanders honed tactics in counterinsurgency against irregular Confederate forces, it was William Sherman's broad punitive warfare against the people of the Deep South that most illustrates adaptation of French warfare in North Africa. Tasked to hold territory and protect supply lines earlier in the war than in the East, Sherman's forces in the western theater were more vulnerable to guerrilla attacks. He thus adopted harsh war techniques beginning in 1862 in Mississippi, subsequently moving through Tennessee, Alabama, Georgia, and the Carolinas. Sherman embraced the new Union military emphasis on troop mobility and logically authorized soldiers to supplement, and, in Georgia, replace their rations with food confiscated from the countryside. Beyond that, as a rule, Sherman instructed his forces generally to treat all Southerners not aiding Union troops, "old and young, rich and poor," as the enemy and to consume or destroy everything in their path as they moved.[50] Sherman's forces shelled towns without warning, razed villages, and destroyed farms and railroad lines. Sherman ordered the evacuation of Atlanta, stranding its residents in the countryside or deporting them out of the state by train. Elsewhere, to dissuade Confederate cavalry from mining railroad lines carrying Union supplies, he threatened to load prisoners and civilians on the trains. Approaching Savannah, prisoners were made to walk in front of Union soldiers to explode or detect and dig up Confederate land mines.[51] At the end of 1864, Sherman would interpret these ways of war as markers of the Civil War's differences from conflicts in Europe, as Jomini had anticipated: "This war differs from European wars in this particular," Sherman wrote. "We are fighting not only hostile armies, but a hostile people, and must make young and old, rich and poor, feel the hard hand of war, as well as their organized armies."[52]

The Lieber Code

Union troops' prosecution of the "hard hand of war" clearly went beyond any prewar doctrine of warfare prescribed by Napoleonic French and US military theorists. Some legal scholars have concluded that at least some elements of Sherman's brutal Deep South campaigns violated not only modern laws of war but even the contemporaneous Lieber Code, declared on April 24, 1863.[53] The code's principal author, Francis Lieber, like Jomini, was a veteran of the Napoleonic Wars. But the extent of the Civil War's casualties; its legal ambiguities regarding civilians, spies, prisoners, and partisan troops; and the Lincoln administration's interest in justifying the Emancipation Proclamation and sanctioning the status of people formerly enslaved sparked Lieber's authorship of a "modern law and usages of war" different from Jomini's prescriptions.[54] Lieber claimed that his goal was to differentiate the "modern regular wars of the Europeans, and their descendants in other portions of the globe [including the US military's]" from warfare practiced by "uncivilized people" and "barbarous armies."[55] Lieber, in other words, sought to distinguish the American Civil War from European colonial wars.[56]

Couched in terms of differentiating between Europeans and their descendants and uncivilized people, however, the Lieber Code effectively licensed Sherman's harsh war measures in the Deep South—which were actually characteristic of European forces fighting outside European borders, particularly

French warfare in Algeria. The code identified all "citizen[s] or native[s] of a hostile country" as the enemy.[57] Everyone was therefore susceptible to war's hardships. It allowed the execution of prisoners in retaliation against the enemy's unlawful behavior and execution of spies and irregular fighters. It allowed the shooting on sight of individuals suspected of trying to commit sabotage. It allowed the starving of unarmed enemies and the bombardment of civilian areas without warning. It allowed destruction of all enemy property and "incidentally unavoidable" destruction of any person.[58] Ultimately, it held that the "paramount" consideration of legal warfare was the saving of the nation-state, which, Lieber wrote, "must be maintained at any price, under any circumstances."[59] Thus the Lieber Code sanctioned extreme violence against civilians, many of whom may have shared the perception of Alabamian John Parrish that US forces "would exterminate our race if they could. They will make it a war to annihilation if they can."[60] One Southern periodical's threat early in the war that the people of the South "will become as savage as the Seminoles" and another newspaper's comparison of Robert E. Lee to Abdelkader were perhaps unintentionally prophetic.[61]

Apparently, neither Francis Lieber nor William Sherman had read specific literature on French colonial warfare as a source for shaping military doctrine or practice in the later years of the Civil War. Still, they each had opportunities to learn about that French way of war. Lieber had corresponded in the 1840s with Alexis de Tocqueville concerning the history of American westward expansion, the character of settlers, and their relationship with local and national political authorities. As a member of the French parliament, Tocqueville consulted Lieber to gather information to help formulate Algerian policy near the end of the July Monarchy.[62] Tocqueville, famous as the author of *Democracy in America*, actually hoped Algeria could, like the American frontier, produce democratic opportunity and metropolitan renewal. And Lieber wrote his code at the request of Henry Halleck, general-in-chief of the US Armies, who had visited France to study the French military before publishing the leading US military science textbook, in which he recommended French forces' response to their "savage and undisciplined" Algerian enemy as a guide for the US military's response to "the Indians in this country."[63]

Meanwhile, although published in the Confederate capital of Richmond, Thomas Bugeaud's commentaries on his Algerian war strategy appeared in English in 1863. In addition to principles of infantry tactics, the book also included a section titled "International Law and Usages of War" that had not appeared in the book's earlier French version.[64] Bugeaud's laws of war were similar to those promulgated the same year, 1863, by Lieber, pointing toward a convergence of doctrine shaped, on one hand, by unconventional colonial combat and, on the other, by warfare between conventional armies grappling with the usages of new technology and the degenerative nature of civil war, "so terrible for the sake of humanity," as Antoine-Henri Jomini had warned after witnessing partisan warfare in France and Iberia.[65]

To be sure, both the Lieber Code and Bugeaud's description of international law affirmed that human rights bounded justifiable military action: the Lieber Code stated that principles of "humanity" governed the exercise of martial law and the treatment of prisoners; Bugeaud pledged that "rights of humanity" were "above necessity and rights of war."[66] However, like Lieber's statement that a soldier's obedience to laws of war was subject to whatever was necessary to save the country, Bugeaud declared, "Necessity knows no law. . . . No general, loving his country, hesitates to put himself above ordinary rules." For Bugeaud, like Lieber, the vindication of the nation-state justified resort to various illicit war tactics.[67]

Thus, said Bugeaud, unlike laws of "humanity," laws of war permitted "terrible" and "cruel" actions, including destruction by asphyxia, compulsion of civilians to house and feed soldiers, and taxation or confiscation of "all things appertaining to the enemy . . . [that] belong by right to the conqueror." Bugeaud distinguished, as did Lieber, between "civilized nations" and "barbarians" and indicated that razzias could be a legitimate means of war waged only against the latter group. Bugeaud did not define a razzia, but his description of acts of an enemy that could justify a razzia anticipated Sherman's rationale that all Southerners should suffer what he acknowledged was his forces' "barbarity and cruelty": Bugeaud asserted that razzias were justifiable "when the entire [enemy] population . . . participat[ed] generally in the acts of hostility."[68] Thus, such a justification for Sherman's resorting to "hard war" could be found in the Confederate South as much as in French North Africa.

While Sherman officially prohibited his troops' theft and destruction of private property in the South, he echoed Bugeaud in his interpretation that Southerners collectively were savages—"all of the people are now guerrillas. . . . The entire South, man, woman, and child are against us, armed and determined."[69] As a consequence, Union forces needed to "imitate" Southerners' resorting to terror as the necessary means to "colonize the country."[70] Sherman anticipated that Southerners should "dread the passage of troops through their country."[71] The Union general here echoed Jefferson Davis's antebellum praise for the French cavalry's power to instill "such respect . . . that it has seldom been found necessary to chastise" Algerian tribes more than once. More to the point, Sherman echoed Bugeaud's report of an attack on stubborn Kabyle tribes in Algeria's Tell Atlas mountains. For Bugeaud, the French troops' "appalling work of destruction is undoubtedly cruel," yet "the information we have received suggests that this incursion has induced a sense of terror in all the Kabyle tribes because it has shown that we can go wherever we want. . . . There are simply no other means of conquering this extraordinary people."[72] Broad acceptance of razzia warfare in the Atlantic military world by the 1860s, and the Lincoln administration's need to justify warfare against all Southern civilians, shaped Union forces' adaptation and rationalization of brutal counterinsurgency techniques honed in French North Africa to conquer the "savage" people of the South on account of their resistance to the preservation of the US nation-state.[73]

The Plains Wars

To be sure, neither US nor French military doctrine during the nineteenth century officially prescribed counterinsurgency warfare strategy or tactics. As late as 1900, General Samuel Young, governor of the Philippines' Northern Luzon military district during the Philippine-American War of 1899–1902, urged that French publications on colonial warfare be made mandatory reading at West Point.[74] Both countries' continued study and planning for conventional warfare happened for several reasons. French and American military planners deemed Arabs, Indigenous Americans, Southern rebels, and Filipinos "uncivilized" and not worth acknowledging through doctrinal reform. Unconventional frontier warfare remained controversial, expensive, and unheroic, prioritizing adaptability, not technique. The need to transport supplies and forage by wagon train to support territorial forces exacerbated the inherent frustrations of subduing much more mobile irregular fighters. And in France and the United States, the fortification of the nation's borders against a conventional enemy's invasion remained the priority.[75]

Nonetheless, Sherman, promoted to commanding general of the army in 1868, sanctioned "hard war" practices in the Plains Wars of the late nineteenth century that bore the markers of counterinsurgency warfare practiced during the Civil War and reflected a renewal of antebellum efforts by the federal government to incorporate the West.[76] Several of the most effective commanders of US forces in the post–Civil War West, including

Philip Sheridan, George Crook, and Philippe Régis de Trobriand, extrapolated Sheridan's techniques in the Shenandoah campaigns and Sherman's practices in his Savannah and Carolinas campaigns of waging war by relentlessly attacking Indigenous peoples' foodstuffs and shelter. In 1869, Sheridan was charged as commander of the Division of the Missouri to drive the Comanche in Texas and the Sioux and Cheyenne on the Northern Plains onto reservations. To guide his accomplishment of these orders, he drew on experiences in Virginia in 1864, when General of the Army Grant instructed Sheridan to invade the state's Shenandoah Valley in order to turn the region into what Grant said should be a "barren waste."[77] Sheridan was to ensure "that nothing should be left to invite the enemy to return" and to inform Virginians "that so long as an enemy can subsist among them recurrences of these raids [could] be expected." On the principle that poverty, not death, was war's great punishment, Sheridan destroyed all food, forage, farms, and livestock—actions that a participating officer described as both "horrors" and "necessities of war."[78] Sheridan's order to raid Virginians suggested the suddenness with which Union forces were expected to attack anyone merely near insurgent activity and to destroy their livelihoods—an example of the principle of collective responsibility that had become central Union military doctrine, linking conduct of the French war in Algeria with the Civil War and the Plains Wars.[79]

Especially after the end of Reconstruction, the US military size was severely reduced to an annual average of twenty-five thousand troops who became widely scattered west of the Mississippi River.[80] Partly to overcome the sparse number of his troops and the slow mobility of conventional travel by wagon trains, Sheridan readily adopted razzia tactics on the Plains. To gain an element of surprise, Sheridan organized his cavalry into columns to descend on Indian villages from different directions. Different from most Civil War campaigns, Sheridan's cavalry attacked in the winter, when the tribes' horses were weak from lack of forage.[81] Sheridan advocated extermination of bison to destroy Indians' food and clothing supply.

Sheridan believed that because of their race and cultural background, Indian peoples of the Plains were too cowardly to stand and fight against US cavalry. Other US commanders, including General George Custer, shared this belief, which, as shown at the Battle of Little Bighorn, was sometimes proven false. That hubris was not the attitude of George Crook, who served as a lieutenant in California and Oregon in the 1850s and then fought principally in the Civil War's eastern theater. In 1864 he commanded the Army of West Virginia in Sheridan's Virginia campaigns. Crook's experience trained him as a sort of counterinsurgency specialist; while committed to conquest, he, more than Sheridan (and Custer), sought to understand Plains Indians' societies. Like French officers who learned Arabic language and Algerian peoples' cultural ways to develop counterintelligence, Crook endeavored to learn tribal languages in order to learn "all these little secrets of the inner Indian which control his baser part." In 1861, as a colonel of the 36th Ohio infantry regiment, Crook enacted what he called "Indian country . . . kind of warfare" to deal with guerrillas in West Virginia's Greenbrier Valley. He used spies to identify guerrillas and enforced a no-quarter policy toward anyone captured.[82]

Besides acquiring actual experience, Crook probably learned the practice of irregular warfare through knowledge of War Department publications about French warfare in Algeria, including the studies of Phil Kearny and Randolph Marcy. After the Civil War, Crook developed tactics in the Sioux War of 1876 and the Apache War of 1886 that eschewed wagon trains for mules to gain mobility and recruited Indians to serve with him against their own tribes, which not only assisted in tracking a moving enemy but served as a psychological weapon when tribes learned their own people were providing Crook assistance.[83]

Finally, Philippe Régis de Trobriand was a French immigrant whose uncle served as a general in Algeria in the 1830s. De Trobriand arrived in New York in 1841 and led the New York 55th infantry regiment, the Lafayette Guards, at least one of whose companies was a Zouave unit. He rose to the rank of brigadier general by 1864 for distinguished service in the Army of the Potomac, including commanding the repulsion of Confederate assaults on the second day of the Battle of Gettysburg.

De Trobriand did not gain the experience of "hard war" acquired by Sherman, Sheridan, and Crook during the war but learned quickly after he was appointed in 1867 to command military forts in the Dakota and Montana territories. De Trobriand embraced the extension of "hard war" to encompass the annihilation of tribes as a means of warning others about resistance. In reporting on an expedition against Blackfeet people encamped on the Marias River in January 1870 that resulted in the killing mainly of women, children, and elderly men who were members of a tribe that had already submitted to the reservation policy, de Trobriand wrote that the attack had manifested US "power on the whole of the Blackfeet nation . . . who henceforth will carefully avoid bringing upon themselves a similar retribution." Echoing the mixed reaction provoked by inhumane actions by the French military in Africa—praise among European settlers accompanied by criticism among

Paris-based critics of colonialism—de Trobriand was feted with torchlight parades in the territory for "rid[ding] the territory of its fiendish foes" while "philanthropists in the Eastern states opened a crusade of denunciation" against him, Sheridan, and Sherman over what is now known as the Marias Massacre.[84] Perhaps in response to civilian critics in Washington, and in contrast to his candor as a general in the saddle about the draconian nature of his campaigns in Georgia and the Carolinas, Sherman wrote Sheridan that reports of military butchery of the Blackfoot people should be suppressed.[85] But de Trobriand openly acknowledged the likelihood, if not intent, of such surprise raids to end in atrocities: "The confessed aim is to exterminate everyone. If extermination were not achieved, just another burden would be added—prisoners."[86]

De Trobriand, meanwhile, emulated General Crook in enrolling in volunteer companies Indigenous Americans at war with hostile tribes and those who were "familiar with [their] habits, ideas, and languages."[87] De Trobriand used native people not only as scouts and trackers but also as regular soldiers, although in combat he authorized them to fight according to their custom. "In this way," he wrote, "the red [sic] companies would render the same services to the government as the native tribes of Algeria rendered to France."[88] Here de Trobriand referred to French deployment of Algerian *goum* ("people") native troops, principally cavalry auxiliary forces. *Goumiers*, incentivized mainly through promises of plunder, like the US military's Indian Scouts, provided vital service in tracking Algerian fighters beyond the range of European troops and in enabling French infantry to surprise and destroy whole civilian encampments. "Cries of alarm are shouted, shots are exchanged, terror spreads throughout the valley," recalled a veteran of one such razzia. "Women, men, and children flee toward the only exit which the terrain offers them, but they find the *chasseurs* [*d'Afrique*] and the *goumiers*. Bullets fly in all directions, the sabers of the cavalry kill a large number of the enemy. . . . No one escaped death."[89] Both the US and French militaries continued the goum tradition of attempting to develop loyal military units from local national communities, with both success and failure, into recent time.

In 1870, General Philip Sheridan visited France as a military observer of the Franco-Prussian War, on the Prussian side. The United States declared neutrality during the war, but Sheridan's location reflected unofficial US support for Prussia in the wake of the earlier French invasion of Mexico and the more recent transatlantic impact of the Paris Commune.[90] Sheridan had been the chief practitioner of the Union's brutal warfare in Virginia during the Civil War's latter stages and became central strategist for the renewed

American Indian Wars. In France, Sheridan took it upon himself to advise Chancellor Otto von Bismarck that he should take the lesson of Sheridan's Shenandoah Campaign to deal with the *Francs-tireurs* who were carrying out guerrilla attacks on Prussian supply lines during the siege of Paris. Bismarck thereafter gave the order to burn all French villages and hang their male inhabitants found near guerrilla activity and to bombard Paris with heavy artillery despite the presence of children. Witness to Sheridan's counsel of Bismarck, future Chief of the German General Staff Alfred von Waldersee recalled Sheridan's comment that the Prussian army had "hit" the French enemy but "not yet learned how to annihilate him. One must see more smoke of burning villages, otherwise you will not finish with the French."[91]

The irony of Prussian forces' usage of counterinsurgency tactics to subdue the French Second Empire, prescribed by a US general, himself drawing on French practices in North Africa that US forces had borrowed and adapted, was probably lost on Sheridan. On the other hand, the outcome illustrated how counterinsurgency warfare, from development in Algeria to adaptation in the American South and West to deployment in Paris's suburbs, was "highly imitative" long before the turn of the twentieth century.[92] This example of a transimperial, if contextualized and contingent, military tradition bolsters arguments against a singular US "way of war" ingrained from early in the country's history.[93] In this period of "endemic, world-wide violence" of "dispersed" yet severe and sometimes total warfare, colonial wars, postcolonial wars, and wars of national unification were connected not only by nation-state building but by expansion of military targets and the erasure of Westerners' assumptions of differences between civilized and savage military forces.[94] From this perspective the American Civil War did not become different from "all the wars of Europe," as William Sherman later characterized his campaigns.[95] Seen as an extension of Americans' earlier settler wars and Americans' selective adaptation of French military doctrine in terms of the Union's development of strategy and legal treatment of insurgents in the South and West, the Civil War era was, in fact, far more like a European colonial war than has been previously acknowledged.

Chapter 3

The Limits of Republican Citizenship

In the spring of 1919 representatives of people of color in Africa, Asia, and the Americas descended on Paris during the Paris Peace Conference to lobby for the exercise of rights that US President Woodrow Wilson had declared to be inalienable to all peoples. Most representatives, including those of Egypt, Vietnam, India, China, and Cuba, requested independence or an end to foreign military occupation to restore real sovereignty to their governments. Two other delegations, however—those speaking for natives of French Algeria and for African Americans—requested not independence but simply full citizenship. Khaled ibn Hashimi, or Emir Khaled, led a group of *jeunes Algériens* reformers who called for representation of Indigenous Algerians in the French parliament, the abolition of the Code de l'indigénat, which instituted specific offenses that denied Algerians the due process guaranteed to French citizens, and the naturalization of Indigenous people as French citizens without the renunciation of their personal status.[1] Khaled's petition called French rule a "so-called republican regime" whose special laws would "shame the barbarians themselves."[2] Meanwhile the African American scholar and Pan-Africanist W. E. B. Du Bois, of the National Association for the Advancement of Colored People, led the drafting of resolutions calling for equal rights for persons of African descent who were "civilized and able to meet the tests of surrounding culture."[3] While Du Bois elsewhere called for Germany's former African colonies to become independent under the stewardship of the League of Nations, both Khaled's Algerian and Du Bois's African American documents instead merely emphasized republican rights of representation as a means of individual assimilation into the nation-state.[4] In response to the jeunes Algériens, French Prime Minister Georges Clemenceau made it easier for certain Algerian men to become French citizens and raised to one-third the fraction of Algerian local government councils open to Muslims, but no evidence suggests that President Wilson, despite his leadership of the United States and enunciation of self-determination of all peoples, met with Khaled or Du Bois or seriously considered their arguments.[5]

Important roots of Khaled's and Du Bois's respective petitions for citizenship and Wilson's ignorance of them lay in the mutually constitutive history of French Algeria and the American South in the half century before the Paris Peace Conference. This perspective provides a useful context for appreciating the similarly ambiguous status of Algerians and African Americans by locating their stories within the broader consolidations of territory by the French and American empires in the last decades of the nineteenth century. Previously, historians have determined that in terms of men receiving the right to vote and a promise of equal protection under national law, former slaves in the United States were generally better off than their counterparts in Haiti, the British Caribbean, and southern and eastern Africa but less well off than in Cuba and Brazil, where a larger proportion of non-white people resided.[6]

In its post–Civil War civil rights and land policies toward the freedpeople, the United States resembled not only other postslavery societies but also France, specifically in French ideas and practices of citizenship in Algeria that Emir Khaled wished to bring to Woodrow Wilson's attention. Of course, the two situations had several notable differences. In the antebellum United States, slavery had legally separated the races in the South, and black codes did so in parts of the North. In contrast, in keeping with the national principle of universal equality, until the mid-1860s, French policy was that European settlers and Algerians, in the words of Marshal Thomas Bugeaud, the colony's governor-general from 1841 to 1847, were "everywhere to intermingle," not to live separately, under a policy of *rapprochement*.[7] The US South, about three times the size of French Algeria in 1870, comprised a thriving economic system of the United States whereas Algeria remained economically sluggish. After four decades of military rule, by 1870 Algeria had attracted only some 270,000 Europeans, including 150,000 French people, among some 2.1 million Algerians.[8] In contrast, two-thirds of US Southerners were white.[9] Officially, for most of the nineteenth century, French policy distinguished between the peoples of Algeria on the basis of religions, Christian and Muslim, and made renunciation of Islam a basic requirement for Algerians to gain French citizenship.[10] In the United States, white and Black inhabitants of the South were largely Protestant Christians, and obviously no American could renounce his race.

Likewise, where French imperialists repeatedly insisted that France should "assimilate" Algeria as a trans-Mediterranean French department (actually, beginning in 1848, the three departments of Alger, Oran, and Constantine), there was never a premise for the US government to call for assimilation of the contiguous Southern states or their inhabitants, before or after the Civil War (1861–65).[11] In the United States the traditional federal system and the South's white majority, similar to the North, obviated the question of assimilation, even during its military occupation. To be sure, from 1866 to 1870, Radical Republicans orchestrated the "restoration" of the former Confederate states to the United States, meaning moving gradually from military occupation at the end of the war toward Southern states' regaining congressional representation through ratification of the Constitution's Fourteenth Amendment. In this process Radical Republicans sought to utilize "war powers to hold open the possibility of revolutionary change" in the South.[12] While *assimilation* seemed to exaggerate the extent to which Algeria could be treated as an integral part of France, *restoration* was a euphemism for the subordinate status that, in the 1860s, Radical Republicans intended for the postwar authority of the national government over the Southern states. In the United States, the South, strong or weak, stood apart.

Yet even given all of these differences, French Algeria and the US South were similar imperial spaces, and not only as regions sharing a common tropicality of climate, topography, and kinds of diseases, viewed by outside reformers in need of gradual uplift.[13] Before the 1860s they were both loosely administratively connected to their respective national governments, even though Algeria was under military authority. Antebellum Southern elites, in fact, studied the French army's occupation of North Africa for lessons on territorial conquest, and some proslavery Americans interpreted the French conquest as an encouraging sign that American slavery's expansion was in step with European imperialists' appetite for coerced labor.

The Civil War's destruction of slavery, however, as scholars have shown, inspired reformers across the Americas and Europe about the possibilities of republican government and nourished hopes for universal emancipation among plantation slaves and urban workers alike.[14] The abolition of slave property in the United States vindicated free labor as the basis of a nationally integrated economy, marked the triumph of the new US state, and provided an ideological and moral premise for the extension of national jurisdiction into formerly remote areas of both the American and French republics.[15]

This chapter's argument, however, is that the late French Second Empire and early Third Republic and the post–Civil War United States together retreated from such liberal measures. Both the US and French governments declared new policies of republican government and equal citizenship—different from the colonial practices of Britain, to which scholars have compared each regime.[16] Practice of this egalitarian policy, however, became limited by other priorities of republican ideology and rule that diminished enforcement of national citizenship rights. Specifically, the prioritization of local or provincial rule elected by qualified citizens, accomplished through the disenfranchisement of de facto colonized peoples, created a system of contingent citizenship for people of color in areas of the country newly under national law.[17]

Thus, if policies in the late 1860s in both the French and US empires promised to use new national power to protect the civil rights of people of color, the 1870s reversed that momentum. French defeat in the Franco-Prussian War in 1871 sprouted the short-lived Paris Commune. From the wreckage of the Second Empire and the Commune emerged the French Third Republic, whose paradoxical policies of *fusionnement* and the Code de l'indigénat coincided with the end of Reconstruction in the United States, when new national rights began to erode.

Thus, a view of the policies of incorporation developed in the United States and France from 1865 to World War I shows the commonality of their administration of citizenship among African-descended residents of conquered territories as well as their occasional but important inter-imperial exchanges and adaptations. In the period, US state-builders' anxieties over French socialism dampened support for central government authority in the South. French imperialists, meanwhile, were determined to integrate Algeria with France no less than they perceived that the United States had stitched the American West and East together through migration and agriculture. To do so, however, they needed to make Algeria more like the American South than has been recognized.[18]

French Views of the American Civil War

French opponents of Emperor Napoleon III praised the Union during the Civil War and the first years of Reconstruction on account of the exercise of power by the US government, an elected civilian regime, to defeat secession and destroy slavery.[19] Agénor de Gasparin, a liberal Protestant reformer living in exile in Switzerland due to his opposition to the French emperor, quickly published two books upon the war's outbreak that an American woman, Mary Booth, translated into English for publication in New York City. Gasparin hailed the Northern cause for two reasons: its defense of minimal government, "that form par excellence of liberalism," but also its establishment of a new kind of confederation, a "nation with a central preponderance" of force, sufficient to conquer secession. Gasparin considered the proslavery South, before its military defeat, to have been beholden to a "reign of terror." The slave power, said Gasparin, "sought to force the nation into the path of socialism," not merely for spreading slavery but also, in a transparent analogy to the French Second Empire, on account of its opposition to civil liberties of thought, the press, and religion.[20] Likewise, Auguste Laugel, US correspondent for the newspaper *Revue des deux mondes*, emphasized that the Civil War had "put an end to the fatal contradiction between servitude and liberty" by restoring "to the executive power the force which the democratic school had deprived by decrees."[21] Many French liberals considered the abolition of slavery and preservation of the Union in 1865 a triumph of national civil rights development in the United States.[22]

Other French commentators, however, foresaw problems that would thwart meaningful practices of those rights. The conservative *Le Monde* newspaper interpreted the Civil War as a conflict of sectional interests that military conflict had not resolved. Although slavery was abolished, Northerners' interest in African Americans' welfare was, likely, hardly genuine. "Their philanthropy is a mask which they will put aside when they will no longer have need of it," warned *Le Monde*.[23] Gustave Paul Cluseret, a Paris-born mercenary who served as a Union general before returning to France to join the Paris Commune as its deputy of war, reached the same opinion. Writing to US Senator Charles Sumner in the spring of 1865, Cluseret called for land to be confiscated from rebels and sold to the freedpeople and Union veterans. This would constitute the only true fulfillment of a second American "revolution."[24] Cluseret was not confident, however, that President Andrew Johnson, whom he considered a counterrevolutionary no less than Napoleon III for his defiance of Congress, would allow that possibility.

Another skeptical French voice was that of Georges Clemenceau, writing for the newspaper *Le Temps*.[25] A recent medical school graduate, Clemenceau arrived in New York City in 1865 after fleeing the Second Empire for publishing a newspaper that commemorated the 1848 Revolution and criticized Napoleon III. Clemenceau did not travel in the South other than to Richmond, Virginia, yet he advocated for the freedpeople's economic empowerment. He agreed with the demands of Gustave Cluseret and US Congressman Thaddeus Stevens, a Radical Republican, that former slaves should be granted land as well as voting rights. Later an advocate of Algerian people's rights, Clemenceau described the freedpeople as "a nomad population," destined to be "forced to submit to the harshest terms imposed by their former masters" unless awarded land by the national government. He warned, "There cannot be real emancipation for men who do not possess at least a small portion of the soil."[26]

On the other hand, Clemenceau believed that the freedpeople's civic ignorance, combined with an essentially conservative Reconstruction policy and encrusted segregation in the South, would limit any real change from conditions of bondage.[27] In January 1867 he declared the South was an "area uninhabitable for men with ties to the Union," but already he could not imagine the United States confiscating and transferring former Confederate land to the freedpeople. This was the central demand of Sumner and Stevens, but not even the bulk of Radical Republicans favored such a redistribution of wealth.[28] Foreshadowing the doubts of Liberal Republicans in the 1870s, Clemenceau thus believed that "blacks" were "deluded . . . to imagine" that former slaveholders' property "ought to belong to them."[29] Their reluctance to follow rules of the Freedmen's Bureau, a US Department of War agency intended to provide relief to and ensure labor rights of freedpeople, made "it seem difficult to confer citizens' rights" on them because they had not "come to a wholesome appreciation of the duties entailed by citizenship."[30] Clemenceau further predicted that Southern whites would reject the "political servitude" induced by the military occupation of the South during Radical Reconstruction while the former slaves learned the duties of citizenship (and he did not indicate how the freedpeople were to learn those duties).[31] Clemenceau, enamored of Thaddeus Stevens but also more perceptive of US postwar conditions than French observers who had not seen those conditions firsthand, anticipated the problem that land inaccessibility and embittered race relations in the South posed for meaningful exercise of Black citizenship.[32]

Algeria at the End of the Second Empire

Even as only a possible vindication of a liberal, centralized authority curbing the prerogatives of states-rights aristocrats, the outcome of the US Civil War created pressure for France to reform the rule of its own provincial territory, Algeria. That response was tentatively signaled when Napoleon III, returning from an African tour where he learned of the end of the US Civil War, declared a new policy toward France's North African departments.[33] In 1863 the French emperor had written that Algeria was not a colony but an Arab kingdom under the French Empire, where European colonists and Algerians should be separated. A national Sénatus-consulte of the same year made "the tribes or fractions of tribes the incommutable proprietors of the territories that they currently occupy and claim as their traditional homes."[34] In 1865 Napoleon wrote to the Algerian people a promise to put them in the same "class" as the French, and a Sénatus-consulte on July 14 of that year reiterated protection of Algerians' religious expression and claims to land they occupied and declared that Indigenous Muslims were French, to be governed by Islamic law.[35] Beyond this, however, Algerians, upon renunciation of Sharia law, could leave the Arab kingdom and be admitted "to enjoy the full French citizen rights," meaning public employment, education, medical care, and eligibility for voting and office-holding in local government councils, as well as military service.[36] An 1866 directive praised Berbers particularly as potential French citizens, "enterprising as Protestants . . . [and] as democratic as Americans."[37] The Second Republic had declared Algeria an integral part of France in 1848 and, in its short-lived era, offered rights of citizenship and suffrage to the few Europeans then resident in Algeria.[38] Napoleon's decrees in the 1860s went substantially further than these previous measures.

Scholars previously have noted that the US Emancipation Proclamation may have helped to spark Napoléon's interest in intervening in Mexico, in anticipation that the US Civil War was likely to embroil North America in a race war.[39] But two years later the Union victory, accomplished, as President Abraham Lincoln insisted, via slavery's constitutional abolition, provided context for the French emperor not only to abandon the prospect of a Francophilic Mexican monarchy but to redefine French Algeria. The North African departments would be segregated, but French national law now outlined a path, albeit tortuous, to French citizenship for Algerians. The 1865 Sénatus-consulte occurred one year before Congress, overriding President

Andrew Johnson's vetoes, passed the country's first Civil Rights Act and granted Black men in the District of Columbia the franchise.[40]

In other words, suggesting the transnational impact of the beginning of Radical Reconstruction, the Civil War's promise of equality to the freedpeople through centralization of power provided momentum for the French government to confirm the opportunity for Algerians to enjoy equal treatment under French law with European *colons*, and to have land they occupied sequestered from European settlement. Though fitted to different territorial circumstances, one broadening national law by enforcing land reservation, the other replacing plural state laws with standard national law, both regimes declared national civil rights for people previously disenfranchised.

In imposing a moratorium on Europeans' territorial settlements in Algeria, Napoleon III rationalized that Algerians, though they were a "warlike" race, were also, or might become, an "agrarian" people, an important part of French designs for Algeria. During the American Civil War, Algeria's potential value as a cotton-growing enterprise had, indeed, attracted heightened interest as the Union embargo cut France off from southern cotton and then the war destroyed cotton's American slave labor.[41]

Yet French settlers on the ground did not share Napoleon's confidence in Algerians' capacity for large-scale agriculture. Analogous to many white people's attitudes about freedpeople in the American South, European settlers believed nomadic Arabs were "ignorant, vulgar, lazy, [and] lying," in the words of a wealthy colonist, the comte de Raousett-Boulbon.[42] Europeans "rail against the Arabs and constantly talk about driving them out into the desert, but nonetheless trust them to do all the work," lamented Elisée Reclus, a geographer and tutor on a Louisiana plantation in the 1850s before he returned to France in 1871.[43] Resentment of Napoleon's declaration of Algerians' right to naturalization thus grew among the European *colons*— less ethnically united than white Southerners but likewise suspicious by the 1860s of a distant metropolitan government. Views among Europeans critical of Arab indolence and incapacity for farming land that they presumed to possess mirrored prejudices against Black capacity for free labor in the American South.

These factors, coupled with the prospect of the failure of US civil rights policy during Radical Reconstruction, which Georges Clemenceau warned of in *Le Temps*, sparked imaginative solutions to France's problem of sparse white agricultural settlement in North Africa. Although French observers doubted that the freedpeople were likely to gain equal treatment in the United States, they recognized them as reliable agricultural laborers and

Christians—qualities that French imperial planners had been keen to emphasize in attracting Europeans to Algeria since the 1840s.

Thus, some surprising ideas emerged among advocates of French expansion in Algeria in the 1860s, even including resettlement of African Americans there. The promotion of these ideas intertwined schemes of empire-building and republican assimilation and citizenship, a variation on what the British writer James Bryce called "qualified democracies" in the British colonial system, and what scholars have previously considered distinctive practices among the "Anglo-Wests" of Australia, North America, and South Africa.[44]

One such promotion of an American colony in Algeria, probably the first, was expressed in a pamphlet published in 1866 by Pierre-Charles de Saint-Amant, a former French diplomat and chess champion who retired to Algeria in 1861. Earlier in his life, Saint-Amant had been the secretary to the governor of French Guiana before being dismissed for condemning the colony's slave trade. He was an officer in the National Guard formed by the provisional government of the Second Republic in 1848 but then threw support to Louis Napoleon when Napoleon was elected president in December of that year. For his loyalty he was appointed as the first French consul in the state of California and published a memoir of conditions there.[45]

Saint-Amant did not witness US slavery or the conditions of freedpeople firsthand, yet his sense of incurable post-emancipation land competition and race animosity resembled the views of American supporters of Black colonization, possibly shaped by his reading of *Le Monde* and the sober observations of Georges Clemenceau in *Le Temps*. "The Negroes in the United States are entwined with whites, are linked with them without being able to be equal. These two races of different colors, which can never unite, must separate." In his pamphlet, Saint-Amant traced the history of US colonization projects, citing the support of presidents Thomas Jefferson and James Monroe, and the history of Liberia, the West African republic originally established by the American Colonization Society, although he regarded Liberia as a failure. He declared that the US federal government's assertion of authority to emancipate the slaves was a "revolution" against the Southern states' sovereignty. But he anticipated the coming rejection in the United States of Radical Republicans' plans for racial integration, and he shrewdly predicted how white Northerners and Southerners would reconcile their differences, to Blacks' exclusion and subordination.[46]

Saint-Amant appeared aware of writings since the days of Alexis de Tocqueville among French observers of the United States anticipating the extinction of American Indians as well as of predictions, based on this analogy, of the fate of Indigenous Algerians.[47] His pamphlet appeared in the wake of earlier writing of Eugène Bodichon, a physician and ethnographer in Algeria who, in the 1840s, had observed that despite what he saw as Euro-American benevolence, the precarious conditions of American Indians, as a predictor of the future of Algerians, "ran quickly towards the extinction of their race."[48] Indeed at the end of the Second Empire in 1870 the Muslim population of French Algeria was at its lowest ebb.[49] American writers who after the Civil War called for separation of the "Anglo Saxon and Negro" races cited, for comparison, Bodichon's theory of autogenocide among Algerian Arabs.[50]

Like other critics of the excessive government centralization of the Second Empire, Saint-Amant opposed Napoleon III's philanthropy toward people on France's Mediterranean frontier to save them; here his loyalty to the French emperor ended. Saint-Amant argued that Algerians' uncivilized ways after a generation under European rule resembled the squandered "wandering and adventurous life" of Indigenous Americans. But he refocused previous French arguments about autogenocide of minority peoples residing in white-occupied national territory. For Saint-Amant, disappearance would be the fate of the American freedpeople if they were to remain in the United States, on account of heightened white hostility to the national government's declaration of their US citizenship: "If [white and Black Americans] continue to tread the same ground, the smaller will perish."[51] He anticipated American emigrationists' arguments as late as the 1890s, that life in the United States would cause Black extermination.[52]

Resettled in Algeria, on the other hand, Saint-Amant predicted that American freedpeople would flourish. France's history of abolitionism showed a long commitment to former slaves whereas for him the American Civil War "addressed the issue of slavery with less preparation than it had been at home in 1848," when the French Second Republic declared the end of colonial slavery. Saint-Amant envisioned settlement on land south of the Tell Atlas mountain range that traditionally marked the edge of European settlement. There, he predicted, "sands [will be] transformed into lush vegetation."[53] The fields of North Africa would yield readily to farm laborers skilled in agricultural work and removed from scenes where the work had been extracted by force and without compensation. African Americans and European colonists shared the common bond of the Christian faith, a "guarantee of union between us" as opposed to the "idolatrous and barbarous" Indigenous laborers of Africa. In his cultural attraction to the freedpeople, Saint-Amant imagined Algeria not only as a "space of conviviality" where Black immigrants would receive better treatment because they were American but as homesteading equals to white settlers.⁵⁴ "We call the free people of color from America, who [will] prefer our commitment in Algeria with the title of French identity, to remaining American without free enjoyment of political rights." Noting antebellum discrimination against Northern Black men who were technically US citizens on the basis of having voting rights, Saint-Amant, like other French observers, perceived as a chimera American reformers' pursuit of the right to vote as the central attainment of citizenship, more than land possession.⁵⁵ On the more open French frontier, he predicted, American freedpeople could start anew and there serve as "honest and free citizens."⁵⁶

Saint-Amant's plan to offer the freedpeople French citizenship was novel, but his resettlement scheme was not entirely unique. Other French Algerian writers, like Bodichon, had encouraged the resettlement of sub-Saharan Africans in Algeria as farmers. He and others wrote that under French supervision they had more of a chance of civilization and an embracing of a work ethic than under Muslim control. As Jean-Jacques Baude, a deputy during the July Monarchy, had written in support of French use of slave labor in Algeria, "Immersion in white society seems to be the means by which Negroes become capable of liberty." If Saint-Amant's and others' schemes as possible policy in Algeria were not debated by metropolitan policymakers, their vision provided a rationale for recruitment of Black soldiers and farmers, whose programs were adopted by the Algiers Chamber of Commerce and many civil administrators from the 1870s.⁵⁷

Likewise, Saint-Amant's intended destination of the freedpeople and their means to travel echoed previous American schemes of colonization. President Lincoln and Congress supported colonization of free Black Americans as late as 1862, and about sixteen thousand black emigrants left the United States for Liberia during and after Reconstruction through the American Colonization Society and similar organizations.⁵⁸ Interest in emigration was greatest among lower-class African Americans.⁵⁹ Meanwhile Algeria was not the only African destination for which European imperialists would court American Blacks. In 1901 Booker T. Washington's Tuskegee Institute was invited to send an expedition to the German colony of Togo with the purpose of transforming the region into a cotton economy similar to that of the post-Reconstruction South.⁶⁰ W. E. B. Du Bois took note of Saint-Amant's pamphlet in a 1905 bibliography of works on African Americans selected from "all the great collections of *Americana*."⁶¹

But Saint-Amant's pamphlet does not seem to have circulated in the United States. In the early twentieth century Du Bois and other pan-Africanists did not quite see French Algeria as a part of Africa, particularly in the context of other Black migration schemes to Togo and Liberia. Saint-Amant's publication lacked a level of detail and realism to be considered a real possibility for African Americans at the time. It remained unclear in the pamphlet how European settlers in Algeria would respond to Black colonization, despite their alleged religious kinship.

How the American freedpeople were to acquire land was also unrealistic. Saint-Amant advocated African Americans' expatriation to Algeria because there they could become citizens through land settlement, presumably undisturbed by neither central government administrators nor racist neighbors with too vivid a memory of old times not forgotten. Anticipating that US central government power wielded during the Civil War could also aid his scheme to ensure that free African Americans could gain the benefits of French citizenship outside the United States, Saint-Amant ingeniously imagined his plan unfolding through a French-American treaty negotiated for the purpose. But this was public support for expatriation that the US government showed no inclination to offer after ratification of the last of the Reconstruction amendments in 1870. Americans' passage of national laws abolishing slavery, declaring equal protection under the law, and barring race requirements for voting eligibility, saluted by liberal French observers interested in the United States as an imperial model for France, actually began the end of US federal protection of freedpeople's civil rights; definition and maintenance of those rights would soon revert to US state authorities. Saint-Amant's stillborn plan for a North African American colony suggests the frustrated boundaries of Atlantic and West African "spaces of conviviality" for people of color in the late nineteenth century.

Still, Saint-Amant's pamphlet was significant for its realistic appraisal of the problems of citizenship likely to arise among African Americans, absent access to easily accessible land. In its idea to use the freedpeople to make France's African frontier prosper via land-based citizenship, it confirms how the freeing of American slaves fired the imagination of ideologues in the 1860s willing to consider Algeria a heterogenous French imperial region.

1871 as an Inflection Point

Historians have dated the problems of Reconstruction to which Saint-Amant alluded to the early 1870s—a turning point in postwar policy. The Republican war hero Ulysses Grant won the US presidency overwhelmingly in 1868, but by 1871 political terrorism and violence enacted by the Ku Klux Klan became widespread. The Panic of 1873 influenced voters to return a Democratic majority to Congress in 1874. Grant's second term was marked by federal judicial decisions that restricted African Americans' rights and Democrats' consolidating their white voting base by emphasizing white supremacy and lower taxes. At the same time, the free labor doctrine of the Republican Party became clarified to mean principally the need for workers to remain employed. Meanwhile, industrial labor strife in the 1870s and efforts to maintain wartime federal power bled into hysteria that disaffected or unmotivated African American workers might prove dangerous to the American republic. In the words of one white Southerner who might have inadvertently anticipated the attitudes of European colonists who were witnesses to American freedpeople settling near them in Algeria, "Negro commonwealths" on which African Americans might be experimentally situated could be used for "mak[ing] war upon our own [white] countrymen."[62]

Parallel political events—people of color's reactions to the specter of violence—occurred in Algeria. In reaction to steps toward unification of the German states following the Austro-Prussian War of 1866, France declared war on Prussia on July 19, 1870, but the war was a disaster for the Second Empire. Napoleon III was quickly captured, and, following the French army's surrender to Prussian forces in January 1871, rural French people, the church, and the military supported the conservative government of the Third Republic that was reestablished at Versailles. But socialists, urban workers, and anarchists founded the Paris Commune at the traditional revolutionary center of Paris, the Hôtel de Ville, and refused peace terms. Hoisting the red flag of revolution, Commune leaders Auguste Blanqui, Félix Pyat, and Louis Delescluze declared a workers' republic, setting government salaries at the level of a skilled worker and taking unused private property to house the homeless and to enable trade unions to establish cooperative workplaces. In May 1871 the French Third Republic was proclaimed as the French army sought to subdue the Commune, whose partisans built barricades, executed the archbishop of Paris and thirty priests, and destroyed various monuments of the Second Empire. In response, government forces shot over one thousand Communards, precipitating a struggle for Paris that left some twenty-five thousand people dead. The Commune, many partisans of which were exiled to Algeria, became principally associated with the bloodshed.[63]

While the role of the Paris Commune in the decline of the political fortunes of African Americans has been noted by a few scholars, the similar ways its perception undermined rights of people of color in the American South and French Algeria has not been recognized.[64] In both places the Commune's revival of a "reign of terror," a common literary phrase during the 1870s, defeated confidence in central government authority to define and enforce national, equal citizenship in areas of the two republics where people of color were most populous (even as the same fears rationalized military crackdowns on striking industrial workers).

To be sure, some Americans praised the Paris Commune as an analogy justifying Radical Reconstruction governments headed by African Americans, accompanied by nominal US military forces in the South. They did so by invoking a typically ephemeral American sympathy for new French republics on the basis of their likeness to the American founding. For example, the Radical Republican Benjamin Butler declared that "the Commune of Paris were [sic] fighting for the right of local self-government. . . . The commune had the example of our fathers as a precedent." Indeed, the Commune's Central Committee's Declaration to the French People stated that Paris had simply claimed municipal rights as a free autonomous and sovereign body and invited other communes to do the same.[65] Butler's confidence in nascent African Americans' political power was not shaken by the Commune's assertion of radical democracy.

But more widespread American views were expressed by journalists Horace Greeley, E. L. Godkin, James Shepherd Pike, and Edward King, who condemned, in King's words, "African communists . . . consummating, as a Commune assembled in Paris . . . infamy which it effects as a Legislature in South Carolina" and other Southern states.[66] Taken as a foreign analogue of what Black politicians in the South were pursuing during Reconstruction, the Commune thus encouraged mainstream American commentators and policymakers to define legitimate self-government more as *local* government than as *representative* government in the postwar South—the two attributes of republicanism were not necessarily compatible. For these observers the conflict in France in 1871 was illustrated by the arrogance of the Communard republicans "to dictate a form of government" to the majority of the country outside the metropole.[67] This same kind of conspiracy, necessary to implement the freedpeople's interests as new citizens, seemed to be taking hold in the US South. At the extreme, African American leaders appeared "as if they belonged to a foreign nation," wrote *The Nation*; indeed, they seemed to "bec[o]me . . . French"—clearly a pejorative association.[68]

Suggesting the reverberation of the Commune in US jurisprudence, in 1873 the US Supreme Court determined in the *Slaughterhouse Cases* that only very limited rights of national citizenship were protected by the new Fourteenth Amendment to the Constitution. The case, decided amid the political and economic "chaos" of Reconstruction and "recrudescence of revolution in Europe," helped strengthen institutional opposition to national civil rights laws.[69] In France the Paris Commune actually represented an assertion of the rights of local government, but its impact in the United States, paradoxically, was to discourage centralized enforcement of civil rights: Freedpeople's citizenship rights were to be determined by local civilian governments.

The similarity of the Paris Commune's signaling of an important pivot in French colonial policy and US civil rights policy is striking. Certain Republicans in Congress and commanders of the South's military districts during Radical Reconstruction were able to extend military rule in parts of the former Confederacy, including arrest and trial of Klan terrorists, oversight of fair elections, and even outright replacement of state officials with ones more sympathetic to Black civil rights. This regime, creating "a geographically expansive sense of national sovereignty," continued through the fall of 1870, when the elected representatives of Georgia, the last "restored" state, were seated in Washington. Congress's recognition of civilian rule independent of military—meaning federal—authority meant the erosion of representative government in the South. In the summer of 1865 the *Army & Navy Journal* opined, "Force . . . is the constitutional means of establishing republican government." But within five years most Americans' fears and fatigue about a standing military began to thwart Reconstruction's "republican revolutionaries."[70]

The same period saw the French Third Republic renounce the centralizing policies of Napoleon III in order, it could be said, to redeem Algeria in response to demands for home rule by French and other European settlers in North Africa. Policies adopted in Paris were driven by an uprising in Algiers among disaffected settlers generationally exiled to North Africa by the Second Republic and the Second Empire. Alienated by a lack of representation in the French Parliament, rule by centrally appointed military governors, and restrictions on land settlement, settlers reacted to the Prussian war defeat by establishing a Committee of Public Safety, called an "Algiers Commune."[71] In the name of liberal republicanism, the Algerian communards, like their namesakes in Paris, advocated civilian, not military, and local, not national rule.[72] Like American redeemers of the South they rejected socialism, expressed in ridicule of Napoleon's Arab kingdom and demand for land privatization.[73]

Home Rule and the Irony of the Statue of Liberty

A leading ideologue for this reform was Édouard Laboulaye, a constitutional scholar and antislavery activist who was famous as a proponent of a statue as a French gift to the United States, later known as the Statue of Liberty. After the Civil War, Laboulaye completed the three-volume *Histoire des États-Unis*, in which he argued that colonial American history could be a model of self-government for French rule in Algeria, replacing martial law. He wrote, "Give the province of Algiers independent representation . . . [and] imitate the wise provision that began the prosperity of Virginia: leave the colony to its laws, subject to the veto of the metropole." Likewise essential to Algeria's redemption would be the ending of collective property rights. In colonial New England as well as, again, in Virginia, wrote Laboulaye, when settlers had acquired land, they became inspired to be "very industrious, and they tried to outdo each other in . . . [erecting] buildings and other amenities of life."[74] Lately historians have argued Laboulaye was prompted by the US Civil War to advocate for stronger French imperial authority in Algeria to, "at least in theory, expand the rights of those [Algerians] brought under the nation's sway."[75] But in the early Third Republic the practice of French republicanism, parallel to similar developments in the United States, would be to undermine Algerians' potential fruits of citizenship. This was the irony of liberal democratic institutions at the time: their application gave assertive white residents in territorial areas the opportunity "to create their own independent power base."[76]

Indeed, in response to the Algiers coup d'état, and under the strain of the Prussian army's siege of Paris, the Third Republic quickly announced sweeping reforms in Algeria. It replaced military with civilian rule, expanded European Algerian deputies' representation in the Parliament, declared French citizenship for Algerian Jews (but not Muslims), extended European *colons'* authority over previously self-governing tribal reserves, and disavowed the Second Empire's guarantees of grain replenishments for Muslim farmers.[77]

These measures, intended to end what one critic of Napoléon's 1863 Sénatus consulte had labeled "Arab communism," precipitated the insurrection of Muhammad El-Mokrani, a Kabyle Berber sheik, involving some 150,000 Algerian troops.[78] Indicative of the stakes posed by the triumph of local white civilian authority over the liberal nationalism of the Second Empire, El-Mokrani requested that Prussia release the captured French emperor, Napoleon III, from prison, even offering to pay ransom, and to restore him to his throne.[79] Mokrani's rebellion was put down in January

Figure 3.1. From Adolphe Messimy, *Le Statut des indigènes algériens* (H. Charles-Lavauzelle, 1913). Bibliothèque Nationale de France.

1872 after French forces that earlier had crushed the Paris Commune could be deployed in Algeria. In the aftermath, French authorities exiled leaders of the rebellion to French New Caledonia and punished the Muslim population wholesale, confiscating in the next two decades some 1.5 million acres of land and placing the Kabyle region of northern Algeria, where the rebellion had started, under a *régime d'exception* (extraordinary rule).[80] In 1881 the régime d'exception would be codified under the Code de l'indigénat (see fig. 3).[81]

Echoing how the former Confederate states achieved national reconciliation and economic integration via subordination of African Americans,

France thus moved toward assimilation of Algeria through cohabitation of its peoples under race-segregated laws and subject to the caprices of local officials who could flout national citizenship prescriptions.[82] The Code de l'indigénat criminalized acts not punishable under French law, including insolence and unauthorized assembly, and empowered the governor general to jail non-European suspects without trial and then force them to labor. Representation of Muslims in Algerian communes was limited to one-quarter of the municipal councilors.[83] Meanwhile anecdotes circulated of Algerians who requested naturalization to be told by local bureaucrats, "Why do you need to get naturalized? You will have difficulties in your family, your wife is not likely to [sic], your son-in-law will seek quarrels."[84] Similar to the US Census of 1890, which produced racial categorization by instructing enumerators to identify individuals as "Black," "Mulatto," "Quadroon," or "Octoroon," by 1900 the French census used "Muslim" as a racial category to identify Arab, Berber, Mozabite, Moroccan, Tunisian, and "Other" Algerians, including Christians.[85]

African American and Arab leaders who negotiated for greater civil rights in this era adopted some similar strategies of resistance to their respective republics' laissez-faire turns. Both groups declared their loyalty to the state, but both also rejected assimilation, instead embracing their racial differences from whites. They also utilized national patriotic days as moments to call attention to their respective people's disenfranchisement. Educator and orator Booker T. Washington, for example, like W. E. B. Du Bois at the time, emphasized that African Americans should take pride in their race and should study their own history as essential elements to "aspire to the highest and best things in life" and to win white people's respect.[86] Similarly, Emir Khaled, brought as a teenager to Algiers in 1892 but educated at a prestigious French military college, declared that he was French "in his heart and soul" yet remained "proud of [his] race" and jealous of his religion.[87] George Washington Williams, a Black military veteran (including, coincidentally, service with Mexican republicans against the French puppet Emperor Maximilian) and historian, used a centennial address in 1876 to show African Americans' role in founding the United States and to recall Black troops' vital defense of the Union during the Civil War. After slavery had "wasted our army and emptied our national treasury," said Williams, the enslaved African American "threw down his hoe, took up his musket, and saved the country."[88] Likewise the jeune Algérien Taïeb Morsly argued that protest against French settlers' and administrators' discrimination was "imbued with the ideas and great principles of the Revolution of 1789."[89]

Algerians, like African Americans, sought equal rights by locating their contemporary circumstances in the national history of the republic.

Yet, as in the United States, restrictions in Algeria on citizenship of people of color, legal and extralegal, remained until after World War I a means of ensuring equal citizenship among white populations interested in maintaining provincial distinctiveness, grounded partly in pride, distinctive from the larger country, and in maintaining rustic or "folk" traditions.[90] Known as a marker of the US federal government's sanctioning of Jim Crow law, the 1896 case *Plessy v. Ferguson* used language that French officials might also have expressed, honoring "the established usages, customs, and traditions of the people [of the state of Louisiana]" and "the preservation of the public peace and good order."[91] At this time, French citizens in Algeria (as well as the colonies) were covered by the *Code civil*, while natives, still the majority of the population, were governed by local custom. Officially not colonies but instead outlying areas being incorporated into the metropolis, the post–Civil War South and French Algeria, alike in their practice of local white rule, gave "an aura of normality to other colonial practices," albeit in the language of republicanism.[92] Both regimes manifested patterns of tenant farming among people of color, a shortage of funding for public education, and erection of a segregated society.[93] The similarity was inadvertently acknowledged, for example, by a criticism levied by Louis Vignon, a former cabinet minister for colonial affairs and professor at Paris's École colonial, of French government spending on Algerian children. In 1887, Vignon noted, French spending on indigenous education in Algeria amounted to 219,000 francs whereas, "according to a U.S. Indian Affairs report for 1878, the Five Civilized Tribes in Indian Territory, Cherokees, Criks [sic], Choctaws, Chickasaws and Seminoles," benefited from "about 690,000 francs ... [spent on] 198 schools with 5.993 children."[94] Vignon meant to criticize the French government's relatively low financial investment in territorial secondary education by contrasting it with the American public investment in American Indian education. But Vignon missed the fact that US government spending on education in the South during Reconstruction ended in 1870, reflecting a public hostility suggested by the *New York Evening Post*'s comment that continued federal aid for education in the South would promote "mendicancy."[95] The French and US regimes were alike in only gesturing toward national civic education in areas where most people of color on the margins of citizenship actually resided.

Occasional American eyewitnesses to French Algeria's racial organization also commented on the two regimes' similarity and attested to their connections. An example was Poultney Bigelow, a student and son of former US Minister to France John Bigelow, and the artist Frederic Remington, who traveled together in Algeria in 1893. Transported by train to the southern edge of the Atlas Mountains, Bigelow noted how the train's segregated cars, separating white passengers from Berbers, Jews, and Arabs, resembled "our Jim Crow cars in the former slave states."[96] The pair then rode horses into the Sahara Desert, an escape that they, like a few other visiting romantic American literati, falsely envisioned as an "ahistorical place seemingly untouched by the modern era."[97] In the desert the Americans met a French cavalry force. Recognizing their fascination with the exotic native troops of the Armée d'Afrique, a French officer, "Capitaine du Moulin," unaware of the history of Americans' borrowing of French irregular military practices, offered the Americans some advice: "You would have equally good results with your North American Indians if you treated them as justly as we do our Arabs."[98] Inspired by exotic scenes of these rifle-wielding Arab horsemen—a model "Mustafa . . . stood . . . straight as a Mohawk, and equally inscrutable"—Remington rendered several paintings in the Orientalist style, romantic linkages he envisioned between Plains Indians and Algerian Bedouins. A more material, if ironic, linkage of Arab and American that Remington painted was that the Arabs' rifles were probably produced by Remington Arms, which proliferated in North Africa via sales from the company's direct customer, the government of Spain.[99]

In an article for *Harper's Magazine*, Bigelow, meanwhile, deftly countered Captain Moulin's assertion of the "just" French treatment of Algerian Arabs, suggesting that he, at least, was not oblivious to French depredations that embedded what one scholar called "instabilities in the colonial order."[100] The Americans visited an Arab "chief," "El Hadj Ahmed Ab d'el Kader ben el Hadj Mohammed," probably a *qa'id*, or local administrator co-opted to enforce French authority. After a lavish meal of roasted goat, Bigelow wrote, he fell asleep and dreamed that el Hadj Mohammed had sentenced him to die on account of his mistreatment of Algerians. Bigelow recalled the Arab's damning words: "For fifty years you have kept my people in slavery," making war, encouraging moral debauchery, and stealing livestock. "This night you die." Bigelow awoke just as el Hadj Mohammed's tribesmen lifted swords to dismember him, surely as a surrogate culprit for French crimes.[101] Not as psychologically troubled as Bigelow, philanthropic French imperialists claimed that "just" treatment of Indigenous peoples was symbolized through the opportunity for Algerian men to perform military service, as in the United States—an early justification for providing rights of citizenship to men of color.¹⁰² More generally, Algeria, with a non-white population density more like the American South than the West, became reconstructed like the former American region, even if intrepid tourists like Remington and Bigelow did not fully perceive the similarity.

Thus, specifically, in Algeria the Code de l'indigénat of 1881 offered citizenship to Algerian men who renounced rights and responsibilities under Muslim law. But this era also signaled the Third Republic's new commitment to a policy, following the arguments of the liberal reformer and imperialist Paul Leroy-Beaulieu, of *fusionnement*, or the careful commingling of different racial populations. Like contemporaneous US policy toward African Americans, the policy was designed to make the Algerians Arab French. This meant situating them within the national boundaries, subject to local laws and economic expectations and especially attachment to the soil and development of agriculture as a means of education and assimilation, *all the while* segregated politically from white society and without expectation of immediate citizenship. In 1903 Leroy-Beaulieu's counterpart in American society, Booker T. Washington, called this process "the secret of civilization" that African Americans should accept in order "to start [their] upward course" from de facto colonial citizenship.¹⁰³

Dedicated in New York Harbor in 1886, the Statue of Liberty, the fulfillment of Édouard Laboulaye's admiration of US constitutionalism and salvaging of liberal political principles suppressed by Napoleon III, symbolized the fruition of the Civil War's inspiration of reformers during the French Second Empire to hope and strive for the triumph of democratic institutions in France and elsewhere. Democracy did recover in both France and the United States. However, its compromises in liminal spaces of central state authority undermined practices of national equal rights and citizenship for non-white inhabitants. It is no surprise, then, that by the early twentieth century the Statue of Liberty became a symbol of rights of immigrants, not of native-born peoples of color.¹⁰⁴

In the long era of Reconstruction, empire-builders in the United States and France undertook analogous practices. Each regime selected evidence and images from the other's experience to shape its territorial policies: US policymakers and ideologues sought to avoid French-style socialism in rebuilding the post–Civil War South; their French counterparts sought to replicate US frontier conquest in Algeria. The outcome was two regimes of liberal republican rule, meaning rights of constitutional citizenship bound by national governments' deference to provincial political authority, fostering racially mixed, agriculture-dependent societies under segregated conditions: analogous, central locations of their countries' particularly republican empire-building.

Such a paradoxical triumph, sparked by the abolition of slavery and erected via racial ordering, is a cautionary tale about the triumph of race-blind citizenship in the Atlantic world after slavery. It suggests that the defeat of Radical Reconstruction, giving way to the South's redemption, while perhaps the historical nadir of African American citizenship, was not unique in the era; US policies in the post–Civil War South both shaped and were shaped by French incorporation of Algeria for settler development as *La France nouvelle*.[105]

Chapter 4

A French Wild West

At the 1889 Paris Exposition the official US proceedings were overshadowed by the impact of Buffalo Bill and the Wild West Company. The showman William Cody's spectacle of Indians, white Americans, African Americans, Mexicans, and Canadians packaged a fictional space called the Wild West, which, according to Mark Pottinger, for French spectators *"was* American history." A dual attraction of Buffalo Bill's Wild West was its symmetry with France's own dazzling display of racial and cultural diversity of colonial peoples under French hegemonic—"civilizing"—authority.[1]

The symbolic kinship of civilizing conquest shared by the US and French exhibitions in Paris in 1889 is part of a larger American story of frontier ideology, grounded in territorial expansion, that the two countries shared in the late nineteenth century. Territorial expansion has lately been shown as a type of Anglo-American settlement, part of a "settler revolution" that occurred during the long nineteenth century.[2] In that period the English-speaking world boomed in population and prosperity. Frontier areas came to be seen as scenes of opportunity and symbols of empire, not places of exile or anarchy. Steamships and railroads moved people and trade goods between the metropolis and the colony. Canada and the Australian colonies of Great

Britain passed homestead acts shortly before and after the US Homestead Act of 1862, offering similar land opportunities for white settlers. Indigenous people, earlier treated as trading partners and strategic allies, became seen as illegitimate occupiers of underdeveloped land. Among Anglo-American settler societies encompassing both rural and early urban development, the United States most rapidly integrated new states with the homeland.[3]

This chapter shows that while the US territorial empire shared commonalities with its Anglo-American cousins, it also shaped ideas about territorial expansion of imperialists in France, a similarly ambitious, expanding republican empire. From the 1830s through the turn of the twentieth century, French writers interpreted images and urged adaptation of specific policies of the United States concerning territorial integration. The imperial neighborhood of the United States was not only English-speaking.[4]

To be sure, the two countries came to their similar circumstances following different paths, and their territories remained different in important ways. The US western territories were part of the North American mainland, and US policy from the country's founding was to treat new territories as areas where white settlers enjoyed the same rights as citizens. The French occupation of Algiers initially treated Algeria as royal "possessions" delegated to military governors general; only in 1848 was Algeria declared an "integral," if trans-Mediterranean, part of France, and only in 1889 did European settlers gain French citizenship.[5] Moreover, an essential challenge for French imperial ideologues was the fact that the Algerian population continued to outnumber and live near all European settlers from France and elsewhere, despite early projections that it would, like the Indigenous population of the Americas and Australia, suffer precipitous population decline or flee beyond contact with white settlers. From 1850 to 1900 the European population in Algeria rose by 575,000 to nearly 700,000 settlers who lived alongside some 3.6 million Algerians. That was about a third of the population growth rate over the same period of the US trans-Mississippi West, where the 1900 US Census recorded more than 18 million residents, including 237,000 American Indians, about 123,000 of whom lived on western US reservations.[6] Comparing the two territorial spaces on the basis of their legal treatment of settlers and Indigenous populations emphasizes their differences.

Nonetheless, the two countries shared imperial attributes. As a means of territorial assimilation, they both offered national citizenship to people of color via naturalization beginning in the 1860s—in France through the Sénatus consulte of 1865, in the United States through the Constitution's

Fourteenth Amendment.[7] Both saw frontiers as areas for producing or resurrecting democracy. Both suffered national trauma through wars that toppled conservative regimes and established in their place governments more committed to liberal republican rule: The Civil War destroyed the Confederacy; the Franco-Prussian War toppled Emperor Napoleon III.[8]

More than showing similarities, several French reformers interested in regenerating France's *mission civilisatrice* sought Algeria's development based on their perceptions of Americans' experiences. French interest in the United States rose, particularly after the Franco-Prussian War, in a sort of jilted response to new American enthusiasm for German methods and out of concern that "blue-water colonialism" was the best option for France in the face of emerging German power in Europe.[9] Somewhere between wishful thinking and concrete policies, these reformers' ideas and practices ran parallel to the French public's fascination with the US West as an affirmation of their own country's imperial power and "cultural renewal," expressed, for example, in response to performance and visual representation by visiting American artists and actors and Indigenous Americans.[10]

While various examples of Anglo-American territorial settlement patterns interested ambitious French imperialists during the nineteenth century, there were two notable issues in Americans' experiences that gained attention concerning Algeria. One issue concerned the question of what should happen to the land in Algeria, particularly concerning how and where it could be peopled by European settlers. Who from Europe, France particularly, could be expected to make a "New France" in Algeria, and what answers to that question could land usage provide? A second issue was the question of what would happen to the Algerian people under French rule, given the example of the fate of Indigenous Americans after the arrival and expansion of Anglo-American settlement in North America. Were Algerians likely to become extinct? If not, should they be separated from Europeans, or should the two groups assimilate?

These two questions were debated during much of the first forty years of French occupation of Algeria. They then intersected beginning in the first years of the Third Republic, established in 1871, when advocates of civilian governance of the territory, principally as an instrument to achieve that end, called for assimilation, not separation, of Algerians through broad privatization of Algerian land. And, somewhat paradoxically, the US Homestead Act became a focus of attention at this time for how it was perceived to offer egalitarian, orderly, and attractive private land ownership in Algeria.

French-American Land Reforms 1830s–1850s

In the United States, both the practice of selling public land for cheap prices—$1.25 an acre under the Land Act of 1820—and the land reform movement had begun in the early republic, accelerated by President Andrew Jackson's removal of Indigenous Americans from the southeastern states and the Panic of 1837.[11] In the antebellum era, Southern lawmakers, some of whom raised the specter of French socialism as a warning against government regulation of property, thwarted efforts in Congress to adopt a western homestead law.[12] Still, advocacy for free distribution of public land to homesteaders emerged in the 1840s. In 1844 pamphleteers for the National Reform Association emphasized that opportunities in the United States should be kept "remote . . . from the arbitrary constitutions of Europe," which they feared encouraged land monopoly.[13] That same year an Illinois representative first introduced a homestead resolution in Congress.[14]

From nearly the beginning of the French occupation of Algeria, meanwhile, there were connections between it and the US frontier. The second French governor in North Africa, General Bertrand Clauzel, had farmed in Alabama from 1815 to 1820 and in the 1830s drew on his experience to publicize Algeria as a "Mediterranean Alabama," meaning a potential supplier of cotton, sugar, and other colonial products for Europe. Clauzel's advocacy assumed that landowners would actually cultivate these goods, which was not always the case. The problem of land speculation in the US West and French Algeria resulted in land being left fallow in its owners' hopes of its value appreciating, a problem that in the United States provided the spark by the mid-nineteenth century to land reform activism.

In the 1840s, the French goal in Algeria expanded to attempt occupation of its Tell and northern Sahara regions, which required planning for a settler colony committed to agricultural development. In 1846 the European settler population in Algeria was some one hundred thousand and for the first time outnumbered French soldiers. Mixed French recruitment efforts resulted in half of the colons arriving from Spain, Malta, and the states of Italy and Germany, suggesting how French Algeria would, from its origins, have a European diversity similar to that of the US West.[15]

Probably three-quarters of the first settlers remained in or near fortified towns, however.[16] Upon first glimpsing Algiers in 1841, Alexis de Tocqueville, ten years earlier a visitor to the United States and a notable supporter of the French conquest of Algeria, remarked on the "prodigious mix of races and costumes . . . tossed together in a space much too tight to contain them."[17] Tocqueville meant to applaud the arrival of Algiers' new inhabitants, but his observation also suggests that most of them stayed near established coastal urban areas. Reflecting on his visit to the United States in 1835, Michel Chevalier, an imperial advocate like Tocqueville, expressed this tendency to congregate in a different way: "The Yankee alone in the woods, with no companion but his wife, is all-sufficient for himself ... [whereas the] Frenchman cannot become interested in any industrial enterprise except in connection with others. ... It is quite impossible for him to fall in love with a *clearing*."[18] Tocqueville and Chevalier, writing in the first years of the French presence in Algeria, revealed the challenge that a significant hostile Algerian majority population would pose to attempts to transform the region into a frontier of self-reliant farmers.[19]

Shortly after its establishment upon the February 1848 revolution, the French Second Republic passed various radical reforms, including the abolition of colonial slavery and establishment of labor workshops for the unemployed. But regarding Algeria, the Second Republic reaffirmed the imperial commitment of the July Monarchy, declaring Algeria an integral part of France and organizing it into the three departments of Algiers, Oran, and Constantine. And, indeed, most French deputies quickly proved more interested in simply relieving revolutionary Paris of its unemployed masses than in building a socialist society in North Africa. As a pragmatic first step toward accomplishing the linked goals of political stability and Algerian incorporation, the French Second Republic sent some twenty-five thousand of those arrested in the revolutionary uprising of the June Days of 1848 to Algeria, after the abolition of the death penalty for political criminals. Suggestively, Algerian war veterans Generals Eugène Cavaignac and Louis Juchault de Lamoricière presided over the suppression of the socialists and workers who erected and fought from the barricades of the June Days as well as the North African resettlement scheme. Frontiers toughened soldiers, and received rebels.[20]

Reiterating their antisocialist animus, Americans generally grew suspicious of the French Second Republic upon news of the June Days, which they blamed on "red republican" violence.[21] But American observers found merit in the deportations of urban laborers from Paris: French colonial investment offset the perception of metropolitan social upheaval. The *Atlantic Monthly*, for example, named Algeria "the safety-valve of France, giving active employment to the idle, the discontented, and the revolutionary."[22] French Algeria's functioning as a receptacle for radicals and the economically deprived resonated with Americans, particularly those who had earlier encountered Michel Chevalier's implicit comparison of the American and French frontiers in terms of their functioning to dissipate threats to political and social stability: Chevalier anticipated that Algeria would function as "a West" where "excess population . . . may overflow," thus keeping working men from both starvation and civil war. "This is . . . the reason why France is right in keeping Algiers."[23]

In light of the Second Republic's effort to establish *colonies agricoles* in Algeria in 1848, French emigration to Algeria was nearly double the emigration to the United States that year, reversing a general trend to that point.[24] Meanwhile, however, scattered information about the availability of cheap public land in the United States had begun to circulate. For example, Guillaume Poussin, who traveled in the United States before serving as Ambassador of the French Second Republic to the United States in 1848–49, published *De la Puissance américaine* in 1843, in which he observed, "No individual in the United States can be so poor as to be unable to hope that at some future day he may become a proprietor in the vast solitudes of the west. The price of government lands is one dollar and twenty-five cents per acre." A prudent emigrant from Europe with a "disposition to labor," he wrote, could "become a landed proprietor in the immense western regions of the United States, where 370,500,000 acres of excellent land are available."[25] Poussin's encouragement of Atlantic, not Mediterranean, emigration is a reminder of the challenge that the allure of the US West posed to French advocates of converting Algeria into a European agricultural colony.

On the other hand, Poussin remarked that many American immigrants "are so often destitute of resources that they find it impossible to reach the interior of the United States. . . . [Therefore] in the great cities in which they are obliged to remain they abandon themselves . . . even with more facility than in Europe, to debauchery and idleness."[26] Poussin's warning was echoed in French periodicals' accounts that contrasted the optimism of émigrés headed for Algeria with the desperation of those set to cross the Atlantic.[27] Thus, when French sources began to report on the US homestead movement in the late 1850s, they viewed it as a calculated Republican Party platform, not a possible Algerian exemplar. The conservative *Annuaire des Deux Mondes* echoed proslavery Southerners' skepticism in describing Congress's debate of the bill on the eve of the Civil War, calling it merely "a maneuver . . . to ensure electoral support of new citizens and needy classes."[28]

Seen in this way, the United States was not simply a beggar's paradise, and French territorial policymakers Cavaignac and Lamoricière were bolstered in developing a settlement scheme embraced by Louis Napoléon upon his election in December 1848 as a domestic imperial alternative. Under a policy of *cantonnement*, Algerian tribes received collective title to part of the land they possessed in exchange for ceding to the French government tribal *arch* lands, meaning unfenced land worked collectively by a village or tribe, or land left fallow, by enabling officials to claim those lands in order "to make them productive," in the words of Algerian Governor-General Jacques Louis Randon, echoing a key justification for native land-taking in Anglo-American history that French imperialists reenacted.[29] Under cantonnement, some 1.25 million acres were acquired, helping attract some 200,000 European civilians to Algeria by 1860.[30] And beginning during the Second Republic, free land, on average some fifteen acres within militarily fortified villages, was given to each European colonist, with the requirement that he improve it within three years or face eviction.[31] While the July Monarchy had offered wealthy prospective settlers Algerian land grants of ten to thirty acres, the awarding of small lots of free land to ordinary civilian settlers on condition of its development, preceding the US Homestead Act by over a decade, was novel at the time.[32]

Shortly after the establishment of the Second Empire in 1852, Napoleon III declared his interest in Algeria as a "vast kingdom to assimilate to France."[33] But despite this proclamation, inconsistent land settlement policies by the state, from awarding small land lots to settlers to retaining land to making selected large concessions to *grandes companies*, all accompanied by continued military command of Algerian natives within the territory's political integration to France, made prosperous settlement and agricultural development impossible for many ordinary settlers.[34] Shifting French approaches continued through the early 1860s, despite attention showered on Algeria at Paris's Universal Exhibition of 1855 and Napoléon's establishment in 1858 of a Ministry of Algeria and the Colonies, removing Algeria from under the Ministry of War.[35]

French-American Policies Toward Indigenous Peoples, 1840s–60s

In 1860, after a North African tour, and impressed by the tribal chieftains he met, Napoleon III called for a halt on the expansion of European settlement beyond the coastal zone and restriction of contact between Muslims and the colonists, whom he considered to have a corrupting influence on the Indigenous population. Motivated in part to protect the Algerian people from what he called "the fate of the Indians of North America . . . a thing both inhuman and impossible," and reiterating that Algeria was not a colony, Napoleon asserted a particular French humanitarian mission, self-consciously different from Anglo-American rapaciousness.[36]

Napoleon's moratorium drew upon writings by French travelers and settlers earlier in the century who had witnessed the situations of both Indigenous Americans and Algerians. French observers expressed pity for Indigenous Americans for their wretched condition and condemned white settlers' violence against them, although they did not condemn American expansion or conquest and tended to see collapsing Indigenous societies as an inevitable outcome of the advance of democratic civilization. Alexis de Tocqueville concluded that the "aborigines of North America" were destined to perish. Persisting in "barbarous ways" they would be forced to migrate, "wandering from waste to waste." Attempting to "civilize their manners" and settle, the "contact of a more civilized community subjects them to oppression and destitution."[37]

French colonial writers in Algeria, meanwhile, anticipated that Algerians would meet a fate—extinction—similar to the fates of native peoples elsewhere under colonial rule. A French deputy, Amédée Desjobert, actually an anti-colonialist, noted in 1838 that France was following the example in British America of "partial extermination and complete dispersal" of local populations; this approach, he noted scornfully, was "the only logical thing to do in seizing the country in order to plant a European population there."[38] In 1845 Eugène Bodichon, a physician and ethnographer in Algeria, observed that despite what he saw as Euro-American benevolence, Indigenous Americans, as a predictor of the future of Algerians, "ran quickly towards the extinction of their race." The North American Indigenous population had dropped to an eighth of its precolonial level, and the same phenomenon was happening "in Tahiti, New Holland, New Zealand, and on the other islands of Australia and Polynesia," according to Bodichon, who predicted this phenomenon's replication in Algeria.[39]

Indeed, French land expropriation during the July Monarchy mimicked Anglo-American practices. Expropriation became justified as retribution against Abdelkader, the emir of Oran who led resistance to the French until his capture in 1847, as well as on account of the "vacancy" and "lack of improvement" of Algeria's land under native occupancy. For example, an official bulletin of the French colonial government in 1840 determined that since Algerians had "abandoned their property to join France's enemies [Abelkader]" and "houses, lands, and gardens cannot remain vacant," it was important to award land grants to European migrants in order to generate colonial revenue.⁴⁰ This support for putting "vacant" land to use to encourage settlement replicated European arguments to justify colonial agriculture in the Americas as well as Australia. In the latter country, similar to Algeria, the first contact was made by imperially armed expeditions, which felt little need to purchase native land and thus developed the doctrine of *terra nullius*, under which the land was owned by no one and was therefore available for the taking.⁴¹ Generally, meanwhile, the United States government sought to purchase Indigenous American lands rather than simply seize them, although, similar to French actions in Algeria, Americans on such significant occasions as the War of Independence and the Creek War of 1813–14 took land from Indians without compensation, in retaliation for war-making.⁴² French practices of taking "vacant" land as retribution against Algerians were similar to Anglo-American models even though, in light of the relatively large Algerian population, the claim that the land was vacant was more fictitious in North Africa.

While some French writers saw the disappearance of native peoples beyond Algeria as a predictor for the outcome of Algerians, others saw this tragedy only as a warning. The "suffering Indian," not destined for extinction but worthy of "saving" by analogy to the Algerian through a distinctively humanitarian French gesture, resonated in French society by the 1840s and may well have struck Louis Napoléon's fancy before he came to power. During that decade, nearly a half century before Buffalo Bill more famously brought Lakota, Cheyenne, Arapaho, Pawnee, and Crow peoples to France in his romantic portrayal of the pre-civilized Old West, American artists and ethnographers visited France, making appeals about the Indians' plight.⁴³ The artist George Catlin, for example, brought a group of Iowa and Ojibwe peoples to Paris in 1845–46 as a living "Indian Gallery" for display in the Louvre, to call international attention to the fact that they were dying out.⁴⁴ And in the summer of 1848, during an Algerian debate in the National Assembly, Minister of War Lamoricière emphasized the cost of US treatment of Indigenous Americans, contrasted with France's putative higher "mission":

> What has become of the Indians? . . . You all know it—they have been massacred. They have been poisoned by rum and strong liquors. Thus have done the Anglo-Americans with the Indians. We do not wish to dispose of the Arabs in the same way. . . . Such proceedings—such means—such crimes, we utterly repudiate. We abjure them in the name and honor of France. . . . Yes, in the name of honor—of the honor of our country—of that mission

which we are fulfilling in the world, in the name of Christianity. We mean that the noblest of God's creatures shall be respected, whatever religion they may profess.[45]

If US "land for the landless" would soon provide inspiration for French liberalization of land laws in Algeria, the French Second Empire portrayed US treatment of native peoples as a mistake to be avoided and incorporated its dire effects into an argument for French exceptionalism.[46]

Napoleon III thus decreed an Arab kingdom in February 1863, separated from the colonists and French military garrisons. Napoleon's land reservation reform was influenced by the arguments of certain Saint-Simonian reformers, particularly "Arabist" military officers serving in the Bureaux of Arab Affairs who supported French annexation of Algeria, yet, like American missionaries working among the Five Civilized Tribes before their removal in the 1830s, thought it best accomplished not through rapid annexation and population immersion but study of Indigenous society and culture and governance of native peoples through their own institutions. To be sure, a subsequent decree, the April 1863 Sénatus consulte, confirmed retention of land earlier confiscated by France from the dey of Algiers (beylick), declared Algerian tribes to be "proprietors" of territories that they traditionally used and certified the "proprietors" to have "legal title" to land, an intended step in the evolution of Algerian society toward the realization of individual property rights. Still, the Second Empire also renounced French claims to tribal lands not considered beylick and suspended settlers' speculation in them. Unlike President Jackson, who notoriously demanded that American Indians vacate their homelands for reservations to accommodate white settlers, Napoleon declared a separate homeland for the Arab population where they already lived, one that would protect native land tenure practices.

American observers were skeptical of news about Napoleon's philanthropy in Algeria, quickly suspecting, in the context of the Civil War, that its motivation was to shift French military forces from the Mediterranean to the Gulf of Mexico. The US Minister to France, John Bigelow, warned in 1865 that eight Algerian regiments were being transferred that year to Mexico in support of Marshal François Bazaine, deployed to place the pretender Maximilian on the throne of the Mexican republic.[47] Meanwhile, perhaps reflecting an Anglo frame of reference from which many Americans perceived the French Second Empire, a periodical surmised that Algeria was henceforth "to be [like] India and not Australia," meaning it would function as a French administrative possession and source of wealth extraction but not a destination for an extensive settler population.[48] And American observers, other than missionaries who sometimes tried to defend the rights of Indians by comparing them to minority groups elsewhere in the world, generally ignored French references to the dismal fate of Indigenous Americans under US rule.[49]

Still, American accounts could be found that praised the pragmatism of Napoleon's new anti-assimilationist approach toward Algeria for offering Algerians a chance to become yeoman farmers. "The Arabs, hunted and dispossessed, are to be restored to their lands, to settle down, if possible, as cultivators," concluded one sympathetic commentary. Apparently, judging from the relatively small immigrant population in Algeria as well as North America, "Frenchmen [were] not good colonists," and this change promised to be "a most able one."[50]

The US Homestead Act and Algerian Land Reform, 1860s–90s

With the exodus of Southerners from the US federal government as a result of the South's secession in 1860–61, Republicans in Congress passed the 1862 Homestead Act, which offered any adult citizen, or intended citizen, who had never borne arms against the US government 160 acres of surveyed government land. Claimants were required to improve their plots by cultivating and building a dwelling on them. After five years on the land, the original filer was entitled to the property after paying a small registration fee. Title could also be acquired after only a six-month residency and improvements, provided the claimant paid the government $1.25 per acre. During and after the Civil War, land that the federal and state governments distributed to railroads, universities, and Indian tribes considerably surpassed the amount granted to homesteaders. However, the Homestead Act's motto, "land for the landless," became synonymous among many Europeans during the nineteenth century with how the prairie states were settled.[51] US diplomats and consuls promoted the Homestead Act abroad to attract European immigrants, following Secretary of State William Seward's circular number 32 of February 8, 1863, for that purpose.[52]

Immediate French official opinion, however, downplayed the possible resonance of the Homestead Act in the French Second Empire, instead emphasizing the reaction among migrants in the rival German states. There, "more than any other measure," opined a colonial periodical, it was likely to trigger an "emigration crisis."[53] Treated as a competitor to, not a blueprint for, settlement in Algeria, the Homestead Act thus appeared as an annoyance to French officials. In 1863 the US consul in Tunis, nominally an autonomous Ottoman province but under French influence, reported to the State Department that a government journal had published excerpts of American news from the "liberal journals of France," including Secretary of State Seward's homestead circular letter.[54] Soon the US commissioner of immigration, a position established in 1864, sent a similar circular around Europe, highlighting the advantages of the 1862 homestead law. The US consul in Marseilles sought to distribute the circular in Southern France as a pamphlet, but in 1866 this provoked a complaint by the French government to Bigelow, the US minister. "There would be inconveniences," wrote Foreign Affairs Minister Edouard Drouyn de Lhuys, "in authorizing the distribution through the departments of the empire such documents, which . . . appeal in favor of emigration . . . among native-born operatives."[55] Information about the Homestead Act was immediately welcomed in areas of overpopulation in Europe, such as Scandinavia.[56] However, the act's appeal to the "native-born operatives" of France to come to the New World assured its cold welcome by French statesmen, undeterred by the emperor's recent setting aside of lands strictly for Indigenous Algerian occupation and intent to encourage migration within, not beyond, the French empire.

The quite different perception of the Homestead Act among French imperial observers was brooked by the demise of Napoleon's controversial Arab kingdom, a result of the catastrophic Franco-Prussian War, the toppling of the Second Empire, and the establishment of the Third Republic. Following the defeat of Sheikh Muhammad El-Mokrani's insurrection in the Kabylia region of northern Algeria in the summer of 1871, the French Third Republic declared the replacement of military authority with civilian rule in Algeria. Meanwhile, refugees from Alsace and Lorraine, French provinces lost to Prussia, arrived in Algeria, transforming and magnifying its purposes to become, in the words of one writer, a "New France," offering the promise of "offsetting losses in Europe."[57] The French Third Republic reasserted the full assimilation of Algeria, this time extending the colons' authority over previously self-governing tribal reserves through confiscation from Algerians, by the end of the century, of some two million acres of farmland and forest.[58]

The principal instrument of the Third Republic's reinvigorated land privatization in Algeria was the Warnier Law of 1873, named for Dr. Auguste Warnier, a physician and settler who first went to the Oran Province in 1834 and later represented Algiers in the French Parliament. Based on a study of

Arab culture while serving the ambulances of the Armée d'Afrique, Warnier decided that France should assimilate North Africa by developing a loyal regime of European independent landholders. As early as 1846 he expressed his cynical desire that Algerian laborers be pressured into the marketplace in order to become the "docile instruments" of French settlers.[59] The Warnier Law abolished traditional proscriptions of sales of *melk*, precolonial landholdings maintained by families or tribes, and accelerated the speed with which the 1863 Sénatus consulte scheduled tribal land to be made individually alienable, through a reform allowing an individual to sell a part of communally held land. A subsequent law in 1887, the *petit Sénatus consulte*, expanded on the reach of the Warnier Law by fragmenting additional tribes into smaller administrative *douars* and allowing plots of undeveloped *arch* land, not already claimed by the state, to be converted to private property upon initiative by a prospective buyer.[60] In 1863 Warnier had denounced Napoleon's reservation program for "confining the Europeans, maintaining barbarism . . . [and] stifling civilization" and preventing Algeria from becoming a "transmediterranean France."[61] He anticipated that the 1873 law would "recover the productivity of the past" and stop "land inequality between local residents and French and European immigrants" by the leveling mechanism of universal land privatization.[62]

As context for the Warnier Law, territorial expansionists like Warnier studied Anglo-American settler policies and history, not, as in the past, seeking analogies predicting the inevitable decline of the Algerian population but for evidence of the positive impact on territorial settlement of orderly land privatization. French territorial planners faced two peculiar challenges, different from perceptibly more successful Anglo-American settlement schemes. The first was the failure, according to proponents of colonization, of the Second Empire to realize the potential of Algeria as a major European settler destination. In 1875 Paul Leroy-Beaulieu, France's leading freetrade economist and advocate of expansion (and son-in-law of Michel Chevalier), lamented Napoleon's Arab land reservation scheme as an obstacle to the seemingly simple route to the Europeanization of North Africa: a "thoughtless measure," he called it, "very philanthropic thinking, but also very unrealistic."[63] Others echoed his criticism. In a widely read study of French Algeria, Maurice Wahl, a Third Republic official in charge of colonial education and a historian, criticized the reservation law of 1863 for impeding immigration by creating "the uncertainty of tomorrow for the settlers."[64] And French senator and minister of finance Jean-Jules Clamageran, a native of New Orleans, Louisiana, who toured Algeria in 1873 and 1881, wrote that if the French government, rather than "procrastinat[ing]," had appealed to immigrants from any country, it would have diverted some of the "current which then poured into the United States each year" to Algeria. "We [have] in this country a Wild West to discover, a California to exploit; we have to create and renew."[65]

The philanthropy of Napoleon III had envisioned a regulated Algeria differently from a "Wild West," which in the French imaginary meant a North African settler frontier. Under a more free-market approach, Jules Duval, founder of the important *L'Économiste français* newspaper and a colonial administrator in Oran was intent to enforce a common nationality in Algeria as a means to make it commercially profitable. Duval expressed confidence that "nothing, in law or in fact, [now] prevents alienating land as quickly and surely on the banks of the Habra or Isser as on the banks of the Ohio and Missouri."[66]

The other challenge, related to the first, was the persistence of the Indigenous population of the French territory. French writers, beginning during the July Monarchy, had prophesied the disappearance of Algerians, and indeed the Algerian population declined by one-third from the time the French arrived in 1830 to the end of the Second Empire.[67] But at the empire's end, this cynical expectation was clearly proving unrealistic, and imperial advocates were citing the large Algerian population to rationalize, not criticize, the French investment.[68] Jules Duval showed a close familiarity with the US Preemption Act of 1841 in emphasizing the peculiarity of the French Algerian situation. Duval explained that the "American method" of preemption—"the right, for those who took possession of a wasteland, to retain ownership" by buying it once it entered the marketplace—could not be practiced in French "possessions in Africa" since Algerians had not abandoned land but returned to its possession during the Second Empire.[69] Likewise, Émile Levasseur, president of France's Society of Commercial Geography and a pioneer in French economic history, acknowledged the reality that unassimilated Algerians obviously were still present in North Africa, a "far more serious problem than in other colonies" where aboriginal people had fled the approach of settlers, who had "only to take possession of the land." But in Algeria, "France found itself in front of an energetic breed, having a religion, language, manners, and family organization who never allow it to blend with the Europeans, keeping deep in his heart the common hatred of the vanquished against their conquerors, civilized enough to resist eviction, too uncivilized to accept our customs and to transform to our image."[70]

In the 1850s Levasseur had authored an important study of the impact on global currency of the Californian and Australian gold strikes and perhaps hoped Algeria could produce similarly sensational wealth.[71] For him and Duval, stubborn Algerian occupation of the territory thwarted French attempts to imagine and promote North Africa as empty, similar to how Anglo-American writers and settlers treated frontier territories.[72]

Nonetheless, Algeria's redemption could be accomplished, especially if land policies enacted elsewhere could be adapted to facilitate land distribution. Duval hailed the fixed-price option of the Homestead Act, although he argued that land in Algeria should first be sold at auction, with unsold land then being put on the market for twenty francs per hectare. This price, he calculated, would allow French Algeria to compete with the United States.[73] Likewise, Clamageran noted how the United States had spread "from the banks of the Atlantic Ocean to the Pacific . . . [meanwhile] remain[ing] faithful to the principle of land for sale at a fixed price or auction."[74] Canada in 1850 and Australia in 1831 had also successfully adopted the principle, Clamageran calculated. Leroy-Beaulieu declared, "The model of colonization is no longer undiscovered, it is found. It exists in the western states of the American Union, and it shows in Australia."[75] Although the Indigenous populations in Anglo-American colonies and territories were much smaller, French writers emphasized the similarities of those circumstances to Algeria as a basis for arguing that aggressive land alienability would be the solution to sluggish European settlement in Algeria.

Thus, references to the US Homestead Act, optimistic rather than critical, began to appear in French colonial literature of the 1870s and 1880s. "In America," wrote Leroy-Beaulieu, "everything is arranged so that the settler . . . has in his pocket . . . a paper guaranteeing his property, having paid a low price, 16 francs per hectare [$1.25 per acre], or even without paying anything, if he wants to take advantage of the law known as the homestead." The policy was both "reality" and "the ideal of perfection."[76] Appraising the Warnier Law in 1878, an Algerian government commission declared that establishing "a strong French population in the three Algerian provinces" had required appealing not only to Alsace-Lorrainers but to "French emigrants" everywhere, as well as "a fair share of the Algerian agricultural element." In thus "break[ing] entirely with the mistakes of the past, we borrow[ed] resolutely from the American system of colonization[,] *almost* as it is formulated in the so-called 'Homestead Act'."[77]

Territorial land development invoking a "homestead" principle served different purposes in Algeria than it did in the United States, however. More

Figure 4.1. Henri Dormoy, 1830–1930, *L'Algérie. Pays de grande production agricole* [Algeria: Country of Great Agricultural Production] (n.p., 1930). Archives nationales d'outre-mer, FR ANOM 0009Fi64.

than protection of land from monopoly, as in the US West, in French North Africa the practice meant protection of land from Algerian tribal reservations and accelerating its availability in the marketplace. Through land sales at fixed or, after that, market prices, conducted even "among Arabs," according to Leroy-Beaulieu, the "aberrations" of previous land reservations for Algerians could be corrected by establishing a reliable process for Europeans to own Algerian land as well as a legal fiction for assimilating Algerians.[78] Leroy-Beaulieu argued that Indigenous Americans' assimilation in the United States was a better prologue for French Algerians than was the fate of the "Australian negroes, tracked down and murdered by English settlers."[79] The Warnier Act launched the French Third Republic's policy of *fusionnement*, designed to make the Algerian people "Arab French," not citizens but subject to French laws and customs, especially attachment to the soil and development of agriculture (see fig. 4).[80]

The Mythology of the Frontier Farm

Both the American West and French Algeria in the late nineteenth century became settled through largely unregulated privatization of land, giving rise to golden ages of speculation and corporate ownership: Homestead laws in both places could not possibly sustain yeoman farming.[81] Over time, other elements of "how the West was won" entered the French imperial imagination. Although not until the twentieth century, French planners scrutinized irrigation projects in the US West—particularly in California—for how they represented the arrival of "civilization" in the desert to save it from "the Arab or any other nomad," as an 1889 US agricultural report put it, and an assumption that echoed earlier French attitudes toward Algerians' apparent failure to make the Sahara Desert cultivable.[82]

More immediately, as had happened on the US frontier a generation earlier, the first decades of the French Third Republic saw a surge in passenger railroads in Algeria for the first time, from three hundred to over three thousand kilometers by World War I, reflecting both a redefinition of how people could become "civilized" through embracing technology and recognition of the proven importance of railroads elsewhere to populate territories with white civilians.[83] Adolphe Duponchel, an engineer and author of *The Transsaharian Railway*, reminded an audience in Paris in 1879 that the "golden spike" driven in to complete the intercontinental railroad in 1869 symbolized US national unification.[84] Stanislas Lebourgeois, head of the French ministry of education, likewise remarked that US "wonders" in agricultural and commercial development were owed to the role of the railway "in the colonization of a country." Specifically, Lebourgeois pointed to the laying of railroads preceding, not following, settlement into "large uncultivated land." Via railroads, "settlers arrived, cities arose as if by magic, the land was cleared, and in a few years acquired considerable value."[85] Lebourgeois's analysis exaggerated the ease with which cities emerged from American woodlands, prairies, and mountains. But his comment also suggests an evolution in the French imperial imagination of the US frontier from an example of an agricultural countryside to a network of urban areas and how land value appreciation became a marker of the arrival of "civilization."

Yet while both the US and French frontier territories saw the beginning of industrial consolidation, the images of both remained similarly romanticized. A primary source of this mythmaking in Algeria was the land that was distributed to 1871 war refugees from Alsace and Lorraine. These land distributions, like those made to the exiles from the June Days uprising of 1848, were free on condition of residence. While Alsatians and Lorrainers had to show possession of at least five thousand francs, the requirement that they simply had to live on and farm the land for five years became the stipulation that at least one writer remembered in 1897 in commemorating the land grant as "borrowed from the American Homestead Law."[86]

Though their situation was quite different, like homesteaders in America, the opportunity in Algeria for these refugees to re-create themselves became celebrated, their construction of humble homes on the frontier folkloric. Charles Lavigerie, the bishop of Algeria, declared to Alsatian and Lorrainer migrants in 1871 that "la France africaine" was "a home no less French than the one you have lost. It awaits you, and its love is as great as your misfortune."[87] The French writer Augustine Fouillée similarly celebrated the Algerian homeland by setting her 1887 novel *Les enfants de Marcel* there. In the novel, the grandmother of a resettled Alsatian family declared, "Blessed land. . . . After so many trials and tribulations, my children owe you their safety, their happiness, and their health. When my time has come, I will take my final rest in your soil without regrets, my new Alsace."[88]

Likewise, the Kansas homesteader Brewster Higley romantically evoked the Homestead Act in his 1873 poem "My Western Home," later adapted into the famous anthem of the US West "Home on the Range."[89] But the American homesteaders' loneliness in struggling to make the land bloom was more often lamented in such songs as "Starving to Death on a Government Claim" and "Little Old Sod Shanty on the Claim."[90] Willa Cather's *O Pioneers* explored the tragic effects of "prairie madness" on a settler family in Nebraska.[91] Both American and French settlers, as well as frontier soldiers, struggled with what was known for most of the nineteenth century as a pathological condition of "nostalgia," a longing for the homeland. Yet in French folklore the colons of Alsace-Lorraine were united by their re-creation of the *pays*, or native country, and concomitant social and racial separation from Indigenous Algerians who surrounded them; in American song and story, isolated settlers lamented the land's emptiness.[92]

While the Homestead Act hardly drained the American population westward or relocated the poor on the land, its settler saga, like the French myth of pioneering *colonies agricoles*, became part of the national folklore by 1900, though as a place of exile as well as opportunity.[93] Like western settlement pursuant to the Homestead Act, French settlement in Algeria after 1870 was accelerated because of a national war. While in the United States Republicans in 1860 insisted that "land for the landless" was not a program for destitute "paupers or suppliants for public bounty," destitute refugees ultimately enabled France to assert national unification through territorial expansion, similar to American homesteaders. Thus, both migrations gained legendary status. As a salve on wounded national pride after the Franco-Prussian War, French Algeria resembled how the US West's consolidation offset the large-scale failure of visionary Reconstruction policies in the post–Civil War South.

Land reform in the United States, as an influence on French ideas about imperial development in Algeria, illustrates how territorial settlement ideas were shared and reconfigured not only within the Anglo-American settler world but beyond it. To be sure, liberal ideas for French Algerian land settlement during the early Third Republic diverged from their example in the United States, an unsurprising evolution from the US West to the French Mediterranean. As French writers eventually acknowledged, French Algeria did not fit closely with the Anglo-American type of territorial land largely emptied of its Indigenous population. Yet they considered how the mythology of US land reform might invigorate territorial settlement anyway.

The US Homestead Act culminated decades of work by American reformers to restrain capitalistic speculation and absentee land ownership of the public land. In its partial success, it was a triumph of anti–laissez-faire groups in the United States concerned that, left to private hands, the West would succumb to the same historical forces that first pushed Europeans to the New World. Paradoxically, the meaning of US homestead law in French Algeria in the late nineteenth century reflected something quite else, adopted and adapted as it was by French imperialists hopeful to bolster arguments for privatization of Algeria, critical of earlier "philanthropic" state regulation of the North African frontier's development. The US West and French

Algeria alike served multiple national functions. Like the West as envisioned by American land reformers, French Algeria functioned as a vision for egalitarian agricultural opportunity, but rapidly, and unsurprisingly, it remained a field for brutal exploitation and profit-making. As a French "West," it, like the American frontier, came to represent national rebirth, state-building, and individual enterprise.[94]

Chapter 5

Algeria, Puerto Rico, and the Philippines

Gonzales v. Williams was the first of the Insular Cases heard by the US Supreme Court that dealt with the question of the citizenship of the people who lived in the overseas territories the United States acquired by warfare with Spain and the resulting 1898 Treaty of Paris. William Williams, the New York state commissioner of immigration, prevented Isabel González, a Puerto Rican woman who arrived in New York City in August 1902, from entering the United States, classifying her, under the 1891 Immigration Act, as an alien, likely to become a public charge.[1] González found lawyers who filed a petition of habeas corpus in court. A US circuit court ruled against her petition that she would not become a public ward, a condition of entry into the United States from abroad at the time. González appealed the decision, arguing that she was not an alien. Her lead attorney at the Supreme Court, Frederic Coudert, argued that González was neither an alien nor a citizen but an American "national."

Coudert drew on international law for his argument, principally the example of laws of nationality in French Algeria. This aspect of his argument, and the extent to which it shaped the Court's somewhat ambiguous opinion, marked the formal arrival of French rule in Algeria as a precedent for US law. Americans had studied French Algeria episodically since the 1830s for analogies, and sometimes warnings, on how to shape their own burgeoning continental empire. Scholars recently have shown how US empire-builders sought to emulate as well as compete with the British Empire around the turn of the twentieth century, though they have not explored Americans' attention to the second French colonial empire.[2]

To be sure, US expansion until 1898 was different in important ways from European empire-building in the nineteenth century. Settlers in US territories, like counterparts in British and French colonies, were denied representation in the national government, though they gained the right to vote in local elections. Yet other than Alaska, US territories shared borders with states, and US state-building practice was to admit territories to statehood upon attainment of required populations and submission of an acceptable state constitution to Congress. White settlers in US continental territories, moreover, relatively quickly became majority populations, different from British South Africa and India and French Algeria, where white minorities ruled large populations of Indigenous peoples.

The Spanish-American War of 1898 and the Philippine-American War of 1899–1902 marked a turning point in US expansion. US acquisition of former Spanish island colonies showed Americans' ambition to compete with European powers for control of land, natural resources, trading partners, and naval stations beyond North American shores. The Philippines, Puerto Rico, and other new possessions would be the first US possessions to which large numbers of settlers did not migrate. But US establishment of democratic institutions in these places—"liberal exceptionalism" as the United States's version of liberal empire—suggested the continuance of putative US differences from traditional European powers.[3]

This chapter joins other recent literature that has studied US territorial policies after the acquisition of the former Spanish colonies of Puerto Rico and the Philippines from a comparative perspective. That literature has identified similar or analogous aspects of the French and US territorial frontiers. Within and outside those comparisons, scholars have focused on the discrepancy between claims about democratic institutions in these US possessions and actual practices, a problem actually endemic among imperial powers claiming to bring civilization to other peoples.[4]

This chapter, instead, explores how, at the turn of the twentieth century, US expansionists often referred to European empires to contextualize arguments that the United States needed overseas possessions to be a great power, as well as to uphold its alleged responsibility as a civilized country to help uncivilized others progress. Scholars have concluded that in the Insular Cases the Supreme Court enabled US legal treatment of "other peoples" similar to practices "among European imperial powers."[5] To be more specific, however, the chapter shows that American writers, military and civilian policymakers, and jurists studied French Algeria, even in an era when Americans either doubted French capacity for colonizing or, according to Ambassador Jules Jusserand, simply lacked interest in French international affairs.[6] US war-making in the Philippines proved similar to the French experience in unconventional war in Algeria. Native Algerians, moreover, like those in the new US territories, were racially different from the metropole yet were ruled under republican principles that they were officially assimilable through the prospect of gaining national citizenship. The chapter asks historians to consider the role of the southern shore of the Mediterranean Sea, what a scholar of eighteenth-century Ottoman history aptly called a "forgotten frontier," in Atlantic history at the turn of the twentieth century.[7]

Arguments for Annexation

In the Treaty of Paris of 1898, Spain merely relinquished sovereignty over Cuba but ceded Puerto Rico, Guam, and the Philippines to the United States, areas coveted by US national strategic planners. Particularly since the Depression of 1893, the value of stable offshore markets had become clear. The four Spanish islands provided demand as well as supply, there and in China, and provided coaling and naval stations in the Caribbean and Pacific for the navy's use to protect the trade (Americans' work on the Panama Canal, envisioned to speed this trade, began in 1904).

US acquisition of Spain's far-flung colonies also was attributable to a surge in popularity of the beliefs that the United States needed overseas possessions to be considered a great power and that expansion by powerful countries would bring civilization and peace to the world. In speeches during 1899, New York Governor Theodore Roosevelt emphasized the global service done by powerful nations—France in Algeria, Britain in India and Sudan, and Russia in Central Asia—when they "took" nations that were "savage." Concerning France, Roosevelt noted, its occupation of Algeria ended both the piracy practiced by "Moslem bandits of the sea" and the tribute that had been paid by European countries as well as the US government to protect trade in the Mediterranean. The same kinds of "foolish sentimentalists," said Roosevelt, who "celebrated the Algerian freebooters as heroes

96   Chapter 5

who were striving for liberty against the invading French . . . now write little essays in favor of [Filipino revolutionary leader Emilio] Aguinaldo against the Americans." But the French had persevered, applauded Roosevelt, and as a result, "Algiers has thriven as never before in its history." Thus, anyone who subsequently abetted revolts in Algeria "would be traitors to civilization (see fig. 5.1)."

Figure 5.1. Exhibit portraying a street in Algiers, Algeria, Exposition Universelle 1900, Paris, France. Look and Learn, Valerie Jackson Harris Collection, Bridgeman Images LLH6032492.

Roosevelt here possibly alluded to the 1871 Mokrani Revolt in Algeria, when a third of the Algerian Muslim population rose up against French rule after the Third Republic declared European civilian rule in Algeria, ended protections of Arab land from European settlement declared by Emperor Napoleon III, and offered citizenship to Algerian Jews. Foregrounding Roosevelt's imperial language, French commentators on the suppression of the 1871 Algerian uprising had inscribed it "as a victory for modern civilization" by which Algerians, ironically, could benefit, even though, in retribution, France redistributed a million acres of Algerians' land to European settlers in order to expand commercial agriculture and industry, rationalized as markers of the spread of civilization.[8] Earlier, in his multivolume history *Winning of the West*, Roosevelt had hailed only "Teutonic conquests in alien lands," except for which "the world would have halted."[9] Now he reasoned that US overseas expansion was like the self-sacrificial colonial undertakings of various European great powers, France prominently among them.[10]

Significantly, in light of Roosevelt's argument that it was time for the United States to act like a great power by civilizing "barbarous" nations, the Treaty of Paris did not refer to the citizenship status of the native inhabitants of the territories ceded to the United States. Instead, their "civil rights and political status . . . shall be determined by the Congress."[11] This was the first such omission among US treaties concerning territorial annexation.

The novel idea of legal treatment of the overseas territories first appeared in an 1899 article written by a Harvard professor of government, A. Lawrence Lowell. Based on a review of the Federalist Papers, the Constitution, prior treaties, and Supreme Court rulings, Lowell found that before 1898 inhabitants of territories, upon annexation, had generally gained citizenship rights but only on the basis of specific language in relevant treaties or federal legislation. Lowell thus dismissed the possibility that international law, dictating that conquered possessions fell under the conqueror's full legal authority, might apply to the United States. Since neither the Paris Treaty nor any subsequent act of Congress had placed the newly possessed areas fully under the Constitution, Lowell reasoned that the United States could acquire territory without the territory forming part of the sovereign country, meaning that only some or even no constitutional guarantees might take hold there. Lowell speculated that some constitutional limitations on Congress's authority might be "universal," but these stood "upon a different footing from the rights guaranteed to the citizens." "Guaranteed rights of citizenship," he concluded, anticipating arguments soon to be made in Congress, were "inapplicable except among a people whose social and political evolution has been consonant with our own."[12] Ironically, given exceptionalist discourse emphasizing US anti-colonialism, Lowell grounded his rationale for what became known as the doctrine of territorial incorporation in a "career of colonization" practiced by the United States.[13]

Yet in the time between the publication of Lowell's law article and the arrival of Isabel González in New York Harbor, the treatment by foreign powers of persons in conquered countries became more a part of Americans' debates about the status of Puerto Ricans and Filipinos. Filipinos declared their independence in June 1898 and named Aguinaldo as president. But in August a US military general, Wesley Merritt, assumed authority over the islands. On February 4, 1899, the Philippine Republic declared war on the United States, two days before the US Senate ratified the Treaty of Paris. After US forces soundly defeated Filipino troops in set battles, in November 1899, Aguinaldo authorized usage of guerrilla warfare, provoking US adoption of a counterinsurgency strategy that became controversial. The military and subsequent political treatment of the territory became the focus of anti-imperial critiques of Americans' actions in Spain's former colonies. These provided the context for US commentators' and policymakers' consideration of French Algeria in coming to an understanding of the United States's new imperial status, including, eventually, reformulation of citizenship law.

Arguments Against Annexation

While much of the anti-imperial movement emphasized that the new territories would allow the indigenes of those territories deemed racially inferior people to become Americans, another important aspect argued that acquisition of unincorporated territories would violate the principles of US republican origins. Anti-imperialists criticized the actions of the modern European powers broadly, including France. In a commentary that shortly took on more relevance, an American magazine in 1895 observed that the military, political, and moral costs to France of building an empire in Africa and Asia would exceed any benefits. The sociologist William Graham Sumner, likewise, wrote that French militarization had stifled the rebirth of its democracy after the Second Empire.[14]

Among opponents of annexation, however, Britain often fared worse. France, if only because it shared a republican history with the United States, retained a sort of ancestral sympathy. For example, in an 1899 essay urging

Americans to remain neutral in the developing conflict among European powers and Japan over territory in China, the industrialist Andrew Carnegie acknowledged the strength of affection of the "English-speaking race" and pointed out that the United States had taken the Philippines partly because of the friendly neutrality of the British navy. Yet Carnegie warned that Britain hardly forged permanent alliances with any country. It was thus possible that the United States, "grasp[ing] the phantom of Imperialism" and placing faith in an Anglo-American friendship, could become a British "catspaw." A probable casualty of this development would be the United States's relationship with "the sister Republic of France," said Carnegie. France, unlike Britain, had proven "a close friend" of Americans since the American War of Independence. The French-American relationship was a cost too high, Carnegie argued, for any other US alliance.[15]

Likewise, US senators hoping to derail congressional ratification of the Treaty of Paris emphasized Britain's sordid colonial history and capacity to manipulate Americans. Senator Augustus Bacon recalled the impact on him of images in American magazines of British executions of Indian sepoy rebels in 1857 by tying them to cannons and blowing them up.[16] Senator George Vest asked suspiciously why Britain, "the great apostle of the colonial system of Europe," now "welcome[d] with open arms the Republic they attempted to destroy." In the British Empire, save Australia and Canada, where there was limited self-government, 322 million people lived "without the right to govern themselves even locally." For Vest, France was hardly more virtuous than Britain, based on its colonial population. But France was a "nominal" republic, and its colonial possessions, he noted, had been acquired before the Third Republic's establishment.[17]

Perhaps most famously, although appearing only a month after the first Supreme Court argument of the Insular Cases and a month before Aguinaldo's surrender in the Philippines, Mark Twain offered his own anti-British critique of imperialism. In his famous essay "To the Person Sitting in Darkness," Twain condemned the European powers and the United States alike for interventions in Africa and Asia. Like Europeans, Americans had taken up illegitimate war for resources while professing to bring civilization to non-Western peoples who "sit in darkness"—his satirical usage of a Bible verse, Matthew 4:16, often invoked by Christian missionaries.[18]

Americans now, Twain said, were engaged in "the Chamberlain game," a term he coined in reference to British Prime Minister Joseph Chamberlain's leadership in the ongoing Second Boer War, which pitted British imperial forces against Dutch-speaking settlers in South Africa seeking independence. Emphasizing the connection of British imperial practice to US corruption, Twain also quoted American newspaper headlines from November 1900, which had declared "Kitchener's Plan Adopted!" to report US forces' increasing resorting to counterinsurgency warfare in the Philippines. "Kitchener's Plan" was a reference to British Chief of Staff Horatio Kitchener, who, to combat Boer commandos, established concentration camps, destroyed materials of and arrested or killed individuals providing sustenance to the resistance, and executed prisoners. Twain wrote satirically, "Kitchener knows how to handle disagreeable people who are fighting for their homes and their liberties, and we must let on that we are merely imitating Kitchener, and have no national interest in the matter, further than to get ourselves admired by the Great Family of Nations." Twain dramatized the folly of Americans' alleged pursuit of recognition by Europe as a legitimate powerful country by quoting letters written by British and US soldiers describing the bayoneting of enemies who had surrendered or were wounded. Like earlier critics, his anti-imperialism emphasized the British example as negative and, because of the popularity of Anglo-Saxon ideology, particularly infectious.[19]

The French Example in American Annexation Debates

While anti-imperialists focused on the risks to Americans' republican heritage stemming from the toxic influence of the British Empire, other commentators supportive of annexation, or at least resolved to its inevitability, drew attention to distinctive French colonial practices that were actually worthy of Americans' emulation in incorporating the new territories. A Washington, DC, newspaper made an argument for Puerto Rican representation in Congress by noting Algeria's representation in the French National Assembly since 1848 and recalling later reforms that provided representation in the French parliament to the colonies of Guadeloupe, Martinique, Reunion, Senegal, Guiana, and French India.[20] Carman Randolph, an attorney and Columbia University law professor, cited the same evidence in a book that argued that unless the United States was ready to offer eventual statehood to any country, it could not annex it. For Randolph, the fact that "the French Constitution is not restricted, in theory, to France in Europe" but extended to the French Empire was relevant to prospective US territorial policymaking, including regarding citizenship. Neither France nor Britain "pretend[ed]" that new territories or dominions had nationalities different from those of the metropole, Randolph observed. His argument was different from that of A. Lawrence Lowell, not only in its conclusion regarding the necessity to offer citizenship to territorial inhabitants but also, in its reference to French colonial doctrine, its legal reasoning.[21]

These commentators emphasized that the more democratic aspects of French rule in Algeria and the colonies should be the standard for an emerging US policy of incorporation. Alternative stories, however, about the French empire's *failure* to assimilate its colonized peoples also appeared, suggesting the diverse ways that Americans interpreted the practices of its "sister" imperial republic during debates over Puerto Rico and the Philippines. Indeed, one report—an account by Robert De Caix, editor of the *Journal des débats* and member of France's national committees of French Africa and French Asia—actually appeared in both anti-annexation and pro-annexation newspapers.[22] Starting with debates over annexation of Hawaii, the *San Francisco Call* had argued that Anglo-Saxons had no aptitude for tropical colonization. In 1899 it published Rudyard Kipling's poem "White Man's Burden," which beckoned the United States to become a colonial power, only to repudiate Kipling with an anti-imperialist editorial questioning Britons' motives to "divide the glory of civilizing the Orient" with Americans and asserting that "the white man's burden is to set and keep his own house in order."[23] The *Minneapolis Journal*, meanwhile, supported the McKinley administration's foreign policy. Its editors argued that the United States occupied the former Spanish island colonies "by conquest" and had a civilizational duty to remain there.[24]

A paradoxical aspect of Americans' debate about acquisition of Spain's colonies, including Cuba before the United States committed to recognizing its independence, was that advocates and opponents of annexation made similar arguments about the degenerate condition of the islands' inhabitants.[25] Newspaper cartoonists on different sides of the question of the US empire used racist tropes generally to portray subject peoples as Black and infantile, incapable of self-government.[26] In Congress, likewise, members who disagreed over annexation of offshore territories shared a common revulsion toward the people over whom the US flag might sway. Senator William Bate, for one, expressed skepticism that "expanding our authority once to the Europeans living in Louisiana can be deemed as sustaining the incorporation of millions of savages, cannibals, Malays, Mohammedans, headhunters, and polygamists." His sentiment was only slightly more severe than that of Senator Chauncey Depew, who declared that the United States could not "incorporate the alien races, and civilized, semi-civilized, barbarous, and savage peoples of these islands into our body politic as States of our Union." However, Bate was against any annexation while Depew was speaking in favor of annexation of Puerto Rico.[27]

It was in this context that Robert De Caix's description of the operation and challenges of French colonial policy appeared in US newspapers, both for and against the question of the US empire. In one part of his report, on French colonial trade policy, De Caix alerted Americans to consider French colonial trade practice "an experience . . . that should interest the United States," though he described it as a warning, not an endorsement. He complained that France maintained a tariff on goods imported from outside the empire. Required to produce goods locally and to import mainly from the metropolis, colonial inhabitants struggled to have income to pay local taxes, causing colonial governors to ask the national government for subsidies. De Caix observed that French businesses and banks were trying to transform the colonies into areas for capital investment but warned that French treatment of the colonies mainly as producers of raw materials and consumers of finished goods was a practice that Americans should avoid.[28]

Elsewhere it was less clear how De Caix intended for Americans to interpret his description of French imperial development and practices. He observed that Algeria, and to a lesser extent Tunis, a French protectorate since 1881, had solved "the question of peopling the colonies": Seven hundred thousand European colonists, a slim majority French, resided in North Africa. The relationship between French North Africa and France was "about the same," De Caix claimed, as the relationship between Americans and "their old Anglo-Saxon mother country," Britain. By this analogy, he perhaps meant merely (since the United States was obviously larger than Britain and no longer a colony) that white settlers in Algeria and Tunis, whom he termed "neo-French people," supported France because of a shared cultural heritage. Francophilic Europeans "had taken a part of their land" from Algerians and Tunisians, but the sequestration was justified, De Caix maintained, since Europeans had introduced productive farming techniques to native inhabitants on their remaining land and employed native laborers for good pay.[29]

Perhaps astute American readers of De Caix's description of the development of Algeria and Tunis as would-be settler colonies recognized the similarity to US patterns of westward continental conquest in the nineteenth century. And many pro-annexation Americans shared De Caix's faith in the benevolent ends of colonial economic development, even if the means to those ends were violent. However, few Americans who supported annexation of the new overseas territories foresaw them as destinations for settlers who would eventually replace Indigenous populations.³⁰ Thus, De Caix's emphasis that territorial emigrants would project the national mission through land cultivation was likely the least relevant aspect of French colonialism to American readers, whether for or against annexation.

Elsewhere, however, De Caix's analysis was more pertinent. Since most of the French colonies were, in his words, "tropical lands," they had, until recently, received relatively few white settlers; those who did migrate were "overseer[s] of native labor." Such French practices, and similar labor organization in British India, "demonstrate[d] convincingly the possibilities for what one might call the imperial race to govern and administer in very small numbers immense masses of Asiatics and Africans."³¹ De Caix's powerful image of hegemonic white dominance of Algeria as a franchise colony effectively blurred the lines between Anglo Saxon and French imperial capacity, echoing Theodore Roosevelt's arguments about the rights and responsibilities of an imperial master race but displaying the pertinence of the French Empire in greater detail.

Likely most strikingly, however, was De Caix's observation that the French Empire in 1901 had "learned that the granting of citizenship to all our subject peoples would mean submersion." Therefore, France had "renounced the hope of assimilating the natives, even in colonies where a large European element should influence their ideas and customs." Thus, "there is little probability that the French republic will make citizens of her many-colored subjects, at least not in a future the present generation will live to see." Beginning in 1865, the French Second Empire offered national citizenship to Algerian Muslims, although few completed its naturalization requirements. The Third Republic continued the policy and further declared all Algerians to be French nationals, and in 1870 French colonial missionaries, schoolteachers, anthropologists, and engineers, as well as government administrators and even military officials, envisioned Algerians' political assimilation. But the 1871 Mokrani Revolt undermined such ambitions. By 1900 De Caix's statement that the active citizenship of France's "many-colored subjects" was more an ideal of the republic than its policy spoke for the main colonial lobby.³²

It is difficult to say exactly how readers of the anti-annexationist *San Francisco Call* and the pro-annexationist *Minneapolis Journal* interpreted De Caix's accounts of the French Empire. Opponents of annexation may have taken tales of Algeria and other French possessions as warnings about the perils of overseas empire; supporters of annexation may have concluded that French experiences in Africa conveyed former Spanish colonies' need for Americans' tutelage through incorporation. Perhaps as a subtle revelation of the two newspapers' political positions, the pro-annexationist *Journal* inserted in its story a boldface subtitle: "Subjects, Not Citizens"; the anti-annexationist *Call* did not. This *Journal* phrase later would prove predictive. Frederic Coudert, the attorney for Isabel González, would argue that she had a right to remain in the United States by drawing on the history of French colonial law such as that provided by De Caix, particularly how the French republic's incorporation of territory had happened without enfranchisement of its native people—that is, by creating "nationals" but not citizens. It was this aspect of Algeria, reflecting how it was partly settler destination, partly discontiguous trading partner, which made the French territory relevant to the internationalization of US territorial law.[33]

The French colonialist De Caix's account of the French empire appeared in US newspapers at a pivotal moment. Americans had reelected President William McKinley the previous fall on a platform that the United States had a "responsibility before the world" to maintain law and order and establish "good government" among the peoples "rescued" from Spanish sovereignty in the Philippines and Caribbean.[34] The election was a referendum on steps that the McKinley administration and Republicans in Congress had already undertaken to establish government in the new territories. In 1899 the Schurman Commission and its Puerto Rican counterpart, the Carroll Commission, made recommendations concerning territorial governance. Both commissions recommended the development of local political institutions and co-optation and participation of local political elites. The Schurman Commission considered various forms of British colonial governance as analogies for prospective US authority in the Philippines but rejected them in favor of prior US territorial practice, though in a key contradiction to that history the commission concluded, "Adaptation of Territorial system to the islands would *not* . . . mean an extension to them of the Constitution and all the laws of the United States."[35] The Carroll Commission recommended that Puerto Ricans not pledging continued allegiance to Spain be declared US citizens, but the Foraker Act of April 12, 1900, establishing civilian government in Puerto Rico, did not provide for Puerto Ricans' US citizenship.[36]

French Algeria as a Legal Analogy

The status of Puerto Rican and, more so, Filipino peoples remained unclear in mid-January 1901, when arguments were heard in the first of the Insular

Cases, *Downes v. Bidwell* and *De Lima v. Bidwell*. The cases concerned how the Treaty of Paris affected the Dingley Tariff of 1897 on goods imported from other countries to Puerto Rico and a tariff on goods shipped between Puerto Rico and the United States established as part of the Foraker Act. In dispute was the meaning of the US Constitution's Article I provision that "all duties, imposts, and excises shall be uniform throughout the United States."

Although McKinley had campaigned for reelection in 1900 on an annexation platform, the president was reported to be more concerned at this time about these cases' implications for Filipino citizenship than for a ruling on the Puerto Rican tariffs. Specifically, aides in the White House indicated that McKinley worried that the Philippine-American War and its consequences might resemble France's drawn-out, irregular war to establish civilian rule in Algeria.[37] French-Algerian wars, McKinley realized, constituted a conflict between races.

The immediate context for McKinley's concern was a growing perception that Filipino forces interpreted an 1899 order by Philippines Governor-General Elwell Otis that Filipino civilians and surrendered or wounded prisoners were not to be harmed and that private property be protected as signs of Americans' weakness. Shortly after his reelection, McKinley replaced Otis with Arthur MacArthur, who declared a "policy of chastisement," a loosening of Otis's restraints on US soldiers and officers. MacArthur's approach represented a return to Americans' earlier territorial ways of war. Both Otis and MacArthur were veterans of the Civil War and recent Indian wars; Otis campaigned in Montana after the Battle of Little Bighorn massacre; MacArthur, under command of General George Crook, had tracked the Apache warrior Geronimo in Arizona. Both commanders were familiar, therefore, with the elasticity of General Orders 100, the 1862 "Lieber Code" that stipulated laws of war and authorized retaliatory violence for "savage" conduct of Filipino independence fighters.[38] Notwithstanding President McKinley's concern that the Philippine-American War might resemble the French conquest of Algeria, US military strategists had long studied the French occupation of Algeria. General Samuel Young, military governor of the Philippines' Northern Luzon military district, who earlier had urged that French publications on colonial warfare be taught at West Point, wrote to the War Department in December 1900 in support of a scorched earth policy that it "was . . . advisable to pursue the methods of European nations and armies in suppressing Asiatics [sic]."[39]

Considering Young's choice of words, it is possible that he advocated a US approach in the Philippines that would have mirrored a reformed, "population-centric" counterinsurgency strategy against "Asiatics," described at the time by Hubert Lyautey, a French lieutenant colonel and veteran of colonial warfare in Indochina. There Lyautey helped develop an "oil-spot" model in which French patrols circulated around local population centers, gradually extending control until they touched upon the patrol of an adjacent population center. Each center was to become a market that attracted natives, gathered intelligence, and demonstrated that prosperity followed cooperation with France.[40] In effect, Lyautey recommended a broadening of the role of France's *bureaux arabes* in Algeria, a section of the French military composed of ethnographers and intelligence officers specialized in learning about a colonized society's traditions and values and offering economic incentives in order to gain trust. Lyautey wrote a magazine article in early 1900 that described this approach, and the American novelist Edith Wharton, after her escort around French Morocco as Lyautey's guest in 1917, would hail the resident-general's remaking of the country's infrastructure on the basis that "a work-shop is worth a battalion."[41] But given General Young's sense that Filipinos were dishonorable or irrational "savages" and the harsh steps that he urged US forces to take to conquer Filipino resistance, Young probably had in mind the older practices of Thomas Bugeaud, not the revisionism of Lyautey.

MacArthur's institution of irregular warfare therefore signaled the reemergence of Americans' longer-term Algerian connection to the harshening of tactics in the Philippines. The connection provides framing for the observation of the French ambassador to the United States and former governor-general of Algeria, Jules Cambon, that reports of a US commander's holding whole Filipino villages responsible for US soldiers' injuries had been a French North African tactic. Cambon was uneasy with the practice but rationalized, expressing a sentiment that many US annexationists shared, that it "was sometimes the only effective means of action that authority can employ in a barbaric country."[42]

Thus, President McKinley's discomfort at the time of the first Insular Cases may be attributed to the specter, newly significant to him (although in the Civil War he had served under General George Crook, a practitioner of counterinsurgency warfare), of distant long-term wars of conquest in Algeria and the Philippines, whose costs of annexation would be military as well as political. It was possible, thus, at the beginning of 1901, that an alien, hostile population might eventually be defeated—but then offered access to citizenship. France's irregular war in Algeria shaped Americans' rapidly evolving perception of their island territories.

In May 1901, meanwhile, the US Supreme Court ruled that with the Treaty of Paris, Puerto Rico had ceased to be a foreign country, therefore its imports of goods from abroad were not subject to the 1897 tariff. However, the court also found that Puerto Rico was not a part of the United States in terms of treatment as a state or incorporated territory. The result was that "while in an international sense Porto Rico was not a foreign country, since it was subject to the sovereignty of and was owned by the United States, it was foreign to the United States in a domestic sense, because the island had not been incorporated into the United States, but was merely appurtenant thereto as a possession."[43] Reflecting on earlier expansion in which territorial inhabitants gained citizenship, the court found that these episodes were accomplished not by the Constitution itself but strictly through acts of Congress; thus the recent Foraker Act had merely broken tradition, not the law. Critics at the time and scholars since have noted how the court's oblique opinion, admitting concern not to commit a "false step . . . fatal to the development of what Chief Justice Marshall called the American Empire," provided an extra-constitutional device to US overseas expansion.[44] The opinion thus sanctioned, in the words of Christina Burnett, "the idea that the United States could continue to expand its sovereign territory without [necessarily] increasing the ranks of U.S. citizens."[45]

While the dimensions of Puerto Rico's liminal status as an unincorporated territory would be fully realized only over time, its role within the US political system as an analogy to France's Algeria was revealed, if incidentally, nearly immediately. In May 1898 the United States and France had formed a trade agreement providing for reduced duties on imported merchandise comprising "the product of the soil or industry of France." In April 1899, the American Tartar Chemical Company imported tartar from Algeria but was made to pay excise taxes according to the Dingley Tariff. A Board of General Appraisers rejected the company's appeal on the basis that Algerian soil was not French soil.[46]

Meanwhile, the French government instructed its ambassador to the United States, Jules Cambon, to contend that Algeria was a part of France within the meaning of the agreement; thus its products should enjoy the same tariff relief as those of France in Europe. US Secretary of State John Hay replied that "'France' was . . . a well-known geographical and European description, quite distinct from 'Algeria,' an African country."[47] As an incentive to encourage the US government to accept this definition of Algeria's status, however, Ambassador Cambon offered that US products exported to Algeria would be treated with the same trade privileges as they would receive on the Continent.

Additionally, in 1901 the US Treasury Department published a sprawling study of Western European powers' colonial practices during the nineteenth century. The study lauded the British Empire for being "more successful in the management of noncontiguous territory than any other nation" and deprecated the French colonial system, which it dated only from the establishment of the Third Republic in 1870. Less fond of French colonial policy than of Algeria's desert mystique, Poultney Bigelow contributed to the Treasury Department study by observing that France had conquered foreign places but not colonized them, governed heavy-handedly through military force, suspected native people's initiative, and squelched local governance. On the other hand, the study lauded French treatment of Algeria "as a French province and not as a colony in the ordinary acceptance of that term." The report particularly highlighted France's introduction of free trade with Algeria begun during the Third Republic, citing a quadrupling of Algerian exports since 1867. Algeria was a forerunner, the report continued, for the recent trading status of Hawaii and Puerto Rico under the US flag. These free-trade examples were a contrast with a movement in Britain at the time to form an imperial customs union.[48]

Voilà. Hay replied to Cambon that the State Department could regard the inclusion of Algeria within the meaning of "France" to be a "friendly adjustment" to the treaty. Accompanying this concession, Americans requested that Puerto Rico be accorded the same status as Algeria. The two countries adopted both of these in the amended treaty, which President Theodore Roosevelt proclaimed on August 22, 1902. US appellate courts subsequently upheld Tartar Chemical's appeal.[49] Thereafter, drawing on the Tartar Chemical precedent, a 1911 case concerning the kind of tariff applicable to trade between the Philippines and Cuba determined that the Philippines was, like its sister countries Puerto Rico and Algeria, "an other" but not a "foreign" country in relation to the mainland.[50]

No doubt, achieving favorable trade treatment was a motivation for Secretary of State Hay's quick acceptance of France's clarification that Algeria was, indeed, its integral part of France, not a colony—this had in fact been French policy since the Second Republic's declaration in 1848. Yet Americans were newly conversant on the issue of an empire strategically incorporating a territory. Meanwhile, France's recognition of Puerto Rico as "foreign in a domestic sense" to the United States signaled international understanding of the Supreme Court's interpretation. This was so even while US newspaper reports settled on the shorthand phrase "the United States proper" to suggest the part of the country from which the court had excluded Puerto Rico.

Yet it was hardly coincidental that both US and French negotiators treated Puerto Rico as America's Algerian corollary. The two territories formed a reciprocal relationship.⁵¹

The "National" as a Status of Imperial Belonging

Still, like the Foraker Act, neither the first Insular Cases opinions nor the 1902 French-American treaty addressed the citizenship status of the new US territories' inhabitants. In its turn-of-the-century language, the court speculated that such people were "alien" to "Anglo-Saxon principles," but in *De Lima* it declined to rule on their "civil and political rights," declaring, "essentially the whole matter is legislative, not judicial."⁵² This reticence was apparent despite the fact that the attorney for the petitioners in *De Lima* and *Downes*, Frederic Coudert Jr., who also would represent Isabel González, did raise the issue of citizenship. In his brief for *De Lima*, Coudert argued that the inhabitants of Puerto Rico and the Philippines were US "nationals," a term that he claimed fulfilled the intention of the 1898 Treaty of Paris to identify the territorial inhabitants who were not Spanish-loyal "aliens," irrespective of whether Congress had acted to designate their status. *National* was also preferable to the alternative terms *citizen* and *subject*, with whose ambiguity Senator Foraker had wrestled in developing the Foraker Act. At the time, Foraker had explained, "We [the Senate] concluded . . . that the inhabitants of that island [Puerto Rico] must be either citizens or subjects or aliens. We did not want to treat our own as aliens, and we do not propose to have any subjects. Therefore, we adopted the term 'citizens'."⁵³ In his *De Lima* brief, meanwhile, Coudert observed that the term "subject" had become discredited because of "its usual reference to feudal or absolute monarchies where none or few of the subjects are citizens in the sense of possessing political rights" and was "now found in no constitutionally governed nation save England."⁵⁴ For Foraker, and for Coudert, the term *subject* was too closely associated with the status of people under monarchical government for US republican policymakers to adopt.

Coudert, on the other hand, asserted that *national* was a term already in de facto usage in US law to treat groups allegiant to the United States and deserving of its protection, though who, "for a variety of reasons other than alienage, do not possess the political franchise." Specific such nationals were women, minors, and the inhabitants of the territories of Oklahoma and Arizona. Moreover, Coudert also explained that *national* was an appropriate term based on its adoption by Germany and France "to denote all persons subject to the allegiance of the state, i.e., forming a part of the nationality." Coudert would make the concept of the national as practiced in the French Empire even more central in his argument in *Gonzales*. A. Abbott Lawrence Lowell had emphasized in his *Harvard Law Review* article the precedent solely of US territorial practices to justify territorial acquisition, an argument that Justice Edward Douglass White later acknowledged influenced the court's decision in *Downes v. Bidwell*.[55] In contrast, already in the first Insular Case of *De Lima*, Coudert, like Carman Randolph (although Randolph opposed annexation unless territories were guaranteed statehood) emphasized the relevance of *international* law—at least the practices of European continental powers—to US circumstances in 1901.[56]

Thus, when Frederic Coudert had the opportunity to petition the Supreme Court directly on the question of the citizenship of the territorial peoples, he was in fact expanding on his brief for *De Lima*. Given the court's earlier reticence on the point, it was a possible risk to make the same or a similar argument. By the end of 1902, however, the military and political situation in the Philippines had stabilized. The last Filipino forces fighting the US occupation surrendered in April, and President Roosevelt declared a general amnesty on July 4. Congress passed the Philippine Organic Act on July 1, which called for a popularly elected assembly as the Philippines legislature's lower house, the appointment of two Filipinos to represent the Philippines in Congress, and the disestablishment of the Roman Catholic Church in the archipelago, among other measures. As the Foraker Act did for Puerto Ricans, the Organic Act declared Filipinos not declaring allegiance to Spain to be citizens of the Philippines.[57] On August 2, the Puerto Rican woman Isabel González arrived at Ellis Island and was detained as an alien. After Gonzáles brought a lawsuit against her detention, Coudert learned of her case and joined her legal team the following February.[58] Coudert's access to Congressional debates, law journals, popular magazine articles, and news stories about the history of French–American relations and war development and trade helped remind him of French historical and imperial development in the years between the Spanish-American War and his identification of Isabel González as a test case about US citizenship for Puerto Ricans.

Beyond these historical and transimperial contexts, Coudert also had a personal familiarity with France and international law that perhaps predisposed him to ask the Supreme Court to consider its practices to establish a precedent for US territorial law. Coudert's grandfather fought under Napoleon Bonaparte then fled to New York after a failed attempt to return the emperor to power from exile. During the American Civil War he was considered for command of a regiment of French exiles. Coudert's father was an attorney whom President Grover Cleveland asked to serve on the Supreme Court and as US ambassador to Russia, though he refused both appointments. After serving as an army lieutenant in Puerto Rico Coudert joined his father's firm, familiar with French history.

Besides drawing the French Algerian example in his brief for *Gonzales*, Coudert considered other cases heard by the Supreme Court with an eye on French law. In two cases concerning the status of property of the Catholic Church in Puerto Rico and the Philippines after US annexation, the court affirmed the church's title to property it had received from the Spanish government. These decisions appeared shortly after an anticlerical government in France, headed by Prime Minister Émile Combes, partly in response to the controversial Dreyfus Affair, cracked down on the Catholic Church in France. Combes ordered all religious orders to submit to government authorization and closed some ten thousand schools run by Catholic clergy, resulting in the confiscation of some 200 million francs' worth of church property. In this situation Coudert considered the French example one to avoid and applauded the *Ponce* and *Santos* decisions for "avoid[ing] all civil dissension between church and state in Latin countries."[59]

Reflecting his anticipation of a situation like that of Isabel González that could force the Supreme Court to address territorial citizenship, Coudert actually published the substance of his argument for *Gonzales* in an article for the *Columbia Law Review* in January 1903, eleven months before he argued the case at the Supreme Court. Here he again emphasized that for the court to deem Filipinos and Puerto Ricans "subjects" was impolitic because of the term's association with inhabitants of a monarchy. As he did in *De Lima*, Coudert emphasized the attractiveness of an alternative classification as nationals. This time Coudert justified the term using various analogies rooted in US history, though none terribly comfortably. Filipinos and Puerto Ricans resembled residents of the District of Columbia, since they were under the direct authority of Congress, although the district was an incorporated territory while, under the *Downes* decision, the island territories remained unincorporated. The islanders more closely, observed Coudert, resembled free Black Americans before the Fourteenth Amendment, who, as declared in *Dred Scott v. Sandford*, were neither aliens nor citizens. They were also somewhat like Indigenous Americans born on Indian reservations, since in such territories, although they were within the United States, individuals inherited and, even upon leaving a reservation, retained tribal citizenship and could gain US citizenship only through naturalization.⁶⁰

Given the poor fit of various cases that occurred before the United States acquired overseas possessions, particularly how the degrading treatment of "the free Negro and the detached Indian" were precedents "of which we are least proud," Coudert urged the Supreme Court to look abroad, to kindred empires' treatment of colonized peoples. This perspective could inform understanding of the "national" status of Filipinos and Puerto Ricans.⁶¹ Not surprisingly, he highlighted the treatment of Algerians under French rule. In 1839 a French court had determined the Algerians were under French sovereignty, even though the French legislature had not acted to declare it so. In 1865 a decree of Emperor Napoleon III had reiterated that Algerians were French, though unless they were naturalized French citizens they remained under Muslim law. Coudert noted Europeans' large-scale expropriation of land from Algerians partly through exploitation of natives' ignorance of French land laws applied in North Africa. Coudert was no idealistic antiimperialist, dryly imagining that if an Arab chief received a court summons to defend his tribe's land rights, he probably would use it "for the purpose of igniting his pipe."⁶² However, Coudert did urge US administrators in the Philippines to avoid analogous predations, even despite the fact that the Philippines was not a settler colony. He further observed that Algerians wishing for French naturalization underwent a simpler process than did outright foreigners wishing the same, implying that US courts should adopt a similarly liberal philosophy toward the new "other" Americans.⁶³

On January 4, 1904, the Supreme Court announced its decision in *Gonzales*. Again, as in 1901, it declined to say whether Puerto Ricans were citizens of the United States. It also declined to accept Coudert's promotion of the term *national* for territorial peoples, although it embraced the term to describe the territories' collective status. Under the Treaty of Paris, Spanish-born territorial residents not pledging continued allegiance to Spain thus adopted the "nationality of the territory." And on the basis that other Puerto Ricans could owe allegiance only to the United States, it affirmed Isabel González's claim that she was no longer an alien and therefore could not be barred from entering the United States.⁶⁴

The *Gonzales* decision made front-page news in Puerto Rico but did not in US newspapers, many of which simply summarized the opinion's finding that Puerto Ricans were not aliens. Several accounts, reflecting familiarity with the term *citizenship*, pointed out that the court rejected the argument of Puerto Rican Commissioner to the United States Federico Degetau, who had filed an amicus brief that González was already a US citizen. Degetau argued that Puerto Ricans had earned that right by virtue of their level of political development and self-government under Spanish rule, more pronounced than that of the "uncivilized tribes" of the Philippines, for whom the term *native*, used in the Treaty of Paris, was truly appropriate.[65]

While no commentator explicitly discussed Coudert's invitation to embrace the example of French Algeria, several correctly suggested that the court's reticence on the point implied that it had stumbled toward correlating US law with the international practice that transfer of sovereignty conferred the nationality of the new sovereign on the inhabitants of the new territory. One newspaper remarked that the opinion reflected how the new territories had introduced "a good deal of metaphysics into our body of law." A second, under the headline "Queer Status of Porto Ricans," asked rhetorically, "Not being citizens, and yet owing allegiance, can it be said they are subjects?" A law journal's exasperated comment more eloquently attested to the new legal category of belonging in the United States: "The Supreme Court seems to hold that the terms 'aliens' and 'citizens' are contraries, and that the Porto Ricans belong to that vague and indefinable class—the *tertium quid*." Another newspaper acknowledged, perhaps with more insight than it intended, that "the thing [new US territorial law] would not have been thought of prior to the period of present-day republicanism."[66]

This stumbling step of reformulating US republicanism toward an imperial conception of "national" belonging strongly reflected the influence of information that had recently circulated in the United States about nuances of French historical and imperial development. Discussions of the means of establishing US power abroad at the turn of the twentieth century sharpened Americans' resentment of British power at the same time that Anglo-Saxonism fostered a rapprochement between the two countries. Partly as a consequence of that resentment Americans sought lessons, positive and negative, from French practices in Algeria. Like Americans' experience in the Philippines, French Algeria had been conquered by unconventional warfare, which was rationalized as a "civilizing" mission. Its inhabitants were nominally eligible for national citizenship. And native Algerians, like peoples in the new US territories, were racially different from the metropole, yet under republican principles they were officially assimilable through the prospect of gaining national citizenship. Among European colonial empires, the French model best suited Americans' pretensions to liberal colonial rule. This transfer was important in Americans' coming dominance of the relationship between the two empires.[67]

Such an episode in French-American "inter-imperial dynamics and connections" revises two bodies of historical literature. One of these has emphasized the novelty of US imperial policies.[68] The other has explored French interest in US westward expansion to assist development of Algeria as an agricultural settler of overseas territory.[69] Study of the legal treatment of Isabel González puts US and French imperial history in dialogue, showing how French Algeria supplied both the United States and France with imagined legal concepts and facts on the ground to justify overseas territorial expansion and produce the personal status of the "national" within a liberal imperial framework.

Chapter 6

Algeria's Ambiguities Among American Pan-Africanists

The writer and anti-colonial leader Frantz Fanon famously wrote in *The Wretched of the Earth*, concerning what was necessary for colonized people to unite and achieve liberation, that "the practice of violence binds them together as a whole."[1] Fanon's writing has been shown as a major intellectual inspiration for the Black Power revolutionary movement in the United States and one of the most often cited intellectual inspirations of Black militant groups. Stokely Carmichael, a Black Power founder, called Fanon a "patron saint."[2] Huey Newton, a founder of the militant Black Panther Party (BPP), an element of Black Power, recalled how BPP leaders read Fanon obsessively.[3] Fanon's context for his powerful anti-colonial writings was his participation the Algerian War of Independence, 1954–62, as a physician and psychiatrist. Outside of Fanon's work, however, Algeria as an African nexus of American Black nationalists and civil rights activists was anomalous.

This chapter explores that incongruity by tracing the twentieth-century background of African Americans' encounters with French Algeria. The chapter argues that cosmopolitan African Americans struggled to locate Algeria along the "color line," the phrase of W. E. B. Du Bois, constructed by US and French imperial policies from the late nineteenth century through the 1960s, even as the anti-colonial, pan-African movement, a diasporic identification with Africa among African-descended people in Europe and the Americas, slowly emerged. Algeria's liminal status survived the establishment of Algerian independence in 1962, but with the end of its colonial history, Algeria's significance faded. Frantz Fanon's endorsement of unifying violence spoke for a moment of convergence, but that moment's ephemerality was characteristic of this era of complicated transimperial connections between American pan-Africanists and Algerian nationalists, a case illustrating the limits of such connections.

From French Orient to "Perfectible Whites"

In the first part of the twentieth century the United States and France became more alike than ever in their efforts to project imperial power in the guise of republican equality, meanwhile witnessing slowly evolving domestic and colonial upheaval over the denial of that equality to people of color. Nonetheless, in the context of two world wars, Algeria, officially not a French colony and not principally inhabited by Black Africans, steadily disappeared from the attention of most Americans. To be sure, when the US press provided news about the French Empire other than, as has been shown, analogies for US annexation of the Philippines, it was generally negative. US commentators criticized French filibustering in the Congo, Madagascar, Tunis, and Vietnam, and the *Nation* magazine, although it also opposed US overseas expansion, prophesied flatly that the French Empire was destined to cost the country its power.[4]

On the other hand, Algeria's integration as a French department, populated increasingly as it was by European settlers, subtly clarified for many Americans that while the country was in North Africa, it was not *African*. Informed by French international displays of Algeria as both exotic and open to French economic development, Black nationalists and civil rights advocates, like many Americans, considered Algeria a sort of French Orient. Two examples of turn-of-the-twentieth-century world's fairs were such occasions for the display of *French* Algeria, which clearly competed with US displays about its own new territorial possessions but were sharply distinguished from concomitant exhibits showing the status of African Americans.

At the St. Louis World's Fair of 1904 France's enormous investment to modernize Algeria was reflected in an official report of the fair, which lauded a grand-prize-winning French locomotive, displayed in the Transportation building. The prominent customers for which the locomotive's Alsatian manufacturer had built more than one thousand locomotives, the report noted, were nine European countries, including France, as well as the United States and Algeria.[5] The development of Algeria's iron ore deposits and their transport to the coast by rail, and the investment of Alsace-Lorraine refugees resettled in Algeria after the Franco-Prussian War, distortedly situated Algeria among the world's powers.

Elsewhere, the French presence at the St. Louis Fair de-emphasized the exoticism of its colonial empire. Algeria, Tonkin, Madagascar, La Reunion, and Somaliland displayed commercial forestry products and medicinal plants, for example, but not Oriental architecture and much less costumed human specimens.[6] Americans in St. Louis and elsewhere in 1904 were still dancing the hoochie-coochie, a popular vulgarized version of belly dancing or danse du ventre, performed at the 1893 Chicago Columbian Exposition's Algerian Village.[7] A more sober Algerian presence at the St. Louis fair implicitly showed its progress, a development Americans could appreciate partly because US manufactured goods had begun to flood Algeria in the 1890s. The Singer Sewing Machine Company, for example, highlighted its North African presence by including an Algeria card in a set of collectible nations cards it published beginning in 1892. The card showed a traditionally dressed Algerian man standing beside a Singer, accompanied by the caption, "Even on this far off coast of Africa the civilizing influence of our 'Singer' is felt, and our Agent has supplied the native as well as French inhabitants with thousands of Singer Machines." Singer's exhibit at the St. Louis Exposition thus saluted both US and French imperial beneficence.[8]

In contrast, Americans' displays in St. Louis of their new overseas possessions, gained from wars with Spain and Filipino nationalists, were sensational. The most lurid exhibit in St. Louis was a village spanning forty-seven acres in which a thousand Filipinos lived during the fair, a trophy of the US conquest of the Philippines in 1902 (see fig. 6.1). Another exhibit staged reenactments of the 1898 Battle of Santiago de Cuba, which ended the Spanish-American War and temporarily transferred Cuba from Spanish to US possession. Perhaps French officials wished to avoid appearing to compete with US jingoism, and France had supported Spain, as far as many Americans were concerned, in the Spanish-American War.[9] Yet the contrast between the two empires' displays of overseas possessions was pronounced.

The St. Louis World's Fair represented a turning of the tables concerning US and French exhibitors' choices among evidence from history, science and technology, and exotica extracted from overseas territories to display

Figure 6.1. "Members of Uncle Sam's infant class—Igorotte Filipinos, Igorotte Village, World's Fair, St. Louis, U.S.A." International View Co. 1905. Library of Congress Prints and Photographs Division LC-DIG-stereo-1s47789.

national greatness. Four years earlier, Paris hosted its own Universal Exposition. French commissioners spared no effort to showcase colonial goods, people in costume, and traditional—precolonial—architecture. Representations of French possessions in Africa, the Caribbean, the Pacific, and Southeast Asia occupied half of the space the Paris Exposition allotted for colonial pavilions.

To be sure, the quantity of US exhibitors at the 1900 Paris Exposition was exceeded only by that of the hosts.[10] The US presence included a modest exhibition of products and artifacts from Cuba and Hawaii, whose exhibits were located, despite Americans' protests, in the colonial section of the exposition. By far the most unique US content in Paris was an "Exhibit of American Negroes," a joint project of Daniel Murray, the assistant librarian of Congress; Thomas Calloway, a lawyer; and two eminent African American intellectuals, Booker T. Washington, president of Tuskegee Institute, and W. E. B. Du Bois, then a professor of sociology at Atlanta University.[11] Elements of Washington's and Du Bois's different, well-known views of how African Americans should gain civil rights were on display in Paris. Consistent with a general US goal at the exhibition, Washington orchestrated displays demonstrating African American progress and contributions to civilization. The exhibit included four volumes of nearly four hundred official patents by African Americans, photographs from several Black colleges and universities, and some five hundred photographs of African American men and women, homes, churches, businesses, and landscapes. Somewhat like French colonial exhibits' silence about the Code de l'indigénat, the colonial legal code that kept Indigenous people in inferior status, there was no information on lynchings or other chronic racial violence in the United States at the time. The most anticolonial expression was a copy of the Jim Crow laws of Georgia, which Du Bois successfully lobbied for as a marker of the legal inequality that African Americans suffered.[12]

The United States Commission to the Paris Exposition, including Du Bois, insisted that the Exhibit of American Negroes not appear on the Trocadero (on the north side of the Seine River), punctuating its difference from the colonial pavilions (including Cuba and Hawaii) to which that particular space was devoted. The exhibit was in fact located in the Palace of Social Economy, devoted to "social economy, hygiene and organized charities."[13] As such it still could have been perceived, especially by the fair's white patrons, as a display of the benefits of white tutelage for people of color. Indeed, in their appeal to Congress for funding the exhibit, Calloway and Washington (but not Du Bois) speculated that the exhibit could help stir interest among European countries in studying the segregated US South as a model for colonial race relations, an initiative that British and German officials later acted upon in arranging for Tuskegee Institute students to teach Africans in their colonies the ways of US cotton agriculture.[14]

French officials, however, showed no such interest, despite their earlier efforts to replicate in Algeria the US West's agricultural expansion and settlement. In the Paris Exposition, to be sure, the Algerian pavilion was the most prominent on the Trocadero. Algeria was represented as the most exotic site of the colonial world, "where," in the words of a US commissioner, "the remote races of the earth strive to enter into competition with the elements of advanced civilization."[15] The Algerian pavilion was done up to replicate a precolonial Moorish palace and Algiers market scene and offered Algerian and French Orientalist artwork, historical documents about the French conquest, and shops along a mock "tortuous street," a winding Rue d'Alger. But the Algerian Palace emphasized cultural and commercial aspects of old Algeria as mere nostalgia, which French rule was in the process of overhauling.[16] French exaggeration and then erasure of Algeria's precolonial identity, different from US displays of both "savage" Filipinos in St. Louis and "progressive" African Americans in Paris, had the effect of distinguishing Algerians from people of color resident in the US empire.

While W. E. B. Du Bois was in Europe for Paris's Universal Exposition, he spoke at the first pan-African convention, in London. There he first remarked famously that the twentieth century's "problem" would be "the color line," or "how far differences of race . . . will . . . be made the basis of denying to over half the world the right of sharing to their utmost ability the opportunities and privileges of modern civilization." Du Bois posed the issue of bigotry clearly in racial terms, linking the oppression of the "American Negro" with the subordinate status of the "black colonies" of European powers in Africa and the West Indies and the tenuous independence of the "free Negro states" of Ethiopia, Liberia, and Haiti.[17] Ironically, although Du Bois was within walking distance of anthropological information about French Algeria in Paris in 1900, America's founding pan-Africanist did not take note, at the time, of the colonial subordination of Algerians, geographically an African people.

The obscurity of French Algeria even for perspicacious pan-Africanists like Du Bois and other African Americans in Europe diminished slightly in the era of World War I, although the relationship of French Algeria and the US South remained parallel, not connected. Du Bois acknowledged Algeria's subjugated status but still anticipated a different destiny for it and the rest of North Africa than for the sub-Saharan region, which for him was the heart of what he termed in his first autobiography, *Darkwater*, "the Dark Continent," where "the main mass of the Negro race" lived. While the kinship of sub-Saharan Africans and African Americans would grow closer, Du Bois at the time expressed his anticipation that North Africa—Morocco, Algeria, Tunis, and Tripoli (colonized by Italy and renamed as Libya in 1934)—would "become a part of Europe, with modern development and home rule," ironically fulfilling older French imperialists' visions of a greater, trans-Mediterranean southern European continent.[18] Du Bois did not specify who would exercise "home rule" in a modernized Algeria.

Du Bois's focus on racial identity as a basis for exclusion of Algeria from the pan-African movement at the time was not the only factor for the distinction he drew. Along with other African American and even some colonial African leaders, Du Bois maintained a favorable impression of France, Algeria's sovereign authority, during World War I. Du Bois was impressed by the French attitude toward Black soldiers, which appeared exceptional compared to opinion and policy elsewhere in Europe and in the United States and was indeed central to France's justification for drawing on "colored" troops both during the war against Germany and after it, into the 1920s, in enforcing German disarmament.[19] France was the first to arm Black troops to fight against white enemies in Europe. Although all in race-segregated units, some 200,000 African-American troops served in France during the war. French commanders oversaw about 50,000 of them in the 92nd and 93rd divisions of the American Expeditionary Force (AEF).[20] African American troops' arrival followed the nearly half million African troops who fought for France, including West Africans, Algerians (173,000 total, 87,000 in combat), Tunisians, Moroccans, Malagasies, and Somalis.[21] The German Empire, in contrast, circulated images of savage African and African American soldiers slaughtering and raping civilians. Only slightly less cynically, the US military called for strict racial separation of African American soldiers—although they were US citizens—from white people in Europe, soldier and civilian alike.[22] With similar Francophile emphasis, at the first Pan-African Congress in 1919 in Paris, Blaise Diagne, the first West African elected to the French parliament, contrasted social and political inequality in the United States and the "plane of social equality" in France, where members of the "colored race" could marry white women, attend unsegregated theater performances, and hold office in parliament.[23]

Already in 1917, Du Bois was tracking the Great War's impact in Africa for *The Crisis*, the magazine he edited for the National Association for the Advancement of Colored People (NAACP). Contrary to US officials at the 1900 Paris Exposition, who envisioned Germany's institution of racially uplifting economic practices in its African colonies, Du Bois emphasized the resemblance of German atrocities in Southwest Africa to abuses of African Americans in the South. Probably influenced by French propaganda, this was a perspective that was both pan-African and pro-Allies and helped to swell African Americans' military enlistments.[24] Throughout the war Du Bois embraced the cause of France as that of an enlightened civilization assaulted by German racism. In this attitude, to be sure, he was typical of Americans, who generally believed French people were color-blind. Of course, such racial civility may have been a matter of convenience as long as Black soldiers were fighting for France. Nonetheless, when the AEF sent French officials a memorandum discouraging friendly or even equal treatment of African American troops, the French parliament denounced it and affirmed the equality of mankind.[25] Du Bois foresaw that democracy could be expanded with an Allied victory. Shortly after the war's end, he predicted that African American soldiers would love France forever: "There is not a black soldier but who is glad he went,—glad to fight for France, the only real white Democracy."[26]

An early official history of World War I compiled by Emmett Scott, secretary for Booker T. Washington and an advisor in the US Department of

War, illustrated how such affection could linger at the same time that it suggested the particular liminal status of African American soldiers in the post–World War I Black Atlantic community. Scott collected evidence to validate African American soldiers' contributions to the Allied victory. To corroborate his data, Scott obtained a statement from Colonel Edouard Réquin of the French Military Commission to the United States about French colonial soldiers. Réquin made an implicit comparison between Algerian and African American soldiers. He emphasized that "colored troops," meaning Algerian Arabs and Berbers, had fought for France ever since the Franco-Prussian War. Unsurprisingly, Réquin omitted to note that upon that war's conclusion, French colonial forces had gone to war against hundreds of Berber tribes who engaged in Mokrani's Revolt in 1871.[27]

Réquin instead emphasized that World War I was the first occasion for deployment of "black troops" in a European war. "Black" colonial soldiers, of Senegal and Sudan, Réquin explained, had made effective grenadiers but in his view lacked mechanical aptitude for use of machine guns. They "are apt for attack and counter-attack, but . . . are primitive men without civilization—men who cannot be compared from this point of view with colored Americans." Citing the example of wounded white and Black soldiers receiving treatment in integrated French hospitals, Réquin explained colonial soldiers' service paternalistically, as gratitude for France's delivery of them "from African barbarism" and for the gift of "civilization and justice." Wartime France hardly considered Algerians savages any longer, Réquin emphasized, different from the nineteenth century's era of conquest. And France considered African Americans, like Algerians, "colored" but "civilized." What Algeria's governor-general Charles Lutaud said of Algerians in 1916 probably also expressed French people's view of African American soldiers: their gallant military service showed them to be "perfectible whites."[28]

However, neither the grudging acceptance of Algerian soldiers as assimilable to white society expressed by Colonel Réquin nor French affection for Black soldiers had much impact on postwar French reform of its citizenship laws regarding colonial workers. In 1919 France repatriated 90 percent of its colonial and Chinese wartime workers, and French law in the interwar period restricted Algerians who remained in the metropole, the number bulging on account of French settler policies' squeezing Algerians off of land in North Africa to jobs in mining, construction, and dock work and to segregated housing.[29] Likewise, the 1919 Jonnart Law, while enfranchising about 43 percent of Algerian men in Algeria as voters for Muslim members of municipal councils, continued the separation there of Algerian and European legislatures.³⁰ Most Algerians in North Africa remained subject to the harsh Code de l'indigénat until 1944.

Meanwhile, the novelty of French treatment of African Americans as racial equals, different from treatment in the United States, only further obscured French colonial race segregation from the view of African American troops, who considered their fair treatment the most meaningful definition of the civilization that France claimed it represented in the Great War. On this basis, Emmett Scott, like Du Bois, concluded that France was "a land where freedom, liberty, and equality are truly exemplified."³¹

When African American troops returned home, many were more cosmopolitan and politically assertive than before the war; their expectations for equal treatment and intolerance of racist vigilantism were inspired by their memory of fighting for France. Official French gratitude to both African colonial and African American troops highlighted the racial inequities of the United States. A few veterans became leaders in African American civil rights groups like the League for Democracy. But many veterans had to put their war experience to more immediate application in defense of homes, neighborhoods, and businesses amid postwar race riots. Twenty-six race riots broke out in the "Red Summer" of 1919 alone.³² To be sure, veterans' experiences in France, and even occasional French commentaries on US riots, spurred resistance to white vigilantism. For example, under the August 2, 1919, headline "French Give Opinion of Riot," the *Chicago Defender* explained Black Chicagoans' forceful self-defense as an outcome of "encounter[ing] no color line in France." The Chicago race riot and a similar one in Washington, DC the previous month, wrote the *Defender*'s publisher Robert Abbott, punctuated what was "known the world over"—that the United States was "the land of the lyncher and of the mobocrat." The fight for their lives and livelihoods, and their positive view of French society, probably distracted many African American war veterans from seeking ideological kinship with African colonial troops, including Algerians.³³

From Algerian "Negroes" to "I Am France"

Nonetheless, a milestone in Algeria's location in African American activists' consciousness was reached in 1923. That year the Black nationalist Marcus Garvey, nine years after founding the anti-colonial Universal Negro Improvement Association and African Communities League (UNIA), wrote an essay, "Who and What Is a Negro?" Focusing variously on African American migration to Liberia, ridicule of the post–World War I European mandate system in Africa, and support for Ethiopia in its war against Italy, Garvey invigorated thousands of African Americans' sense of connection of their oppressed status with the benighted condition of Africa.[34] But Garvey disavowed W. E. B. Du Bois's aspiration for racial integration; ironically, he shared the ardent desire for separatism of some white political leaders of the day. His complex vision was of a distinctive African nation whose constituencies resided outside Africa.[35]

Garvey's essay drew on the positive image of North African soldiers in France deriving from their service in the recent war. "The *New York World* under date of January 15, 1923," he wrote, "published a statement of Drs. Clark Wissler and Franz Boaz (the latter a professor of anthropology at Columbia University), confirming the statement of the French that Moroccan and Algerian troops used in the invasion of Germany were not to be classified as Negroes, because they were not of that race."[36] As pioneers of the discipline of cultural anthropology, Wissler and Boas were known principally for their opposition to the racial diversification of the world's peoples; in this context, they opined in the *New York World* that North Africans were not Negroid.[37] Boas's claim was consistent with conclusions in a US Department of State Report of 1921, *Colored Troops in the French Army*, in which the US ambassador to France, Hugh Wallace, observed, regarding the Allied forces occupying the Weimar Republic, "Properly speaking, there are no black troops. The Moroccans and Algerians are Arabs of the Mussulman religion and are entirely distinct from the Negro race."[38]

Garvey focused on the acclaim that French African troops had received elsewhere to argue that irrespective of their performance in occupying Germany and saving "the French nation from extinction . . .a black man, whether he be Moroccan, Algerian, Senegalese or what not," remained "a Negro." Consistent with his support for racial segregation and pan-Africans' capacity for civilized behavior without white influence, Garvey essentially argued that Negro troops did not shed their race on account of their environment or accomplishments. Meanwhile, besides merely bringing North Africa within the scope of Negro Africa—the historical lynchpin of which, for African Americans, was Ethiopia—Garvey proclaimed that Moroccans and Algerians were emissaries of the "Negro in Europe," perhaps even harbingers of the "day [when] Africa will colonize Europe."[39] For Garvey, valorous French North African troops' service in postwar Germany both demonstrated a possibility for pan-African military action and enlarged the meaning of "Negroes" that collapsed the distinction between sub-Saharan and North

Africans. Thus, Garvey's sensitivity to anthropologists' diminution of Black soldiers' capabilities perhaps incidentally opened the door to African American activists' recognition of Algerians not only for their military prowess but as exemplars of the merit of Black people for equal citizenship, or even as nationalist allies, thirty years before the Algerian War of Independence.

Likewise, at least momentarily, Garvey's assertion of a common "Negro" identity displayed by military service among African-descended people in the Americas and North Africans was accompanied by similar pan-African activism in France. An Algerian counterpart of Garvey in the 1920s was Messali Hadj, a World War I veteran whose experience, different from African American soldiers, disillusioned him about real French interest in republican equality. Appealing initially to colonized people living in France, Messali formed the Étoile nord-africaine (ENA) in 1926 to demand Algerian independence. In a pamphlet, *Lutte contre l'impérialisme français*, Hadj recounted a previous century's worth of French ruthlessness, involving famine, land sequestration, and mass exile of Algerians to the Sahara Desert. For Messali, French treatment of Algerians in the Great War represented the very nature of imperialism:

> Imperialism enrolls us by force in its army. In order to enrich a few European failures, it doesn't hesitate to have us massacred in fratricidal struggles, we ourselves unconsciously contributing to the enslavement of our Moroccan and Syrian brothers and, through a fatal repercussion, in the reinforcement of our own oppression. Unite your efforts in order to improve our lot. For the suppression of the *Code de l'Indigénat*, for the freedom of the press and assembly, for the equality of military service, for the freedom of immigration, against the sending of native troops to foreign lands! . . . Fight against French imperialism![40]

While for Garvey, common African identity linked people of color in the Americas and Africa, for Messali it was Islam that united North Africans with colonized people elsewhere.[41] UNIA and ENA laid groundwork for transimperial exchange. Although Garvey rejected a proposal by Muslim delegates in 1922 that UNIA adopt Islam as its official religion, UNIA incorporated Islam into its rhetoric. And the newspaper of Messali and other anti-colonialists in Paris, *Le Paria*, reported on Garvey's pan-Africanism.[42]

However, Marcus Garvey was imprisoned for tax fraud in 1925 and deported from the United States in 1927. His exodus did not end African American and Black francophone conversations about self-determination but did quash the possibility of his travel to Algeria (or any part of Africa) to forge an actual connection with Algerian nationalists as newborn pan-Africanists and aborted Algerians' emerging perception as pan-Africanists.[43]

Garvey's exile from the United States meant that African Americans in the interwar period, like African American troops in World War I, would perceive Algeria through a colonial lens. This view was most obvious among African Americans who visited Algeria as an incident of their affection for France. The cabaret dancer and singer Josephine Baker arrived in Paris in 1925 and her mesmerizing performances in "La Revue Nègre" launched a French craze for jazz and African American culture. Suggestive of her racially and transimperially liminal position as a representative of France's "Black" colonies, for the 1931 Paris Colonial Exhibition, the French government named Baker "Queen of the Colonies," and she danced her signature *Danse Sauvage*. In the same year she toured Algiers' theaters, hosted by Racing universitaire d'Alger, a European settler sports club. Baker returned to Algeria during World War II officially as an entertainer for the Free French Army, and unofficially as an Allied spy (conveying intelligence by writing it in invisible ink on her musical scores, passed on to others), and toured the country again in 1956, the occasion for her adoption of two orphans—one Berber child and one French colonial child. But Baker, a French citizen beginning in 1937, did not identify with Algeria's subjugation or later join its resistance to French rule. In Algeria, indicatively, she sang her famous song, "J'ai Deux Amours," meaning, "I have two loves, my country and Paris."[44]

In this way, like Baker, the novelist and NAACP contributor Jessie Fauset visited Algeria as a circumstance of her admiration, ironically, for French culture. Before editing the NAACP's magazine *The Crisis*, Fauset taught the French language in Washington, DC, and New York City. Fauset emphasized in her writing a realistic representation of the African American community, particularly the fledgling middle class. But she also developed a transnational aspect to literature of the Harlem Renaissance. Fauset studied at the Sorbonne in 1914, was a delegate in the US delegation to the Second Pan-African Congress in London in 1921, and lived for eight months in Paris in 1924–25.[45]

Unlike other Harlem Renaissance writers and artists who were inspired by tours of Europe, however, Fauset used the French capital as a point of embarkation to explore Algiers; she was the only writer of the Harlem Renaissance to do so.[46] During a respite from Paris in the Mediterranean city of Marseilles, she and a companion, Laura Wheeler, also a contributor to *The Crisis*, decided to cross the sea to North Africa. "Across the Mediterranean which stretched careless and blue at the foot of the Rue Cannebiére loomed

Africa. Perhaps that dream-land would never lie so near us again. Algiers was twenty-eight hours away." There, at least briefly, they would be "dwellers in Africa." Different from Du Bois, who in *Darkwater* noted his expectation that Algeria would become a part of Europe, Fauset—at least while waiting in Marseilles to embark—imagined the country as a sort of teeming African welcome station, not what Du Bois termed a "French outpost."[47]

In her visit to Algiers, Fauset wrote of a few encounters that invited her to identify with people of color within and beyond Africa. She shopped in a souvenir store on the city's central shopping street, the Rue Bab-Azoun, run by South Asians, the "Pohoomull Brothers, Brahmin merchants." She observed, "the brothers are brown, we are brown, [and] the Arabs [of Algiers] are brown." Elsewhere, while exploring the Casbah, the Arab quarter, Fauset found herself on a "twisting, writhing street, les Tournants de Rovigo" - ironically named for a ruthless French commander in Algeria at the beginning of the French occupation. In conversation with a woman in a bakery, Fauset learned she was mistakenly taken as a native of the Caribbean island of Martinique.[48]

Overall, however, Fauset interpreted Algiers from the perspective of a well-to-do American tourist, a "respectful outsider."[49] Algiers, in person, struck her less as an African or pan-African city and more as a place where "East and West" were brought together by "dark figures clad in European clothes but crowned with red fezzes." The veil covering an "old Arabian woman's" face, Fauset wrote, "lent her mystery and marvel. She was the very savor of the East." In other words, Fauset's self-identity as a person of color shaped her perspective, but it did not become a means of kinship with Algerians she encountered. After leaving the Indian emporium on Algeria's high street, Fauset observed that a "difference in our brownness" perceptibly remained among herself, the merchants, and cosmopolitan Arabs; she predicted poignantly that the longer they interacted, the more likely they were to discriminate against one another. Her mistaken identity as a Martiniquaise actually provided her protection, according to the Algerian baker, because that origin signified that she was "a French woman" for whom "there is no danger."[50] Nonetheless, in her second visit to the Arab quarter, she accepted and paid for the companionship of the wife of a French soldier who counseled her against touring the unoccupied part of the city alone. Appearing a year before the short story of another female traveler to Algeria—the novelist Edith Wharton, her story "A Bottle of Perrier" also a depiction of an American traveler's reliance on European colonial authorities for security against Indigenous North Africans—Fauset's account only partly questioned the orientalist dichotomy between primitive Arabs and civilized Westerners.[51]

Jessie Fauset returned to careers of teaching and novel-writing after her stint as a journalist finished in 1926. As she had in articles for *The Crisis*, in her fiction she profiled men of African descent throughout the world, emphasizing African heritage connections between African Americans and people of color elsewhere. But while, or perhaps because, Fauset remained a Francophile, her visit to Algeria did not clearly shape her literary perspective. French colonialism in North Africa, but not Algeria itself, figured faintly in her imagination. In 1927, while teaching in New York City, she quipped, "Like the French, I am fond of dancing. . . . I should like to see the West Indies, South America and Tunis and live a long time on the French Riviera." Somewhat surprisingly, in novels both before and after her visit to Algiers, Fauset dramatized Black cultural ties across the Americas but not between communities in the United States and Africa or Europe.[52]

Josephine Baker and Jesse Fauset were important transimperial figures in the Harlem Renaissance, and Fauset was likewise so in her role with the NAACP. Their perspectives on Algeria as more of an exotic travel destination than an ideological analogue, however, is suggestive of how those cultural and civil rights groups' takeoff before World War II incidentally weakened ties between African American and Algerian activists, perhaps unsurprisingly in the context of the Great Depression. Although Harlem Renaissance writers Claude McKay, Alain Locke, Langston Hughes, and Fauset met with French-speaking African and Caribbean writers in Paris who were active in the *négritude* literary movement, and probably most mingled at Baker's performances at the Folies-Bergère and the Casino de Paris, the latter group focused on fostering linkages among French-speaking Black writers. Transimperial contact between African American and Algerian reformers remained episodic.[53]

Indeed, the 1930s particularly was a decade in which Algerian activists resembled African American counterparts who focused on achieving full citizenship within white-dominated society, not nationalist separatism. W. E. B. Du Bois resigned from leadership of the NAACP in 1934 amid the organization's focus on lobbying for anti-lynching laws and the end of separate-but-equal US law.[54] This reform agenda was echoed in Algeria in the work of Ferhat Abbas, a secular intellectual trained in French literature and fond of Mustafa Kemal Ataturk's modernization of Turkey. Abbas formed the Fédération des élus indigènes in 1935, committed to forging a federal relationship between France and Algeria, with Algerians fairly represented in the French parliament. Abbas led an Algerian congress in 1936 that called for French citizenship for Muslims, compulsory education, and an end to restrictions against the Arabic language.[55] But that same year he wrote an article in which he declared, "I am France," meaning that after one hundred years of the impact of French culture in Algeria, he as an Algerian, committed to "collaboration," deserved to be treated like a French citizen.[56] French recognition of Algerian civic development, Abbas predicted, would finally emancipate Algerians from peasantry in a premodern society. Although in 1943 Abbas would reverse course and call for full Algerian independence, in his 1931 book, *Le Jeune Algérien*, he envisioned an Algeria finally benefiting from real republican institutions in which colonizers and colonized shared equal rights, where "a culture of work and peace would penetrate everyone's hearts" and "shacks" would be replaced by "white houses covering the mountains."[57] Abbas's emphasis on an interracial collaboration and work ethic and bourgeois housing development resembled Booker T. Washington's agenda of economic assimilation in the US South.

To be sure, the weakness of pan-African ties between African American and Algerian radicals was also a consequence of white authorities simply suppressing radical calls for the autonomy of people of color. Like the United States's deportation of Garvey, which precipitated UNIA's splintering, the French government banned the ENA as a revolutionary group, even though the ENA abjured violence, and deported Messali, first to Switzerland and again later to French Equatorial Africa.[58] Not coincidentally, in 1927 Messali and other ENA leaders had attended the first International Congress Against Colonial Oppression and Imperialism and for National Independence in Brussels, Belgium, also attended by peoples from various colonized countries and the United States.[59]

Thus, while UNIA and ENA planted the seeds of more prominent exchanges between Algerian and pan-African nationalists later, Garvey's and Messali's twin removals solidified the intellectual distance between African American and Algerian pan-African initiatives, not their proximity. In the 1930s the Nation of Islam, founded by a disciple of Garvey, Elijah Muhammad, picked up UNIA's appeal for African American separatism after UNIA's decline. But the Nation of Islam emphasized the distinctiveness of African Americans, not their connections with Africans.

These developments help explain what *pan-Africa* meant to delegates at the last Pan-African Congress before World War II when it was convened in New York in 1927, after French officials forbade W. E. B. Du Bois from holding the congress on African soil. The congress's executive committee defined *pan-Africa* as parts of the world where the percentage of people of African descent was large enough to "cause a so-called 'color' problem." Significantly, it then listed pan-African population centers in sub-Saharan Africa, the Caribbean, and the United States; Algeria was omitted.[60]

From Jim Crow in North Africa to "Equal in Paris"

It would thus take the somewhat incidental arrival of US soldiers in North Africa in 1942, as part of the Allies' effort in Operation Torch to drive German forces back across the Mediterranean, to trigger the movement of Algeria from the periphery to the center of African American radicals' consciousness.

Rising civil rights awareness in the interwar United States, supplemented by information about the nature of German Nazism, perhaps predisposed African Americans in wartime Algeria to notice denigrating French treatment of Algerians, more than their predecessors had done in France during World War I.[61] A prime example of someone for whom the Mediterranean theater of war shattered the colonial lens was Hugh Mulzac, a member of the US Merchant Marine. He earned a master rating in 1918, which should have qualified him to command a ship, but racial discrimination prevented this from occurring until September 29, 1942, when he was offered command of the USS *Booker T. Washington*, a Liberty ship. Mulzac, active in UNIA and a ship captain for Marcus Garvey's Black Star Line, actually signaled his sensitivity to segregation well before he departed for the war, refusing to command the ship unless his crew was racially integrated: *"A Jim Crow ship!"* he remarked. "That's what we're fighting *against*."[62] The *Booker T. Washington*, hailed by *Time* magazine when it launched for serving "not only in the war of ocean transport but in the war against race discrimination," operated in the Mediterranean, carrying cargo and prisoners of war between North Africa and Italy.[63] That service allowed Mulzac not only to identify the ironies that linked US and French racial discrimination but also to express the ambiguous identity of Algerians to African Americans at the time.

Starting in Tunisia, Mulzac detected a bizarre but clear color line that accompanied the grueling French-American liberation of North Africa. His ship damaged in a storm, Mulzac maneuvered the *Booker T. Washington* up a river from Bizerte to a dry dock at Ferryville. Along the way, "we saw one of the most amazing sights of the war—Algerian soldiers digging irrigation ditches along the river under *German* guards!" "Colonialists to the end," surmised Mulzac, the French trusted "captured Nazis more than their own Algerian troops!" Elsewhere, "all along the North African coast," Mulzac witnessed race segregation practiced at American Red Cross canteens replicating discrimination against African American troops in the Jim Crow South. Yet again, on account of the presence of Algerians, racist displays in North Africa took on transimperial dimensions. The Red Cross canteens provided access to white soldiers and African American soldiers on alternating days. Meanwhile French, but not Algerian, women served as hostesses every day. Like the favor that African American troops had enjoyed in France during World War I, Mulzac observed, "The girls were absolutely free of any prejudice toward us." But the illusion was quickly shattered when an African American GI brought an "Arab" woman to the canteen to dance. "French mothers and chaperones threatened to boycott." And Mulzac revealed the conundrum of Algerians' status for himself and Americans' racial constructions. "It was perfectly alright," he observed, for French women to "jitterbug the night away with colored Americans but *never* in the company of 'white' Arabs!"[64]

Mulzac's awareness of French discrimination against Algerians, brought into sharp relief by two kinds of soldiers—first Nazis, then African Americans—surely echoed Algerians' own provocation to seek alternatives to gilded French republican authority. In North Africa, African American GIs cheered for Algerians boxing Europeans, and Algerians cheered for African American troops engaged in street brawls with white soldiers.[65] This context of transimperial race relations on the ground magnified the irony that Algerian soldiers, passing as white troops, marched into Paris on its liberation day, August 25, 1944, while, pursuant to a joint Allied military leadership decision, both African American and sub-Saharan French African troops were excluded from the celebration.[66]

Reaction to upheaval in Algeria among Algerian national leaders, meanwhile, was both clear and considerably more consequential than the effects of the Great War. Mirroring African Americans' inspiration by their impression of an egalitarian French republic during World War I, the US military in North Africa, as a force liberating Algeria not only from German occupation but potentially from Vichy France as well, seemed to offer to Algerians an alternative to the discrimination maintained by French colonialists, to which Algerians were accustomed.

Beginning in 1943, Ferhat Abbas and others began to shift from a goal of equal citizenship in the colonial French Empire to a goal of Algerian independence. On March 31, 1943, four months after the launch of Operation Torch, Abbas published a *Manifesto of the Algerian People* to present to French authorities.⁶⁷ After consultations with Robert Murphy, US Minister to North Africa, about the reach of the 1941 Atlantic Charter, Abbas drew shrewdly on its third principle, which pledged the United States and United Kingdom generally toward decolonization and self-determination, to restore "sovereign rights and self-government . . . to those who have been forcibly deprived of them."⁶⁸ The manifesto reflected Abbas's sense to frame Algerians' independence like liberation causes in the West. The manifesto co-opted both the charter's aim to liberate Europe and African Americans' "Double V" campaign in the United States. It declared that the Algerian people would support the Allies in exchange for support for Algerians' right to self-governance through establishment of a French-Algerian federal government, each with its own legislature and guaranteeing freedom of religion, acceptance of usage of the Arabic language, free and compulsory education, and immediate full participation of Muslims in government. On May 26, 1943, Abbas and others, including the imprisoned Messali Hadj, published an "Addition to the Manifesto" that called for the first time for an Algerian state.⁶⁹ In Constantine in March 1944, Charles de Gaulle, then chairman of the French provisional government, the Comité français de Libération nationale, responded by announcing reforms that gave French citizenship to an additional sixty thousand Algerians without requiring their renunciation of religious belief, opening all office-holding to Muslims, and rescinding the long-lived Code de l'indigénat.

Suggestive of the obscurity among Americans of steps toward independence that Algerian nationalists were taking, disparate US observers struggled to interpret the declaration of Algerian independence on its own terms. Archibald Roosevelt Jr., a US Army intelligence officer stationed in the Middle East, met with Algerian leaders in June 1943. Roosevelt mistakenly dismissed Algerians' capacity for a national identity because the individuals with whom he met called themselves Muslims, not Arabs, the term used by French officials. Curiously, Roosevelt decided that the Algerians' "own heritage had been replaced by an inferior, secondhand European one. . . . They had become denationalized."⁷⁰

In the United States, meanwhile, African American newspapers like the *Chicago Defender* recognized the significance of the Algerian manifesto, even with Algerians' assertion of their "denationalized" religious identity. Attempting to facilitate understanding, the *Defender* reported news of de Gaulle's reform through the milestones of US civil rights reforms. "Emulating the role of Abraham Lincoln . . . General De Gaulle has announced measures that will do for the natives of French North Africa what the 14th and 15th Amendments to the U.S. Constitution were intended to achieve for the newly emancipated Negro peoples in the United States."[71] Perhaps in that context, the *Defender's* qualification, "were intended," suggested skepticism that the application of the 1944 *ordonnance* would match its premise; the halting history of US civil rights enabled the *Defender* to grasp the revolutionary steps that Algerian nationalists were beginning to take.

In any case, the opportunity presented by World War II for Algerians to assert independence invited a renewal of Algerians' ideological significance for American Black nationalists and civil rights advocates. This was true despite the complexities of Algerians' statements of their own identity and the limitations of Americans' understanding of events in Algeria through the context of US history. It was true, moreover, despite continuing disconnection between nationalist leaders in British- and French-controlled African countries themselves. No French-speaking Africans attended the Fifth Pan-African Congress in Manchester, UK, in the fall of 1945, for example.[72]

On the other hand, firsthand accounts of French-American racism on display, like those of the veteran Black nationalist and Liberty Ship Captain Hugh Mulzac, coupled with stark news of violent French suppression of Algerian freedom-seeking, exposed the myth of French liberalism hailed even by cosmopolitan Black Americans since World War I. A massacre of as many as thirty thousand Algerians around the town of Sétif by French police and pied noir settlers in response to demonstrations for independence betrayed the French "mission to civilize." Beginning on May 8, 1945, Victory in Europe Day, the Sétif demonstrations and bloody reprisals they provoked were reported first to Americans by the military newspaper *Stars and Stripes*, which reported a death toll of ten thousand that circulated in the US media. A US newspaper opined that the eruption and aftermath of the Sétif massacre were "very similar to the American Indian wars."[73] This was a misunderstanding, although, surely coincidentally, the Sétif demonstrators had waved the white and green flag of Algeria's forefather, Abdelkader, whom US commentators a century earlier had likened to a Seminole Indian.[74] Nonetheless, the German conquest of France and occupation of North Africa, followed by the brutal French response to this expression of Algeria autonomy at the end of World War II, showed a staggering French Empire mulishly clinging to its race-based colonial system.

Two Algerian nationalist parties formed upon Messali Hadj's release from prison in 1946: his Mouvement pour le triomphe des libertés démocratiques (MTLD) and the Union Démocratique du Manifeste Algérien (UDMA) of

Ferhat Abbas. The MTLD called for Algerian independence, the UDMA for an autonomous Algeria within a federal French system established by the 1946 French Union, by which the French Fourth Republic abolished colonies. Under the French Union local assemblies in overseas territories and departments gained only local authority, and Algeria was now reaffirmed part of Metropolitan France. An attempt to ward off perceived surrenders of overseas possessions at the end of World War II by Britain and the United States, the French Union contemplated a federalized greater France among the metropole and overseas locations. In referendums, however, Europeans living in overseas France overwhelmingly rejected the Union.[75]

The Algerian War of Independence began in 1954, when the radicalized Ferhat Abbas took refuge in Cairo, Egypt, where he helped form the Front de libération nationale (FLN). Abbas's radicalization would be noted by US Senator John Kennedy in a speech in 1957 urging US support for Algerian independence.[76] Kennedy had probably been influenced by publicity for the Maghreb cause of M'hamed Yazid, an FLN representative and husband of an American journalist, Olive Virginia Yazid, stationed in New York by the Inter-Arab Committee for the Liberation of North Africa. While French authorities attempted to broadcast Abbas's more moderate position in US media until he joined the FLN, Yazid publicized instances of French forces' torture of Algerian fighters.[77] Two hundred articles about Algeria appeared in the *New York Times* between 1958 and 1959, manifesting FLN strategy and helping foster pro-independence sentiment at the United Nations.[78] Ruthless French commitment to retaining the North African department titillated Americans not yet humbled by their own attempt to restrain a self-determination movement in Vietnam.

In Paris, meanwhile, Americans witnessed the Algerian war firsthand, once rivalry erupted between the National Liberation Army of the FLN and the MTLD, the latter guided by Messali in emphasizing Algerians' "Arab Maghreb" kinship with Moroccans and Tunisians, more than a national identity.[79] Enabled by a tenfold increase in the Algerian population in Paris between 1946 and 1954, the Café Wars, involving bombings and assassinations in the French capital and other cities, caused thousands of casualties, rationalized French police brutality, and ultimately destroyed the MTLD.[80] Visiting Paris in 1959, W. E. B. Du Bois observed that the city he formerly saluted was beset with "fear, hate, and despair" and thick with heavily armed police who searched Algerian boys on the public streets.[81]

Reflecting well-grounded fear of reprisals by French authorities keen to censor criticism of continuing colonial administration of Algeria, African

American writers residing in Paris, who had expatriated on the assumption that France was more racially egalitarian than the United States, were ambivalent about the revolutionary and counter-revolutionary violence of the Café Wars. The novelist Richard Wright publicly focused on anti-colonial developments in West Africa and Asia and, at times, actually defended French investment in North Africa.[82] Wright's sometime protégé, later rival, James Baldwin, rejected his compatriot's pragmatic Francophilia, writing publicly about his residence in Paris from 1948 in *Notes of a Native Son*. Baldwin expressed how his time in the French capital's streets had figuratively removed him to Algiers; his experience contrasted with Jessie Fauset's earlier sojourn, when she took the opportunity for chance encounters in the Casbah as a destination valuable principally for cultural enrichment. Baldwin echoed W. E. B. Du Bois in shuddering at "what Paris policemen can do to Arab peanut vendors."[83] Baldwin's essay in which that criticism appeared, "Equal in Paris," however, showed only Baldwin's equivocation about his humane treatment by Paris authorities after he was arrested for possessing a stolen hotel sheet. Anticipating the English title of Frantz Fanon's anticolonial manifesto *Wretched of the Earth*, Baldwin described the irony of his kinship with other petty prisoners in a Paris jail, rejoicing that they were soon to be released: Theirs was "the laughter of those who consider themselves to be at a safe remove from all the wretched. . . . I had heard it so often in my native land that I had resolved to find a place where I could never hear it any more."[84] Only in 1972 did Baldwin articulate his earlier empathy for Algerians: "The fact that I had never seen the Algerian casbah was of no more relevance . . . than the fact that the Algerians had never seen Harlem. The Algerian and I were both, alike, victims of this history [of European colonialism], and I was still a part of Africa."[85]

In contrast to Wright and Baldwin, the first African American author to amplify the World War II observation of Liberty ship captain Hugh Mulzac that colonized Algerians' conditions were analogous to African Americans' in a segregated United States was the journalist and novelist William Gardner Smith. A US soldier in Berlin from 1946 to 1948, Smith drew on the experience for his novel *Last of the Conquerors*.[86] Like Mulzac, Smith's protagonist, Hayes Dawkins, a soldier in US-occupied Germany, observes that the US military's Jim Crow system contradicts its rhetoric of supporting egalitarian democracy, which, Dawkins observes, is particularly ironic in post–Nazi Germany. Smith moved to Paris in 1951, where he reported stories for the *Pittsburgh Post*. Unlike its post–World War I charm, Paris now, for Smith, betrayed its similarity to US cities. Reporting his experience in the

Café Flore, for example, he narrated how an "Arab" sought to interest an American woman in a hand-woven rug. "'Buy a rug, lady? Buy a rug?' No one buys, and he walks off, to the next café. . . . And the American woman says to her companion, 'He's an Arab, isn't he? And they're filthy, aren't they? I hear they're all thieves and racketeers.' A bell rings somewhere in your head. Echo from another land."[87]

The tourist's pejorative term *Arab* for the Paris street hawker suggested the continuing obscurity of Algerians among American tourists. Of course, Americans' wholesale evacuation of North Africa after World War II, unlike their establishment of a permanent military presence in Western Europe, as well as the Algerian war and surging tourism in France made Paris's streets the only place most Americans would encounter either Algerian images or people at the time.

The Stone Face, Smith's novel published in the United States in 1963, on the other hand, marked a growing consciousness of Algerian kinship among African American intellectuals. In it the African American character Simeon Brown is disabused of his assumption that France lacks racial prejudice when he witnesses, as Smith did, the 1961 massacre of several hundred FLN demonstrators by Paris police, an event later censored by the French government for decades. In deciding to return to the United States to join its Civil Rights Movement, Brown imagines, "the face of the French cop . . . the face of the Nazi torturer at Buchenwald and Dachau . . . the face of the hysterical mob at Little Rock, the face of the Afrikaner bigot and the Portuguese butcher in Angola, and, yes, the black faces of Lumumba's murderers—they were all the same face."[88] Indicating the complexity of his odyssey in an Algerian Paris, Smith has another character in the novel chastise Brown that "Algerians are white people." Clearly, Algerians complicated Smith's understanding of racist violence at the same time they convicted him of a responsibility to his native country.[89]

From "Fighting the Same War" to Postcolonial Disconnection

France returned Algeria to military rule in 1957, a tacit recognition of the Algerian independence war. In the next few years Algeria's image among American Black nationalists slowly reversed, in ways, from its earlier form. On one hand, notable African American writers, artists, and scholars continued to affirm that sub-Saharan Africa, not North Africa, was the homeland to which pan-Africanists aspired. *Africa Seen by American Negroes*, a 1958 publication of the pan-African American Society of African Culture, for example, categorized Algeria as a part of "Islamic Africa," not "Black Africa."[90] Likewise, perhaps indicatively, W. E. B. Du Bois expatriated to Ghana, not Algeria, in 1961.[91]

On the other hand, by the late 1950s several important US civil rights advocates effectively hailed the sense of William Gardner Smith and James Baldwin that Harlem and Algiers, or at least the North African bidonvilles of Argenteuil outside Paris, were connected spaces. Some drew on brief personal experiences in Algeria; others articulated the new transracial solidarity as a basis for anti-imperial resistance only from a distance. A writer for the Southern Negro Youth Congress called for protests against the lynching of Emmett Till in August 1955 so African Americans could merge "with struggles of the South African, Algerian, Moroccan and oppressed peoples everywhere."[92] Hans Aurbakken, a Methodist missionary with experience in both Mississippi and Algeria, framed Till's murder as a brutal wake-up to Americans newly aware of Algeria's significance: "In the United States only people living in Mississippi in the fifties could really understand what was happening in Algeria."[93] In 1960 the NAACP's *The Crisis* declared that lunch counter sit-ins in the South were the US example of a "revolution now in progress in the world," elsewhere manifesting in mass demonstrations in apartheid South Africa and the war in Algeria.[94] The previous year, the writer and activist Hoyt Fuller, stopping in Algeria en route to the newly independent republic of Guinea, snuck into Algiers' Casbah to meet with a "young freedom fighter." Challenged on his way out by a French guard detailed to stop tourists from the neighborhood, Fuller displayed his US passport, inadvertently resorting to an old means for African Americans to gain French officials' favor. But he also announced to the guard his sense of a new transimperial, transracial solidarity: "I am a black man. The Algerians have no need to harm me. We are fighting the same war."[95]

With the achievement of Algerian independence on March 19, 1962, Algeria as a symbol clearly emerged in American pan-Africanists' consciousness. Algerian people's healing from colonialism was achieved by violent struggle, consummated as the psychiatrist and FLN leader Frantz Fanon prescribed in *A Dying Colonialism*, published in 1959, and *The Wretched of the Earth*, translated into English in 1963. Fanon emphasized that colonial repression of people of color and overthrow of that repression took many forms, and Algeria's example appeared universally adaptable.

In the 1960s, US civil rights leaders frustrated by white resistance to racial integration thus embraced Fanon's writings, witnessed the dramatization of the first years of the Algerian war in film, and made personal contact with Algerian statesmen. Between 1965 and 1970, *Wretched of the Earth* sold 750,000 copies and was required reading among Black Panther Party and Student Nonviolent Coordinating Committee members.[96] These encounters taught them that they themselves were colonized and that shared commitment to revolution, more than race, could bind pan-Africanists in the United States to Africa. As Algeria's first head of state to attend the United Nations, meanwhile, FLN veteran Ben Bella met with Martin Luther King Jr. in New York City in October 1962. Remarking on their two-hour conversation, King declared that "the battle of Algerians against colonialism and the battle of the Negro against segregation is a common struggle."[97] Five years later the iconic film *The Battle of Algiers* debuted in American theaters. Audiences, particularly the Black Panther Party, which screened the film for its members, regarded its neorealist depiction of Algeria's independence war as a sensation, quickly associating its depiction of "people hungry for freedom too long delayed" with US locations of insurrection. The viewer sees "events that have transpired this past summer in . . . Viet Nam, Watts, Newark, Detroit."[98] Quoting the sardonic line of a French officer, "We've gotten along with [Algerians] for 130 years. There's no reason it can't stay that way," a reviewer analogized, "Algeria and Alabama really aren't that far apart."[99]

In the same decade, Algiers famously hosted leading Black nationalists, a distant descendant of Marcus Garvey's early twentieth-century "back to Africa" movement. For the racial justice revolutionary Malcolm X, the Algerian war confirmed that Algerians possessed "credentials," as he put it in 1964, for carrying on a successful revolt against white oppression.[100] That same year Malcolm X visited Algeria during his pilgrimage to the Middle East and Africa. When he returned, Malcolm X renounced the Nation of Islam and founded the Organization for Afro-American Unity as a vehicle to connect the experience of Black Americans to the developing world. Explaining his epiphany, Malcolm X emphasized the signs he saw during a visit to the Casbah in Algiers that Algerians' degradation under French authority was still pervasive. The experience confirmed for him that conditions "that forced . . . the noble people of Algeria to resort eventually to the terrorist-type tactics that were necessary to get the monkey off their backs" were the "same conditions" prevailing "in every Negro community" in America.[101]

Likewise, in 1969 the Algerian government recognized the International Section of the Black Panther Party, about two dozen of whose leaders found political asylum in North Africa, as a liberation movement on par with the peoples of Vietnam and Palestine. Echoing the affirmations of King and Malcolm X and the theory of Fanon, BPP leader Eldridge Cleaver announced at a press conference at the University of Algiers, "Oppressed people need revolutionary principles rather than skin color."[102] Meanwhile, reversing the shunning of Algeria a generation earlier because it was not a "Negro" nation, the Nation of Islam saluted Algeria's sovereignty in its national newspaper, *Muhammad Speaks*, with the headline "Drive On to Free All of Africa!" and American pan-Africanist musicians, poets, and intellectuals met delegates from every African country in Algiers when the city hosted an inaugural Pan-African Cultural Festival in the summer of 1969 (see fig. 6.2).[103] Notwithstanding postindependence Algerians' lack of status as "Negroes," Algeria's flash to the center of solidarity between Indigenous and diasporic Africans, at least in the consciousness of American Black nationalists and civil rights advocates, was complete.[104]

Perhaps inevitably, however, events in the early years of Algerian statehood disabused American pan-Africanists of their image of Algeria as a transnational exemplar. Algerian laws in 1963 made Islam the religion of state and limited citizenship to those whose grandfathers possessed Muslim personal status.[105] Under Houari Boumédiènne, a former FLN commander, the FLN established a one-party state in Algeria, with the military the country's dominant political force through the 1970s. Algeria helped establish the Organisation for African Unity (OAU) in 1963 and pushed the OAU to provide weapons to independence fighters across the African continent; Nelson Mandela first visited Algeria when he was later released from prison to pay tribute for the country's aid against South African apartheid (including Mandela's own military training in 1962) and for other guerrilla liberation movements in the world. But Boumédiènne enforced the "Arabization" of Algeria as a remedy against French colonial legacies. Algeria's contested, postcolonial identification with the Maghreb North Africa and the Middle East, not sub-Saharan Africa, accelerated when it supported Arab countries against Israel in the 1967 Six-Day War. Algeria broke diplomatic relations with the United States over its support for Israel until 1974. In 1971 Algeria nationalized all French oil and gas holdings, part of Boumédiènne's program of Arab socialism. In the next few years, most Algerian land was nationalized and organized into agricultural cooperatives.[106]

Algeria's socialist turn, however, was offset by a desire to export oil and shale gas to the United States, an element in the 1980s of Algeria's shift under Chadli Bendjedid toward an extractive free-market economy and a pragmatic goal that helped chill relations between the Algerian government and the BPP International Section.[107] The relationship was also damaged by a spate of hijackings of US-flagged airplanes by Americans, some of them BPP

Figure 6.2. *The Black Panther*, August 9, 1969. Underground newspaper collection. Western Illinois University, reel 16.

members, to seek asylum in Algeria in the early 1970s. Several times hijackers arrived in Algiers bearing large ransoms paid by airlines to rescue hostages. Disappointing cash-short Black Panthers in Algiers, the Boumédiènne government resolutely returned the ransom money, along with the hijacked planes and their crews, to the airlines, and Black Panthers residing in Algeria were pressured to leave. In 1972 Minister of Foreign Affairs Abdelaziz

Bouteflika told US Secretary of State William Rogers that the Black Panthers made no "effective contribution to Algeria from [a] revolutionary, moral, or ideological standpoint."[108] This was an abrupt change of the two revolutionary groups' kinship over the previous decade. In January 1973 Eldridge and Kathleen Cleaver left Algeria to resettle, ironically, in France.[109]

The exodus of the BPP from Algeria also suggested a poignant parallel between the disengagement with American Black nationalists of Algerian state-builders prioritizing nearby concerns over expressions of solidarity, and similar earlier choices made by African American veterans of World War I and activists in the NAACP and the Nation of Islam, whose domestic priorities had eclipsed Algerians' early anticolonial activism.[110] That is, the Algerian severance with the Black Panthers on the basis of its exceptional situation as a new nation echoed earlier US civil rights advocates who, before World War II, emphasized the singularity of the US's deprivation of civil rights. Algeria's transimperial role for American Black nationalists and civil rights advocates was most pronounced when it was engaged in forcibly overturning French oppression; before and after this status, its connections were more abstract.

At the end of this era of race segregation, world wars, and the violent end of the French Empire, Algeria remained a liminal space for Black nationalists and civil rights advocates—successively a romantic oriental bazaar; a home to meritorious, if ambiguous, Africans; a barometer of US civil rights conditions; a possible self-determining, anti-colonial analogue; and, finally, an alien, capitalist Islamic republic. Not surprisingly, and perhaps fortunately, Algeria's independence marked the end of its transimperial function in French-American relations.

Epilogue

The Politics of Postimperial Nostalgia

This book has traced similarities and exchanges between France and the United States revealed by roles that French Algeria played in their relationship. For much of their history, the two countries acted imperially; studying their actions regarding North Africa illuminates how each country merged national and imperial institutions of governance.[1] Their imperial development, this book argues, was linked through Algeria and the Algerian people, who helped make the two empires in terms of each state's territorial expansion, ways of war, and concepts and practices of citizenship, and in terms of how some ordinary Americans and French people defined themselves and sought or maintained political power. As a form of transimperial history, the book specifically posits Algeria as a kind of "cis-imperial" place, a zone of exchange that helped construct the French and American empires.[2]

Besides connecting the French and American empires, Algeria, or, more specifically, the memory of French Algeria, also offers an opportunity to compare France and the United States in their recent postimperial political development. Scholars interested in the comparative history of empires, partly motivated to critique certain regimes' claims of exceptionalism, have emphasized the opportunity to explore how empires are remembered and forgotten.[3] Imperial nostalgia was, indeed, a political force that riveted Atlantic world politics in the first quarter of the twenty-first century in, among other countries, Britain, Hungary, Russia, France, and the United States.[4]

Elements of a politics of imperial nostalgia often invoke a past that is remembered as more orderly than the present. According to this kind of imperial community's ideologues and supporters, authentic members of the community prospered in that past, partly because the metropole, marking a homeland within the empire, was reliably bounded and therefore protected from civil strife, and the nation's wars were righteous and heroic. Nostalgia politics can interpret current-day leaders' toleration of diversity and humility about historical wrongdoing as signs of betrayal.[5]

By the early twenty-first century, the United States and France shared some common attributes with other countries of nostalgic memory that manifested in political platforms against immigration and cosmopolitan elites, and for recovery of past greatness. In the United States, the Make America Great Again movement of Donald Trump took over the Republican Party by alluding to past eras, particularly the turn of the twentieth century and the years immediately after World War II, when "we [the United States] were not pushed around, we were respected by everybody," traditional values about sexuality were broadly practiced, and most immigrants were not people of color.[6] In November 2024 Trump was reelected president in a close election after promising retribution on behalf of Americans who had been "wronged and betrayed," which would enable the United States to be made secure and restored to greatness.[7]

In France, the politics of nostalgia were enunciated mainly by Marine Le Pen, a candidate of the National Rally (RN) party, and later by her successor, Jordan Bardella. Le Pen won a third of the votes cast for the presidential election of 2017 and 42 percent in 2022; with Bardella as leader, the RN party won most of France's seats in the European Parliament in 2024, and became the biggest party in the French National Assembly. Le Pen was the most popular candidate for the 2027 French presidency at the time, although in March 2025 a French court convicted her of embezzling European Union funds— an irony given her past hostility to the EU—and barred her from running for public office for five years. Le Pen appealed her conviction, and, like Donald Trump, accused the French judiciary of persecuting her in a *"chasse aux sorcières,"* a witch hunt.[8] Bardella denounced Le Pen's punishment as effectively thwarting the will of "millions of patriotic French people."[9]

Both Le Pen and Bardella emphasized that France was in decline and squandering its global status as the world's cultural sine qua non. Like Trump, the RN leaders urged policies that would restore global respect and make "France worthy of admiration . . . a France that is once again conquering and proud of itself."[10] Both Le Pen and Bardella called for deportation of Islamic fundamentalists, reduction of annual immigration quotas—although Bardella's parents immigrated from Italy and Argentina and his great-grandfather from Kabylia, Algeria—and greater French autonomy within the European Union; until 2019, Le Pen, like her father, Jean-Marie Le Pen, the founder of the National Front (FN) party, called for a French exodus from the EU.[11] Donald Trump's election in 2024 provided inspiration for many French voters to elect as France's next president a reactionary change agent bent on revenge.[12]

Besides other factors common to politics of nostalgia on both sides of the Atlantic world, particularly linking the recent success of the movements in the United States and France, was a sense among working-class voters, most not possessing college degrees, that governmental elites, academics, and immigrants were dishonoring military defeats that the core nation had suffered.[13] In the United States this was the Civil War; in France, the Algerian War.[14]

Lost Cause Revival

Americans' reactionary interpretation of the Civil War, it must be said, dates to the early twentieth century. The Dunning School, named for Columbia University historian William Dunning, shaped many Americans' view of the Civil War as a war of Northern aggression against the South; Confederates fought for states' rights in the face of northern oppression. In the postwar Reconstruction Era, Southern "Redeemers," aided by vigilante terror waged by the Ku Klux Klan, thwarted broad political and economic reform of the region by African Americans and white Northern reformers, including token US military forces charged to enforce the US Constitution's Reconstruction Amendments. Dunning wrote of Reconstruction that "southern whites, subjugated by adversaries of their own race, thwarted the scheme which threatened permanent subjection to another race."[15] The Dunning School helped lay the foundation for the myth of the Lost Cause, the idea that the Confederate States of America fought heroically in defense of social stability and local government, not in order to defend enslavement of African Americans or create opportunity for slavery's expansion across the western hemisphere.

A literary group called the Southern Agrarians, centered at Vanderbilt University in Nashville, Tennessee, paralleled the Dunning School's historical defense of the Old South. The Agrarians, most prominently the novelist Robert Penn Warren, condemned modernity, urbanism, and industrialism and, in a 1930 manifesto, *I'll Take My Stand*, held out a superior "Southern way of life" that was traditional, rural, and agricultural as a basis to critique a United States that was becoming more urban and industrialized.[16] The Agrarians sympathized with European fascism in the 1930s and then dissolved after World War II. But beginning in the 1980s Agrarians' writings provided intellectual inspiration for neo-Confederate groups including Sons of Confederate Veterans, evangelical Christians who believed in biblical literalism, Civil War reenactment circles, and media such as *Southern Partisan*.[17]

More prominently, a women's society, the United Daughters of the Confederacy (UDC), founded in 1894 in Nashville, Tennessee, aspired to perpetuate the memory of the Confederacy not as traitors but as defenders of a just cause—the US Constitution—who succumbed, as the UDC historian Mildred Rutherford wrote, to "overwhelming odds." The UDC created neo-Confederate memory primarily by organizing construction of Confederate memorials and statues. Already by 1912 Rutherford could crow, "More monuments stand to the Confederate soldier today than to any other soldier of any other nation who ever fought for any cause." The UDC raised money and helped install over seven hundred Confederate monuments, primarily between 1900 and 1925 and from 1950 to 1970.[18]

Through the 1950s, Civil War scholars largely affirmed this popular understanding of the Civil War as the responsibility of Northern aggressors. In an era of sifting statesmen's mistakes that led to world wars, James Randall and Frank Owsley, for example, attributed the war to fanatical abolitionists whose irresponsible rhetoric, coupled with weak national government, pushed the white South toward secession as the only choice.[19] The Civil War destroyed the South's agrarian gentility and interdependent paternalism between free white people and enslaved African Americans and, in foisting the anarchy of Reconstruction on the postwar South, inadvertently worsened the country's race relations into the twentieth century.

A resurgence of this nostalgic memory of the Civil War manifested during and after the presidency of Donald Trump, elected to his first term in 2016. Trump's salutes to the Confederacy and, more generally, to a United States of racial order, free from multicultural and racial complexity, resembled developments in postimperial France.[20] Trump on several occasions showed a neo-Confederate affinity, using his popular Twitter account, for example, to lambast efforts to remove Confederate statues from public places. Removal of Confederate monuments would "rip [apart] . . . the history and culture of our great country."[21] Inspired by President Trump's tweets, a "Unite the Right" rally in Charlottesville, Virginia, organized in August 2017 to protest removal of a statue of Confederate hero Robert E. Lee, erupted into a riot, killing a counter-protester. "Very fine people," Trump rationalized, were on both sides of the riot.[22] In 2025 Trump reiterated his support for heroic Confederate memory, vowing to ensure that US military bases named for Confederate generals remained so.[23]

In late 2020 Trump launched an education initiative to ensure younger Americans revered the country's heroic but lately unappreciated past, particularly the Civil War's real causes. In early 2021, on the eve of his departure from the White House after losing the election to the challenger, Joseph Biden, Trump issued an executive order creating a 1776 Commission, charged to oppose a "radicalized view of American history" by which "many students are now taught in school to hate their own country" and to advise federal agencies on how to ensure "patriotic education" at the nation's historic sites.[24] In calling for patriotic education, Trump specifically condemned the 1619 Project, a US history curriculum developed by the *New York Times* that emphasized slavery's central, harmful role in American history.[25]

In sharp contrast to the 1619 Project's interpretation, the 1776 Commission's 2021 report emphasized that slavery was an aberration in US history and disconnected from the outbreak of civil war. The report identified US founders Washington, Madison, Jefferson, and Franklin—all slave owners—as uniformly opposed to slavery. The report acknowledged the US Constitution's protection of private property, including slavery, and its clause guaranteeing the return to bondage of enslaved people captured as fugitives but did not cite defense of slavery as Southern states' justification for secession in 1860–61. It described the fugitive slave clause as merely "the most hated protection of all"—though presumably not hated by all the founders—and erroneously denied that it and the three-fifths clause, by which slaves were counted in a state's population for congressional representation, gave sanction to slavery in the states. The report seemed to blame the Civil War on the proslavery statesman John Calhoun, who, as "the leading forerunner of identity politics," played the role of outside troublemaker.[26]

The report then alluded to Calhoun's theory of nullification, which it blamed for conceptualizing anti-American "'group rights.'" In the modern United States, group rights became an important basis for civil rights laws' protected classes. However, for the 1776 Commission, rights-wielding groups, animated, the report warned, by insidious "identity politics," sought to "destroy the established culture" of the "nation that we are blessed to call home." In the early twentieth century "identity politics" then received the federal government's endorsement beginning with Progressivism, which, in its handing power to elites, threatened "America's principles" no less than slavery, communism, or fascism. Following the *1776 Report*'s logic, "identity politics" lay at the root of the American sectional crisis.[27]

A German immigrant's grandson, Donald Trump made deportation of undocumented, "illegal" immigrants the centerpiece of his promise to vindicate native-born Americans and restore order to the United States. Trump warned that the country was bound for anarchy if his 2024 rival, Kamala Harris, a mixed-race woman, were elected, perhaps incidentally evoking a history of US imperialists' struggle to keep disorder out of the "heart of the American empire."[28] Consistent with Lost Cause mythology, Trump vowed to end birthright citizenship for children of undocumented immigrants, encompassed by the Constitution's Fourteenth Amendment. The amendment, adopted during Reconstruction to ensure citizenship rights to the freedpeople, was mocked as such in the early twentieth century by Lost Cause apologists, not only by the Dunning School of historians but also, most famously, in D. W. Griffith's 1915 film *Birth of a Nation*.[29] Early in 2025, Trump ordered federal agencies not to recognize the US citizenship of US-born persons whose parents at the time were unlawful US residents.[30] Trump's position was consistent with his vow of mass deportations of aliens; some commentators compared the difficulties of this operation in hostile US states to the toxic politics of the 1850 Fugitive Slave Law.[31] Expulsion of alien occupants from the US heartland, of course, had its own imperial history, notoriously first launched by President Andrew Jackson in removals of the Indian tribes of the Gulf states in the 1830s.[32]

Lutter contre l'oubli

The French corollary to this US politics of nostalgia, fueled by memory of an epic war lost, has a more recent origin. It was precipitated by President Charles de Gaulle's accession to Algerian independence in 1962, which surprised and humiliated those French citizens on both sides of the Mediterranean who had expected the leader of the French Fifth Republic to use his power to maintain its colonial presence in North Africa, particularly under the circumstance of France's defeat in the Indochina War of 1946–1954. De Gaulle's rationale for conceding Algerian independence has been debated by historians, although his fear of multiculturalism, which he expressed in 1959 with the quip that if Algeria remained French his hometown would be called Colombey-les-Deux-Mosquées, has allowed the RN party to claim that it is the keeper of the true Gaullist legacy.[33]

Algerian independence provoked reactionary responses, both violent and intellectual. In the short term, a few thousand dissident military personnel formed the Organisation armée secrète (OAS), a far-right paramilitary and terrorist organization that through 1963 sought to prevent Algeria's independence from French colonial rule by acts of terror. OAS attacks killed some three thousand Algerians and French forces in Algeria and France, attempted to assassinate de Gaulle, and, in a scorched-earth strategy, destroyed French-built buildings in Algeria to deny their usage by the future government of the National Liberation Front (FLN), including, in July 1962, the Algiers Library and, in Oran, the town hall, the municipal library, and four schools.

Jean-Marie Le Pen was a French intelligence officer in the Algerian War and then maintained contact with the OAS. In the day, ironically, OAS terrorism actually accelerated the flight of pieds noirs, the French-identifying residents of Algeria who made up about an eighth of its population, from North Africa in the 1960s. While only a few of the nearly one million pieds noirs were probably active in the OAS, and the OAS's insurgency did little to undermine the FLN's takeover of Algeria, nostalgic imperialists in France in recent years have remembered OAS insurgents, like earlier white Americans' perceptions of the Ku Klux Klan, as "virtuous heroes, not treacherous outlaws," protectors of the pieds noirs from the FLN, and more like the French Resistance to Nazi occupiers of France during World War II than other terrorists active during the Fifth Republic.[34] In France, as in the United States, reverence for vigilantes who sought to prevent social revolution was an important element in the politics of nostalgia.

An intellectual counterpart to the OAS was the Nouvelle Droite (ND), formed in 1968, whose advocates denounced the Left's protests of that year as fanatical multiculturalism and called for protection of the traditional values of Western civilization. Like some US neoconservatives, the ND denounced US liberal imperialism, and some of its leaders, akin to the Southern Agrarians, embraced traditional Christianity (French Roman Catholicism) and broadly called for preservation of the European heartland against racial amalgamation with immigrants (including former French possessions in Africa). Various ND leaders endorsed and helped shape the FN's platforms in the early 1990s, including ensuring or privileging the rights of white, Catholic, native-born "French French" people.[35]

An important audience of the French ND and constituency of the FN were the pieds noirs, and their descendants, generally resident in France's southern Midi regions. Under the Evian Accords of 1962, the pieds noirs retained full French citizenship.[36] Today, much of the Midi, especially Provence-Alpes-Côte d'Azur, is the largest RN stronghold.

The pieds noirs have a complex status in France. Racially and religiously they and their descendants resembled most other French people. But their North African heritage and their association with a colonial war that France lost and during which, as was alleged during the war and officially acknowledged in 2000, the French military broadly tortured FLN supporters, complicated their assimilation in the metropole.[37] Ironically, while the pieds noirs were privileged beneficiaries of France's two-tiered colonial society in Algeria, in 1970 France officially recognized them as war *victims*, eligible for nominal government indemnification. By the early twenty-first century this self-image fueled the pieds noirs' resentment of Indigenous Algerian residents of France, whom they felt had been strangely welcomed in France despite their alleged peril for French culture.[38] In 1992, Jean-Marie Le Pen, speaking in Nice to the Cercle national des rapatriés (CNR), explicitly tied the epic, futile defense of French Algeria to the prospective defense of a "French France": "Le combat pour l'Algérie française a préparé le combat pour la France française!"[39] The language of Le Pen and his FN acolytes urging fighting to save the "true" France resonated with pied noir organizations whose recruitment slogans framed memory of colonial greatness as a heroic and obligatory struggle: "'Sauvegarder la mémoire,' 'Devoir de mémoire,' 'Lutter contre l'oubli' [Saving Memory, Duty to Memory, Fighting Against Forgetting]."[40]

The Good Negro, the Good Arab

Memory among the pieds noirs about Algeria by the year 2000 bore several resemblances to neo-Confederate memory of the US Civil War and its aftermath, Radical Reconstruction. To pieds noirs, French colonization of Algeria happened through the settlement of European pioneers on France's Mediterranean frontier and wrought from the wilderness a productive agrarian civilization. Mutually reliant Europeans and Arabs had interacted cooperatively, if not equally. An early twentieth-century American analogue was the important icon of neo-Confederate ideology, the "good Negro," an older person held in slavery who willingly accepted their status, loved their owner, and provided folk wisdom and gentle discipline to white children. The most ingrained—though fictitious—characters of this genre were Uncle Remus, the narrator of a collection of African American folktales compiled and published by Joel Chandler Harris in 1881, and Mammy, a woman held as a house slave to raise Scarlett O'Hara, the main character of *Gone with the Wind*, Margaret Mitchell's 1936 novel and the 1939 Hollywood blockbuster film.[41] Walt Disney released a children's film, *Song of the South*, in 1946, animating Uncle Remus's stories and thereafter circulated comic books with the film's characters, although as soon as the film was released, African American leaders in Congress and the National Association for the Advancement of Colored People (NAACP) criticized its inaccurate racial stereotypes.[42]

Among pied noir communities, the specific corollary to the American "good Negro" was the "good Arab" who provided reliable service to European settlers: "selling items to them in the marketplace, working on their land, cooking and cleaning in their homes, looking after their children."[43] Echoing Lost Cause mythologists' bemusement over the Civil War's destruction of slavery by African Americans themselves, in 1967 one pied noir lamented Algerians' revolutionary violence: "Why did they want independence? They were happy with us."[44] Such a memory had roots during the Algerian war, when French commentators who found US encouragement of colonial independence hypocritical had actually contrasted the alleged safety of Arab Algerian schoolchildren amid their Euro-Algerian classmates with racist violence that African American students faced in seeking to attend previously whites-only schools.[45]

In spite of this trope, until the 2000s the pieds noirs, like the French government, disdained the Harkis, Algerians who fought for France in the War of Independence, then fled to France after it. Harkis were kept in reservations on the French Mediterranean or settled in Paris slums, *les banlieues*, in the 1960s and remained unassimilated and less organized in consciousness-raising than the pied noir community. Young French people of Algerian background have come to use the term *neo harki* to mean a sell-out, like the American epithet Uncle Tom, meaning a person of color who accepts subordination or even collaborates in order to curry a white person's favor.[46] In 2012 the FN began to appeal to the Harkis and their descendants—differentiating them from Muslim residents of France not linked to North Africa—on the basis that they shared a history with the pieds noirs as *rapatriés* who supported the empire. For the FN, "a Harki was a good Arab."[47] From this perspective, the Algerian War of Independence could appear as the work of North African fanatics and leftist policymakers in France. The Algerian

Civil War of the 1990s between Islamic fundamentalists, the Islamic Salvation Front (FIS), and the military, making it unsafe for pieds noirs to even visit Algeria, cut short the country's national development and, among pieds noirs, seemed to be long-term evidence of the precipitous mistake of Algerians' sudden award of autonomy in 1962 at the hands of agitators, not the outcome of an internal social revolution as declared by the famed anti-colonial theorist of the day, Frantz Fanon.[48]

This interpretation paralleled explanations of the US Civil War by both early twentieth-century apologists for the Confederacy and, one hundred years later, policymakers reluctant to acknowledge that the war had left legacies of racial discrimination and violence. For example, besides his defenses of Confederate memory conveyed by neo-Confederate statues, President Trump on multiple occasions described the Civil War as an unnecessary conflict brought on by incompetent national leadership—a resurrection of historical opinion of the war from the 1930s. Trump saluted his predecessor President Jackson, a slave owner, as a figure who, had he lived longer, could have averted the conflict, probably by treating slavery amorally and respecting its practice in the South.[49] Similarly, Nikki Haley, a Republican candidate for the 2024 presidency, stated in late 2023 that the central cause of the Civil War was the question of "how [the] government was going to run, the freedoms of what people could and couldn't do. . . . It always comes down to the role of government, and what the rights of the people are." In response to a constituent's question about whether slavery caused the war, Haley responded, "What do you want me to say about slavery?"[50] For Haley, like Trump, the Civil War instinctively was the product of troublemaking bureaucrats; slavery's destructive brutality was irrelevant.

Nostalgic Education

A corollary of this nostalgic view has echoed in various US states that have the authority to develop educational curricula. In the 2010s, Arkansas, Florida, Idaho, Louisiana, New Hampshire, Tennessee, and Texas passed laws that would withhold funding from schools that teach about the enduring legacies of slavery.[51] Countering the 1619 Project, Texas developed the 1836 Project to ensure Texas students received a "patriotic education." Regarding slavery, the project emphasized that "overwhelming[ly]," defenders of a state shrine, the Alamo, whose capture by a Mexican army inspired the Texas War for Independence, were not slave owners. The 1836 Project omitted proslavery provisions of the 1836 Texas constitution.[52] And a middle school standard approved by Florida's education board required students to learn about "skills" learned by slaves that could be "applied for [slaves'] personal benefit." That is, the standard emphasized that some slaves developed specialized trades, "e.g., agricultural work, painting, carpentry, tailoring, domestic service, blacksmithing, transportation." Analogous to French defenses of colonialism in terms of its provision of benevolent "civilization," the standard did not emphasize that the labor of most Americans enslaved in the United States involved coerced manual farming of cotton.[53]

President Trump's 2025 order that a red-ribbon panel develop a patriotic curriculum for schools was likewise the US version of contemporaneous resolutions by governments in Europe responding to demands that education 'return' to lessons about imperial virtue. The British Conservative Party called for education about the British Empire to drop its culture of victimization and identity politics and to teach the empire's benefits.[54] In Hungary, Prime Minister Viktor Orban imposed revisions to school curricula in a bid to restore national self-esteem, hail the country's Christian identity, agrarian genius, and military victories, and downplay its defeats.[55] In Russia, President Vladimir Putin urged the Federal Assembly to amend the country's education law to add "a sense of patriotism and citizenship, respect for the memory of the defenders of the Fatherland and the achievements of the Fatherland's heroes" to the law's definition of proper upbringing.[56] In 2023 a new national middle school textbook differentiated between the Russian Empire, deemed never a colonial power because its contiguous territories became integrated into Russia in a "common economic space," and "classical colonialism," which involved overseas territories.[57]

France's nationalist education in the 2000s varied from other cases described in the United States and Europe in its influence by the pieds noirs, a unique legacy of France's particular experience of a sudden influx of white colonists to the metropole as refugees.[58] The pieds noirs' development of cultural heritage communities in proximity to one another across Southern France from the 1970s, particularly in areas where there were active military veterans' associations among whom calls for duty to the past resonated, provided a springboard to political lobbying of the French government to address public memory of French Algeria in the national curriculum.[59] In the 2002 presidential election the FN candidate Jean-Marie Le Pen, perennially anti–immigration, focused on fears of terrorism after 9/11 and of recent crime sprees that he attributed to immigrants and urged "the small ones, the ones who've been excluded, those of you who've got no recognition" to remember that "France is for the French."⁶⁰ Le Pen lost badly in a run-off against the incumbent Jacques Chirac, but Chirac, recognizing the appeal of Le Pen's nostalgic and pro-colonial rhetoric, committed to a program to recognize the significance of pied noir "sacrifices" for the French nation.

To be sure, Chirac's initiative happened in the context of recent French acknowledgments of the harms for which the French Empire was responsible. A French law in 1999 used the term *Algerian war* for the first time, and acknowledgments accumulated of French soldiers' widespread torture of Algerians during the war. Meanwhile, a 2001 law required that slavery and the slave trade be described as crimes against humanity.⁶¹ But pied noir communities and nationalist defenders of the French military interpreted these gestures as an opportunity to call for "restor[ing] balance" to French history-teaching by acknowledging the benefits of colonialism. Their lobbying efforts culminated in a 2005 French law that recognized the contributions of "repatriated French nationals" and established a public foundation to specifically commemorate "the memory of the Algerian war." It provided compensation for Harkis and their descendants as well as for former OAS activists. Most provocatively, it stipulated that French school "courses must . . . recognise the positive role played by the French presence overseas, particularly in north Africa, and must accord the prominent position that they merit to the history and sacrifices of members of the French armed forces."⁶²

Both the Trump administration's 1776 Commission, established in 2020, rescinded by President Joe Biden, and then re-constituted by Trump in 2025, and the French 2005 pro-colonial school law met with sharp criticism by academic historians; in both countries lawmakers acknowledged they did not consult professional historians in creating the curriculum directives. In a statement, the American Historical Association (AHA) condemned the *1776 Report* for its erasure of "swaths of the American population—enslaved people, Indigenous communities, and women—the way the founders" did. And the AHA pointed out that the report excluded the Confederate States of America, its leaders "clearly guilty of treason," on its list of national threats.⁶³ French historians and activists expressed similar criticism. The anti-racist organization Movement Against Racism and for Friendship (MRAP) said that the 2005 law showed "contempt for the victims" of colonialism.⁶⁴ A historian, Claude Liauzu, characterized the law as "nostalgic revisionism" that presented "French colonials as victims," a highly sought-after status in France's post–World War II commemorative era.⁶⁵ Additionally, citing Edward Said's critique of imperialism, Liauzu warned about "appeals to pure or authentic" nationalism.⁶⁶ French petitions and protests against the 2005 law actually led to the repeal of its school curriculum provision in 2006.

Nonetheless, nostalgic pedagogues, seeking to ensure that schools would teach the histories of respective American and French wars about race from the perspective of well-meaning patriots, persisted in curriculum wars. Repudiating education bureaucrats, the 1776 Commission pledged a steadfast commitment to getting "school boards and students" to read its report. The commission's chairman, Larry Arnn, president of the evangelical Christian Hillsdale College, helped organize a 1776 Curriculum designed to counter the 1619 Project. Republican Party–dominated states invited Hillsdale-connected consultants to overhaul K–12 education in order to help US schools "remember what we used to know," according to a Hillsdale official.⁶⁷ An important historical interpretation of the 1776 Curriculum is that the Civil War's destruction of slavery and establishment of civil rights for African Americans ended large-scale or institutional racism in the United States. Educators who opposed this interpretation thus were deemed to be using classrooms to sow divisions in American society, the prohibition of which twenty-one US states had legislated as of October 2024.⁶⁸

Recently in France, meanwhile, right wing leaders used US anti-racism movements as a foil to call for revanchism in French education. On the eve of his victory in the 2024 European Parliament elections, Jordan Bardella hosted an RN symposium on the danger of "imported" politically progressive ideas about race, gender, and immigration, or *le wokisme*.⁶⁹ In 2021, the administration of President Emmanuel Macron established the Laboratory of the Republic, a think tank intended to defeat the spread of identity politics, particularly "Islamic" identity, primarily focusing on French academia.⁷⁰ Minister of National Education Jean-Michel Blanquer, like Bardella, characterized the growth in France of awareness of the disparate experiences of racial groups and other minorities as a dangerous foreign ideology and acknowledged Donald Trump's provocation of an Atlantic "anti-woke" backlash.⁷¹ Outside French party pronouncements, other evidence showed that many French people recently were pro-American out of a sense of postimperial kinship—that is, that the United States, like France, was a "wounded" country less powerful than it was a half century earlier.⁷² French language and geography textbooks, meanwhile, continued to emphasize the benefits for formerly colonized people of France's earlier cultural hegemony.⁷³

A Triumph of Post-Imperial Nationalism?

In the early 2020s President Macron showed other evidence of acceding to the surging influence of a nostalgic history in France. Echoing nineteenth-century commentators on Algeria in both France and the United States, Macron asserted that the Algerian nation had not existed when it was a loosely affiliated province of the Ottoman Empire before the French invasion in 1830.[74] In early 2023 he declared that France did not owe Algeria an official apology for its colonization.[75] And like Donald Trump earlier, Macron declared that the French government would oppose any attempt to take down statues commemorating the colonial past.[76] Postcolonial, procolonial monuments had first been erected around 1980, the sesquicentennial of the French conquest of Algiers. Then, shrewdly, pied noir advocates invoked the precedent of 1930, the centenary of French Algeria and the apogee of French imperialism.[77]

Despite these gestures to France's right wing, however, in 2025 Macron's Renaissance party was not favored to retain the next French presidency. Instead, polling indicated Bardella was France's leading presidential candidate.[78] In a speech to the European Union, Bardella said that Trump's 2024 election offered a lesson that Europe should defend nations and their interests, that the United States was protecting itself, Europe was not, and there should be a "revolution based on national identities."[79] That year nativist people in the postimperial French and American societies rallied around memories of a racially and religiously hierarchical but productive and stable society that had been irrationally and violently assailed by hypercritical outsiders who, enabled by a too cosmopolitan and overly tolerant government, had displaced the "real" patriots. This international nostalgia was a powerful, politically victorious ideology.

Acknowledgments

Several scholarly journals and presses previously published versions of parts of this book, and I thank their editors for their support to make it possible. They are "The Role of French Algeria in American Expansion During the Early Republic," *Journal of the Western Society for French History* 43 (2015): 153–64; "Republican Citizenship in the Post-Civil War South and French Algeria 1865–1900," *American Nineteenth Century History* 19 (March 2018): 79–102; "'Almost as It Is Formulated in the So-Called Homestead Act': Images of the American West in French Settlement of Algeria," *Journal of World History* 32 (December 2021): 601–29; "The Role of French Algeria in American Incorporation of the Philippines and Puerto Rico," *Historical Reflections/Réflexions Historiques* 48 (December 2022): 90–110; "The French Influence on American Counterinsurgency Warfare," in *Prehistories of the War on Terror: A Critical Genealogy of U.S. Military Empire*, ed. Karen Miller and Yumi Lee (University of Pennsylvania Press, 2024), 19–39; and "The Union's Adaptation of French Counterinsurgency Warfare in the American Civil War," in *Local and Global Perspectives in Military History*, ed. Lee L. Brice and Timothy M. Roberts (Marine Corps University Press, 2024), 131–50. I am grateful for the feedback I received from anonymous readers for these publications and, likewise, for valuable critiques of the book manuscript that readers for Cornell University Press provided.

Additionally, I express great thanks to audiences at conferences where I presented research for this book, including annual conferences of the Society of Historians of the Early American Republic, the Society of Historians of American Foreign Relations, the Society for French Historical Studies, and the Western Society for French History. I also profited from feedback I received at the following additional conferences: "Perspectives on Global and Local Military History," sponsored by Western Illinois University; "The Worlds of 1848: International Colloquium," cosponsored by the Université Paris-Est Créteil, the École des Hautes Études en Sciences, and the Université Paris 13; "Emancipations: Reconstructions, and Revolutions: African American Politics and U.S. History in the Long 19th Century," cosponsored by the Graduate Center, City University of New York, and the McNeil Center for Early American Studies; and "Quels citoyens pour l'empire? La citoyenneté française à l'épreuve de l'empire dans la première moitié du XXe siècle," cosponsored by the Université Paris Lumieres, Université Paris Ouest Nanterre La Défense, Université Paris 8, and the Archives Nationales.

I particularly wish to thank these individuals for their challenging and encouraging conversations about this project: Lee L. Brice, Audrey Celestine, Laurence Cossu-Beaumont, Niels Eichhorn, Van Goss, Karen Miller, Paul Quigley, Emmanuelle Sibeud, and the late Tyler Stovall. I cannot forget Cindy Arnett, who lent her terrific desktop publishing skills for digitization of the book's illustrations. Finally, I am grateful to Sarah Grossman for her initial interest in this project on behalf of Cornell University Press.

Notes

Introduction

1. Martin Thomas, "Colonial Minds and Colonial Violence: The Setif Uprising and the Savage Economics of Colonialism," in *The French Colonial Mind: Violence, Military Encounters and Colonialism*, ed. Martin Thomas (University of Nebraska Press, 2011): 140–74; James McDougall, *History of Algeria* (Cambridge University Press, 2017), 179–81.

2. John Torpey, *Invention of the Passport: Surveillance, Citizenship and the State* (Cambridge University Press, 2000). An international traveler wrote, "The frontiers were nothing but symbolic lines which one crossed with as little thought as when one crosses the Meridian of Greenwich." Stefan Zweig, *World of Yesterday: An Autobiography* (University of Nebraska Press, 1964), 410.

3. For discussion of this aspect of imperial spaces, see Patrick Wolfe, "History and Imperialism: A Century of Theory, from Marx to Postcolonialism," *American Historical Review* 102, no. 2 (1997): 388–420, https://doi.org/10.2307/2170830. See Gavin Murray-Miller, *Empire Unbound: France and the Muslim Mediterranean, 1880–1918* (Oxford University Press, 2022) for a study emphasizing the porous and connected aspects of French imperialism in North Africa and the Middle East.

4. For example, Carl Degler, *Neither Black nor White: Slavery and Race Relations in Brazil and the United States* (Macmillan, 1971); Seymour Lipset, *First New Nation: The United States in Historical and Comparative Perspective*, rev. ed. (Norton, 1979); George Fredrickson, *White Supremacy: A Comparative Study of American and South African History* (Oxford University Press, 1981); Eric Foner, *Nothing but Freedom: Emancipation and Its Legacy* (Louisiana State University Press, 1983); James Gump, *Dust Rose Like Smoke: The Subjugation of the Zulu and the Sioux* (University of Nebraska

Press, 1994); Duncan Campbell and Niels Eichhorn, *The Civil War in the Age of Nationalism* (Louisiana State University Press, 2024).

5. Thomas Bender, *Nation Among Nations: America's Place in World History* (Hill and Wang, 2006); Gerald Horne, *Deepest South: The United States, Brazil, and the African Slave Trade* (New York University Press, 2007); Pekka Hamalainen, *The Comanche Empire* (Yale University Press, 2009); Ian Tyrrell, *Reforming the World: The Creation of America's Moral Empire* (Princeton University Press, 2010); Amy Kohout, *Taking the Field: Soldiers, Nature, and Empire on American Frontiers* (University of Nebraska Press, 2023); Emily Conroy-Krutz, *Missionary Diplomacy: Religion and Nineteenth-Century American Foreign Relations* (Cornell University Press, 2024). A significant earlier work was James Field, Jr., *America and the Mediterranean World, 1776–1882* (Princeton University Press, 1969).

6. Julian Go, *Patterns of Empire: The British and American Empires, 1688 to the Present* (Cambridge University Press, 2011); Atul Kohli, *Imperialism and the Developing World: How Britain and the United States Shaped the Global Periphery* (Oxford University Press, 2020); Paul Kramer, "Empires, Exceptions, and Anglo-Saxons: Race and Rule Between the British and U.S. Empires, 1880–1910," in *The American Colonial State in the Philippines: Global Perspectives*, ed. Julian Go and Anne Foster (Duke University Press, 2003): 43–91; Jennifer Pitts, *A Turn to Empire: The Rise of Imperial Liberalism in Britain and France* (Princeton University Press, 2006); Saliha Belmessous, *Assimilation and Empire: Uniformity in French and British Colonies, 1541–1954* (Oxford University Press, 2013); David Fieldhouse, *Western Imperialism in the Middle East, 1914–1958* (Oxford University Press, 2006); Jane Lahti, ed., *German and United States Colonialism in a Connected World: Entangled Empires* (Palgrave, 2021); Jens-Uwe Guettel, *German Expansionism, Imperial Liberalism, and the United States, 1776–1945* (Cambridge University Press, 2012); Andrew Priest, *Designs on Empire: America's Rise to Power in the Age of European Imperialism* (Columbia University Press, 2021). Two works that focused on French imperial encounters with Americans during the Third Republic were Gilles Matthieu, *Une ambition sud-américaine: politique culturelle de la France, 1914–1940* (L'Harmattan, 1991), and Robert Young, *Marketing Marianne: French Propaganda in America, 1900–1940* (Rutgers University Press, 2004).

7. On circulations as a characteristic activity in transimperial history, see Daniel Hedinger and Nadin Heé, "Transimperial History—Connectivity, Cooperation and Competition," *Journal of Modern European History* 16, no. 4 (2018): 429–52; and Kristin Hoganson and Jay Sexton, "Introduction," in *Crossing Empires: Taking U.S. History into Transimperial Terrain*, ed. Kristin Hoganson and Jay Sexton (Duke University Press, 2020), 6, 18 fn. 26.

8. Azzedine Layachi, *The United States and North Africa: A Cognitive Approach to Foreign Policy* (Praeger, 1990), 13. Osman Benchérif, *The Image of Algeria in Anglo-American Writings, 1785–1962* (University Press of America, 1997), is an anthology of English-language plays, diary accounts, travel narratives, and novels about Algeria, emphasizing their orientalist perspective and negative stereotypes.

9. The other Barbary States that practiced "piracy" were Tripoli and Tunis. The Kingdom of Morocco, a US ally beginning in 1787, was a Barbary State, but largely did not engage in the practice. The word "Barbary" derived from "Berber," a term identifying the non-Arabic, Indigenous peoples of North Africa.

10. Timothy Marr, *Cultural Roots of American Islamicism* (Cambridge University Press, 2006), 135; Robert Allison, *Crescent Obscured: The United States and the Muslim World, 1776–1815* (University of Chicago Press, 2000); Frank Lambert, *Barbary Wars: American Independence in the Atlantic World* (Hill and Wang, 2007); Lawrence Peskin, *Captives and Countrymen: Barbary Slavery and the American Public, 1785–1816* (Johns Hopkins University Press, 2009).

11. Rick Atkinson, *An Army at Dawn: The War in North Africa, 1942–1943* (Holt, 2007); John Bierman, *War Without Hate: The Desert Campaign of 1940–43* (Penguin, 2004).

12. Frank Castigliola, *France and the United States: The Cold Alliance Since World War II* (Twayne, 1992); Irwin Wall, *France, the United States, and the Algerian War* (University of California Press, 2001).

13. Matthew Connelly, *Diplomatic Revolution: Algeria's Fight for Independence and the Origins of the Post-Cold War Era* (Oxford University Press 2002); Jeffrey Byrne, *Mecca of Revolution: Algeria, Decolonization, and the Third World Order* (Oxford University Press, 2016); Mohammed Ghettas, *Algeria and the Cold War: International Relations and the Struggle for Autonomy* (Bloomsbury, 2017).

14. Grégor Mathias, *Galula in Algeria: Counterinsurgency Practice versus Theory* (Bloomsbury, 2011); Douglas Porch, *Counterinsurgency: Exposing the Myths of the New Way of War* (Cambridge University Press, 2013); Terrence Peterson, *Revolutionary Warfare: How the Algerian War Made Modern Counterinsurgency* (Cornell University Press, 2024).

15. For example, Charles Ageron, *France coloniale ou parti colonial?* (Presses universitaires de France, 1978); Yves Lacoste, "La conquête de l'Algérie, un cas très exceptionnel," in *Géopolitique de la nation France*, ed. Encel Frédéric and Yves Lacoste (Presses Universitaires de France, 2016): 139–81. On resituating French Algeria, see Fiona Barclay, Charlotte Ann Chopin, and Martin Evans, "Introduction: Settler Colonialism and French Algeria," *Settler Colonial Studies* 8, no. 2 (2018): 115–30, https://10.1080/2201473X.2016.1273862. The terms are from Wolfe, "History and Imperialism," 419.

16. Nicolas Bancel, "L'histoire difficile: esquisse d'une historiographie du fait colonial et postcolonial," in *La fracture coloniale: la société française au prisme de l'héritage colonial*, ed. Pascal Blanchard, Nicolas Bancel, and Sandrine Lemaire (Éditions La Découverte, 2005), 85; Pascal Blanchard and Sandrine Lemaire, "Introduction," in *Culture post-coloniale: traces et mémoires coloniales en France*, ed. Pascal Blanchard and Sandrine Lemaire (Autrement, 2006), 11; Natalya Vince, *The Algerian War, the Algerian Revolution* (Palgrave, 2020), 185–89; Todd Shepard, *Invention of Decolonization: The Algerian War and the Remaking of France* (Cornell University Press, 2006).

17. James Belich, *Replenishing the Earth: The Settler Revolution and the Rise of the Angloworld* (Oxford University Press, 2011); Walter Hixson, *American Settler Colonialism: A History* (Palgrave, 2013); Steven Sabol, *"The Touch of Civilization": Comparing American and Russian Internal Colonization* (University Press of Colorado, 2017).

18. Ludwig Adamec, *Historical Dictionary of Islam* (Scarecrow, 2009), 110. See a commentary by Kevin Gannon, "The Civil War as a Settler-Colonial Revolution," Age of Revolutions (blog), January 18, 2016, https://ageofrevolutions.com/2016/01/18/the-civil-war-as-a-settler-colonial-revolution. On American wars of incorporation see A. G. Hopkins, *American Empire: A Global History* (Princeton University Press, 2018).

19. *Reconstruction in a Globalizing World*, ed. David Prior (Fordham University Press, 2018); Don Doyle, *Age of Reconstruction: How Lincoln's New Birth of Freedom Remade the World* (Princeton University Press, 2024); Ryan Semmes, *Exporting Reconstruction: Ulysses S. Grant and a New Empire of Liberty* (University of South Carolina Press, 2024).

20. A survey of the racialized meanings of *freedom* that connect American and French history is Tyler Stovall, *White Freedom: The Racial History of an Idea* (Princeton University Press, 2021).

21. Charlotte Legg, *The New White Race: Settler Colonialism and the Press in French Algeria, 1860–1914* (University of Nebraska Press, 2021), 166–68.

22. Janne Lahti, *The American West and the World: Transnational and Comparative Perspectives* (Routledge, 2019); David Wrobel, *Global West, American Frontier: Travel, Empire, and Exceptionalism from Manifest Destiny to the Great Depression* (University of New Mexico Press, 2014).

23. Go and Foster, *American Colonial State*, especially Anne Foster, "Models for Governing: Opium and Colonial Policies in Southeast Asia, 1898–1910," 92–117; Karine Walther, *Sacred*

Interests: The United States and the Islamic World, 1821–1921 (University of North Carolina Press, 2015), 157–239.

24. Edoardo Campanella and Marta Dassu, *Anglo Nostalgia: The Politics of Emotion in a Fractured West* (Oxford University Press, 2019); M. Hakan Yavuz, *Nostalgia for the Empire: The Politics of Neo-Ottomanism* (Oxford University Press, 2020); Radu Cinpoeş and Ov Cristian Norocel, "Nostalgic Nationalism, Welfare Chauvinism, and Migration Anxieties in Central and Eastern Europe," in *Nostalgia and Hope: Intersections Between Politics of Culture, Welfare, and Migration in Europe,* ed. Ov Cristian Norocel, Anders Hellström, and Martin Bak Jorgensen (Springer, 2020): 51–65.

25. A valuable study in comparative nostalgic memory that showed the similarities between early American neo-Confederate ideology and contemporary French attitudes about military humiliation in the Franco-Prussian War is Wolfgang Schivelbusch, *Culture of Defeat: On National Trauma, Mourning, and Recovery,* trans. Jefferson Chase (New York: Metropolitan Books, 2003).

1. A North African Example for Early US Expansion

1. Alexis de Tocqueville, *Writings on Empire and Slavery,* ed. Jennifer Pitts (Johns Hopkins University Press, 2001), 36.

2. See Ewa Atanassow, "Colonization and Democracy: Tocqueville Reconsidered," *American Political Science Review* 111 (February 2017): 83–96; Jeremy Jennings, "French Visions of America: From Tocqueville to the Civil War," in *America Through European Eyes: British and French Reflections on the New World from the Eighteenth Century to the Present,* ed. Aurelian Craiutu and Jeffrey Isaac (Pennsylvania State University Press, 2009), 161–84; Jennifer Pitts, *Turn to Empire: The Rise of Imperial Liberalism in Britain and France* (Princeton University Press, 2009), 189–239.

3. 3 Cong. Deb. 74 (1827); M. Pont, "Traité de Proudhon, sur l'état des personnes et sur le titre préliminaire du Code civil . . . par M. [Auguste] Valette," *Revue de législation et de jurisprudence* 19 (January–April 1844): 673–77, esp. 675.

4. The French action has been explained whimsically as retaliation for Dey's striking a French consul with a fly whisk over France's failure to pay for Algerian wheat it had received. Benjamin Stora, *Algeria, 1830–2000: A Short History,* trans. Jane Marie Todd (Cornell University Press, 2004), 3; Paul Silverstein, *Algeria in France: Transpolitics, Race, and Nation* (Indiana University Press, 2004), 41. In 1830, Egypt again factored in the French invasion of North Africa, this time in Governor Muhammad Ali's war against the Ottoman Empire for control of Syria, which coincidentally increased Algiers' vulnerability. Caroline Finkel, *Osman's Dream: The History of the Ottoman Empire* (Basic Books, 2005), 443.

5. Robert Allison, *Crescent Obscured: The United States and the Muslim World, 1776–1815* (University of Chicago Press, 2000); Lawrence Peskin, *Captives and Countrymen: Barbary Slavery and the American Public, 1785–1816* (Johns Hopkins University Press, 2009).

6. Frank Lambert, *Barbary Wars: American Independence in the Atlantic World* (Farrar, Straus and Giroux, 2007), 157–58; Joshua London, *Victory in Tripoli: How America's War with the Barbary Pirates Established the US Navy and Shaped a Nation* (Wiley, 2011).

7. For example, Paul Ackerman, *American Orientalists* (Art Creation Realisation, 1994); Douglas Little, *American Orientalism: The United States and the Middle East Since 1945* (University of North Carolina Press, 2008), 12; Victoria Thompson, "'I Went Pale with Pleasure': The Body, Sexuality, and National Identity Among French Travelers to Algiers in the Nineteenth Century,"

in *Algeria & France, 1800–2000: Identity, Memory, Nostalgia*, ed. Patricia Lorcin (Syracuse University Press, 2006), 18–32; Edward Said, *Orientalism* (Vintage, 1979), 123–26, 337.

8. Henry Lee to Secretary of State Martin Van Buren, July 28, 1830, in *"Emperor Dead" and Other Historic American Dispatches*, ed. Peter Eicher (Congressional Quarterly, 1997), 98.

9. "Foreign News," *Richmond Enquirer*, October 13, 1835.

10. See Margaret Cook Andersen, *Regeneration Through Empire: French Pronatalists and Colonial Settlement in the Third Republic* (University of Nebraska Press, 2015), 49, 81–93, 200; and Jennifer Sessions, *By Sword and Plow: France and the Conquest of Algeria* (Cornell University Press, 2011), 179–80.

11. Paul Gilje, *Free Trade and Sailors' Rights in the War of 1812* (Cambridge University Press, 2013); Porter to J. P. McCorkle, November 26, 1830, in *Memoir of Commodore David Porter: Of the United States Navy* (J. Munsell, 1875), 396–99. McCorkle was a US naval clerk and father of David Porter McCorkle, a lieutenant in the US Navy charged to evacuate the filibuster William Walker's forces from Nicaragua in 1857, and during the Civil War a lieutenant in the Confederate Navy. Robert May, *Manifest Destiny's Underworld: Filibustering in Antebellum America* (University of North Carolina Press, 2004), 207–8.

12. Actually, French military personnel sent nearly half of Dey's treasures to France, fifteen million francs, covering the invasion's costs, and simply pocketed the same amount. Jamil Abun-Nasr, *History of the Maghrib* (Cambridge University Press, 1971), 238.

13. Porter to J. P. McCorkle, November 26, 1830.

14. William Gallois, "Genocide in Nineteenth-Century Algeria," *Journal of Genocide Research* 15 (February 2013), 69–88.

15. "Four Days Later from Havre," *New York Herald*, April 10, 1837.

16. Quoted in Gavin Murray-Miller, *Cult of the Modern: Trans-Mediterranean France the Cult of the Modern* (University of Nebraska Press, 2017), 11.

17. On the Spoliation Controversy, see Robert Remini, *Andrew Jackson: The Course of American Democracy, 1833–1845* (Johns Hopkins University Press, 2013), 201–88; and Robert Thomas, "Andrew Jackson versus France: American Policy toward France, 1834–36," *Tennessee Historical Quarterly* 35, no. 1 (1976): 51–64.

18. James Leib to Secretary of State, April 30, 1836, in *Despatches from U.S. Consuls in Tangier, 1797–1906*, General Records of the Department of State, US National Archives Microfilm T61/5.

19. For a somewhat similar phenomenon regarding antebellum Americans' shifting attitudes towards the Ottoman Empire, see Tim Roberts, "Lajos Kossuth and the Permeable American Orient of the Mid-Nineteenth Century," *Diplomatic History* 39, no. 5 (2015): 793–818.

20. Quoted in Todd Shepard, *Invention of Decolonization: The Algerian War and the Remaking of France* (Cornell University Press, 2008), 20.

21. Benjamin Brower, *Desert Named Peace: The Violence of France's Empire in the Algerian Sahara, 1844–1902* (Columbia University Press, 2011), 34–50.

22. Abdelkader eventually fled to Morocco, but under French pressure Sultan Abd al-Rahman withdrew his protection and Abdelkader surrendered. He and his family were imprisoned in France until 1852, then freed with great fanfare by Napoleon III; after touring France, Abdelkader was exiled to the Ottoman Empire. He died in Damascus in 1883. "Abdel-Kader," *Dictionary of African Biography*, 6 vols., ed. Emmanuel Akyeampong and Henry Louis Gates Jr. (Oxford University Press, 2012), 1: 33–35; Raphael Danziger, *Abd al-Qadir and the Algerians: Resistance to the French and Internal Consolidation* (Holmes & Meier Publishers, 1977); Wilfrid Blunt, *Desert Hawk: Abd el Kader and the French Conquest of Algeria* (Methuen and Co., 1947).

23. "Foreign," *Richmond Enquirer*, January 16, 1840.

24. "To Abd-El-Kader," *Southern Literary Messenger* 7 (October 1841), 732–33.

25. "Africa," *New York Herald*, March 19, 1840.

26. "Dish of Glory," *Littell's Living Age* 2 (October 12, 1844), 633–34; "Foreign News," *Gentleman's Magazine* 21 (January–June 1844), 82. At this time Bugeaud was governor-general of Algeria.

27. Tocqueville, *Writings on Empire and Slavery*, 37; Barnett Singer and John Langdon, *Cultured Force: Makers and Defenders of the French Colonial Empire* (University of Wisconsin Press, 2008), 61. Bugeaud in fact later justified the beheading, writing that only public display of Embarek's remains for three days before burial convinced Arabs that he, "who had so much influence over them," was indeed dead. Count H. D'Ideville, ed., *Memoirs of Marshal Bugeaud, from His Private Correspondence and Original Documents, 1784–1849*, 2 vols., trans. Charlotte Yonge (Hurst and Blackett, 1884), 2: 99.

28. "Dish of Glory." Americans' focus at this time on French, not Algerian atrocities contrasted with how much of the French press and soldiers described French violence "in the most euphemistic of ways." William Gallois, *History of Violence in the Early Algerian Colony* (Palgrave Macmillan, 2013), 98.

29. "Soldiering," *Littell's Living Age* 6 (September 13, 1845): 503; "French Africa," *American Penny Magazine and Family Newspaper* 2 (February 14, 1846): 27; "Abd-el-Kader and Pelissier," *Living Age* 10 (July 25, 1846): 184: "The Parisians denounce Abd-el-Kader for his recent murder of French prisoners. The barbarian killed them by sword and ball. Now, at the Cave of Dahra, Colonel Pelissier, blessed by the light of civilization, magnanimously used it as a torch." There were four such incidents recorded between 1844 and 1847. Abun-Nasr, *History of the Maghrib*, 246. These incidents echoed through the history of French Algeria, including in an anticolonial film in 1957, René Vautier's *Une Nation, L'Algérie*. Ahmed Bedjaoui, *Cinema and the Algerian War of Independence: Culture, Politics, and Society* (Springer, 2020), 52–53.

30. "Battle with an African Lion," *Southern Christian Advocate*, October 10, 1845.

31. "Foreign Correspondence," *New York Herald*, November 6, 1845; James Crouthamel, *Bennett's New York Herald and the Rise of the Popular Press* (Syracuse University Press, 1989).

32. John Kiser, *Commander of the Faithful: The Life and Times of Emir Abd el-Kader (1808–1883)* (Monkfish Book Publishing Company, 2008), xiii–xiv.

33. Jane Lancaster, *Removal Aftershock: The Seminoles' Struggles to Survive in the West, 1836–1866* (University of Tennessee Press, 1994), 18; J. Fred Rippy, *Joel R. Poinsett: Versatile American* (Duke University Press, 1935), 188.

34. Patrick Malone, *Skulking Way of War: Technology and Tactics Among the New England Indians* (Rowman & Littlefield, 2000).

35. John Grenier, *First Way of War: American War Making on the Frontier, 1607–1814* (Cambridge University Press, 2005), 19; Jeffrey Blick, "Genocidal Warfare in Tribal Societies as a Result of European-Induced Culture Conflict," *Man* (NS) 23, no. 4 (1988): 654–70.

36. May McNeer, *War Chief of the Seminoles* (Random House, 1954).

37. "Negroes, &c., Captured from Indians in Florida, &c," H. of Reps., War Department, H.R. Doc. No. 225, 25th Cong., 3rd Session (February 27, 1839), The University of Oklahoma College of Law, Digital Commons, https://digitalcommons.law.ou.edu/cgi/viewcontent.cgi?article=1220&context=indianserialset; and Thom Hatch, "Osceola Fights to Save the Seminole," *American Heritage* 62, no. 2 (2012): 34–39.

38. W. Fitzhugh Brundage, *Civilizing Torture: An American Tradition* (Harvard University Press, 2020); and Frédéric Mégret, "From 'Savages' to 'Unlawful Combatants': A Postcolonial Look at International Humanitarian Law's 'Other,'" in *International Law and Its Others*, ed. Anne Orford (Cambridge University Press, 2009), 265–317. Long before nineteenth-century imperial forces adopted "barbaric" tactics, European colonial governments were offering cash bounties

for "Indian scalps" in the 1670s. Grenier, *First Way of War*. Bounties paid for the delivery of the severed ears of Algerian fighters were perhaps the French corollary to Anglo-American scalp bounties. Brower, *Desert Named Peace*, 116, 290.

39. President Andrew Jackson's Message to Congress "On Indian Removal," December 6, 1830, Presidential Messages, 1789–1875, Records of the US Senate, Record Group 46, National Archives Building, Washington, DC.

40. The quotations here and in the following paragraph are from "New Instruments of Destruction—War Between Civilized and Barbarous Nations," *Littell's Living Age* 2 (October 19, 1844), 664–67. These references were to the Russo–Circassian War (1763–1864) and the First Anglo–Afghan War (1839–1842).

41. "New Instruments of Destruction—War Between Civilized and Barbarous Nations." A correspondent of President Van Buren apprised the president that the Seminoles were "robbers, incendiaries, and assassins who pillage, burn, and murder at night and then escape into the swamps. . . . Congress should raise a new corps of 2,000 men" that "should use Indian fighting methods." Alfred Bach, Tallahassee, Florida, to Martin Van Buren, May 4, 1840, Joel R. Poinsett Papers, Historical Society of Pennsylvania. Walter Hixson argues that in US-Indian Wars Americans outdid other colonial powers' brutality. Walter Hixson, *American Settler Colonialism: A History* (Palgrave Macmillan, 2013). A broader perspective that contextualizes early US wars with American Indians, though without reference to French Algeria, is James Belich, *Replenishing the Earth: The Settler Revolution and the Rise of the Angloworld, 1783–1939* (Oxford University Press, 2009).

42. In fact, there were about one hundred thousand European and twenty-five thousand Algerian native troops in the French army in Algeria in 1850, by which time, owing to the war, the native precolonial population had declined by over one-third. John Morell, *Algeria: Topography and History, Political, Social, and Natural, of French Africa* (N. Cooke, 1854); Sessions, *By Sword and Plow*.

43. Cuba remained a periodic target for American acquisition throughout the nineteenth century, but before the Civil War, northerners opposed its likelihood to become a slave territory. After the Civil War, American annexationists also considered the Dominican Republic, but anti-annexationists objected to Cubans' and Dominicans' race and religion, among other factors.

44. Kevin Waite, *West of Slavery: The Southern Dream of a Transcontinental Empire* (University of North Carolina Press, 2021); Matthew Karp, *This Vast Southern Empire: Slaveholders at the Helm of American Foreign Policy* (Harvard University Press, 2016).

45. Seymour Drescher, *Abolition: A History of Slavery and Antislavery* (Cambridge University Press, 2009), 274; Lawrence Jennings, "France, Great Britain, and the Repression of the Slave Trade, 1841–1845," *French Historical Studies* 10 (Spring 1977): 101–25, esp. 112. An Anglo-French convention in 1845 abolished Anglo-French pledges to allow searches of each other's vessels but committed each country to police its own merchant ships off the slave coasts. Lawrence Jennings, *French Anti-Slavery: The Movement for the Abolition of Slavery in France, 1802–1848* (Cambridge University Press, 2000), 229.

46. Brower, *Desert Named Peace*, 165; Jennings, *French Anti-Slavery*, 204–18.

47. Seymour Drescher, "British Way, French Way: Opinion Building and Revolution in the Second French Slave Emancipation," *American Historical Review* 96 (June 1991): 709–34, at 718. Mirroring Americans' strategic study of French Algeria, Bugeaud had studied American history for what it might yield about subduing a native people. In 1842 he observed, "It was alcohol that vanquished the [American] Indians, and it will be trade that subdues the Arabs." Quoted in Douglas Porch, "The 'Frontier' in French Imperial Ideology," *Journal of the West* 34 (October 1995): 16–22, at 18–19.

48. Sessions, *By Sword and Plow*, 191; Drescher, *Abolition*, 274; Jennings, "France, Great Britain, and the Repression of the Slave Trade, 1841–1845."

49. Congressman William Boyce quoted in Samuel Sullivan Cox, "Laws of Natural Growth.-Mexican Affairs" (1860), in *American Exceptionalism*, 4 vols., ed. Timothy Roberts and Lindsay DiCuirci (Routledge, 2017), 1: 302. The term "sick man" is attributed originally to Czar Nicholas I in reference to the Ottoman Empire. By the Adams–Onis Treaty of 1819, Spain had relinquished claims to lands east of the Sabine, Red, and Arkansas Rivers, and north of the forty-second parallel.

50. "Official Documents Accompanying the President's Annual Message to Congress: Mr. Calhoun's Letter to Mr. King, Department of State, Washington, August 12, 1844," *Niles' National Register* 67, December 21, 1844, 247–449, at 248.

51. "Official Documents Accompanying the President's Annual Message to Congress." As an example of French ideology about spreading "civilization," the French minister of public instruction, Abel-François Villemain, declared in an 1846 debate on military appropriations for Algeria: "Any system must be good that consolidated French rule on the African soil; France must be powerful for the sake of humanity and civilization; the employment of military forces so considerable was a principle of humanity . . . [E]xtensions of territory were not decreed and proclaimed, they executed and consummated themselves." "Correspondence," *Littell's Living Age* 10 (1846): 338–44, at 341. On the history of French exceptionalist discourse via the spread of 'civilization' by military success, see Olivier Grandmaison, "De l'extermination à la mise en valeur des colonies: le triomphe de l'exception française (1885–1931)," in *Nouvelle histoires des colonisations européennes XIX-XXè siècles: Sociétés, cultures, politiques,* ed. Amaury Lorin and Christelle Taraud (Presses Universitaires de France, 2013): 153–66.

52. On the origins of Americans' sense of entitlement and destiny to the "uncultivated land" of North America, see Jack Greene, *The Intellectual Construction of America: Exceptionalism and Identity from 1492 to 1800* (University of North Carolina Press, 1997).

53. Amy Greenberg, *Wicked War: Polk, Clay, Lincoln, and the 1846 U.S. Invasion of Mexico* (Vintage, 2013), 194.

54. Ralph Waldo Emerson, "Antislavery Speech at Dedham 4 July 1846," in Ralph Waldo Emerson, *Emerson's Antislavery Writings*, ed. Len Gougeon and Joel Myerson (Yale University Press, 2002), 42.

55. Ralph Waldo Emerson, *Journals and Miscellaneous Notebooks of Ralph Waldo Emerson*, 16 vols., ed. Merton Sealts Jr. (Harvard University Press, 1960–1982), 10: 36.

56. John Calhoun, "Speech on the Three Million Bill," February 9, 1847, in *Works of John C. Calhoun*, ed. Richard Crallé, 6 vols. (D. Appleton, 1854–1860), 4: 303–48, at 321, 324, 325.

57. Poinsett quoted in Rippy, *Joel R. Poinsett*, 226–27; Joel Poinsett, January 18, 1847, Georgetown, South Carolina, to Frances Tyrrell, in Joel R. Poinsett Papers.

58. "Proposed 'Civilization' of Mexico," [Washington] *Weekly National Intelligencer*, May 22, 1847.

59. "Course of the Whigs," *Richmond Enquirer*, October 30, 1846. Both the United States and Mexico claimed the area where the incident occurred.

60. "A Precedent of '94 for the Mexican War," [Indianapolis] *Indiana State Sentinel*, February 20, 1847. The original story appeared in the *Boston Post*. For this background on the US Navy's founding, see Ian Toll, *Six Frigates: The Epic History of the Founding of the U.S. Navy* (W. W. Norton & Company, 2008), 24–62.

61. Willard Klunder, *Lewis Cass and the Politics of Moderation* (Kent State University Press, 1996), 142.

62. "Course of the Whigs; "The Three Million Bill. Speech of Mr. Berrien, of Georgia, in the Senate, February 5, 1847," *App. to Cong. Globe*, 29th Cong., 2nd Sess. 302 (1847).
63. Scott Silverstone, *Divided Union: The Politics of War in the Early American Republic* (Cornell University Press, 2004), 180–84.
64. "Proposed 'Civilization of Mexico'," [Washington, DC] *Weekly National Intelligencer*, May 22, 1847.
65. Frederick Douglass, "The 1848 Revolution in France; An Address Delivered in Rochester, New York, on 27 April 1848," in *Frederick Douglass Papers Series One: Speeches, Debates, and Interviews*, 5 vols., ed. John Blassingame (Yale University Press, 1979–92), 2:117.
66. Timothy Roberts, *Distant Revolutions: 1848 and the Challenge to American Exceptionalism* (University of Virginia Press, 2009), chapters 2 and 4.
67. Roberts, *Distant Revolutions*, chapter 6; Frédérique Beauvois, *Between Blood and Gold: The Debates over Compensation for Slavery in the Americas* (Berghahn, 2016), 5; Robin Blackburn, *Overthrow of Colonial Slavery, 1776–1848* (Verso, 1988), 504–05; Drescher, "British Way, French Way," 730–34.
68. Paul Quigley, *Shifting Grounds: Nationalism and the American South, 1848–1865* (Oxford University Press, 2014), 23–25; Roberts, *Distant Revolutions*, chapter 5.
69. At the establishment of the French Third Republic (1870–1940), Crémieux wrote, "In 1848 I was a member of the provisional government, and I used, to a deputation which had come from Algiers, the following words: — 'The Republic desires the assimilation of Algeria to France'." Quoted in Andre Chouraqui, *Between East and West: A History of the Jews of North Africa* (Scribner, 1973), 143. Not surprisingly, even in the revolutionary year 1848, policymakers in the French Second Republic considered the prospect of two separate forms of citizenship in Algeria, the recommendation of Louis Juchault de Lamoricière, an Algerian war veteran and the republic's minister of war. Avner Ofrath, *Colonial Algeria and the Politics of Citizenship* (Bloomsbury, 2023), 33.
70. Wayne Kime, *Donald G. Mitchell* (Twayne, 1985), 10–11; Fayette Copeland, *Kendall of the Picayune* (University of Oklahoma Press, 1997), 151–69. Mitchell became probably America's first war correspondent during the Mexican War, when, as an aide to General Winfield Scott, he sent reports of American advances back to the *Picayune* via an express pony service.
71. Quotations from Roberts, *Distant Revolutions*, 30.
72. Jennifer Sessions, "Colonizing Revolutionary Politics: Algeria and the French Revolution of 1848," *French Politics, Culture & Society* 33 (2015), 75–100, esp. 85–89.
73. *New Orleans Picayune*, July 20, 23, 1848.
74. Larry Reynolds, *European Revolutions and the American Literary Renaissance* (Yale University Press, 1988), 46–48; Copeland, *Kendall of the Picayune*, 242–47, quotation from 246.
75. Ik Marvel, *Battle Summer: Being Transcripts from Personal Observation in Paris, During the Year 1848* (Baker & Scribner, 1850), 285. Ik Marvel was Mitchell's pen name. Lamartine was a poet and historian and Arago a physicist and astronomer. At the time they were both members of the French Executive Commission, the collective presidency of the Second Republic.
76. Antoine Sénard, the National Assembly president, was reported to have said on June 25 that the Paris workers used tactics "borrowed from the annals of the savage tribes of America." Quoted in Sessions, "Colonizing Revolutionary Politics," 86.
77. American odes to Abdelkader would continue after his imprisonment in 1847. Camille Thierry, a poet in New Orleans, Louisiana, praised Abdelkader in a work published in *La Chronique de la Nouvelle Orléans*, April 16, 1848. Cited in Elèna Mortara, *Writing for Justice: Victor Séjour, the Kidnapping of Edgardo Mortara, and the Age of Transatlantic Emancipations* (Dartmouth College Press, 2015), 132, 258. A paean to Abdelkader in a New York magazine in late 1848 again

emphasized his exceptional character and military prowess, allegedly atypical of most savage and impulsive Arabs. "Abd-el-kader," *Eclectic Magazine* 16 (December 1848–April 1849), 267–71.

78. For Fourierism in America see Carl Guarneri, *Utopian Alternative: Fourierism in Nineteenth-Century America* (Cornell University Press, 2018). A Fourierist community was established in Algeria in 1846; it was charged to settle three hundred European families there but failed to achieve that and was evicted from most of its land grant in 1853. David Prochaska, "Fourierism and the Colonization of Algeria: L'Union Agricole d'Afrique, 1846–1853," *Journal of the Western Society for French History* 1 (1974): 283–302. Saint-Simonians believed that science could transform industrial society and help create true equality among all men engaged in useful and collaborative work. A variety of these socialists developed projects in Algeria. Prosper Enfantin, a founder of Saint-Simonianism, participated in a scientific mission to Algeria in 1845 and directed a colonial railway from Paris to the Mediterranean Sea. Enfantin believed the settlement of North Africa by white Christians could help Europe foster harmonious relations with Asia by encouraging racial and religious intermingling and creating a hybrid civilization. Enfantin's compatriot Emile Barrault headed an eight-hundred-person colony near Algiers in 1848, intended to cultivate cotton. For Barrault, "Algeria is the promised land of the chosen people, that is the socialist people." The Saint-Simonian Pierre Leroux, elected to the French legislative assembly in 1849, argued Algeria could be the site of a new society founded on the basis of "association." Osama Abi-Mershed, *Apostles of Modernity: Saint-Simonians and the Civilizing Mission in Algeria* (Stanford University Press, 2010); Kay Adamson, *Political Thought and Economic Thought and Practice in Nineteenth-Century France and the Colonization of Algeria* (Edward Mellen Press, 2002), 182–83, 215–16.

79. "Memoirs of General Cavaignac," *New York Herald*, November 24, 1848.

80. Michael Heffernan, "The Parisian Poor and the Colonization of Algeria During the Second Republic," *French History* 3 (December 1989): 377–403, esp. 384, 393; Ted Margadant, *French Peasants in Revolt: The Insurrection of 1851* (Princeton University Press, 1979), 112.

81. "Correspondence," *The Living Age* 19 (October 7, 1848): 39–44, esp. 43.

82. Marvel, *Battle Summer*, 285; Sessions, *By Sword and Plow*, 313–14.

83. Roberts, *Distant Revolutions*, 23; Jonathan Israel, *Expanding Blaze: How the American Revolution Ignited the World, 1775–1848* (Princeton University Press, 2017), 568.

84. Richard Rush, *Occasional Productions, Political, Diplomatic, and Miscellaneous* (J. B. Lippincott, 1860), 453. Rush's opinion reflected how American and French imperialists alike believed that before white settlers engaged in nation-building, native peoples lived in the wilderness. For alternative views that an Algerian state existed before the French occupation, see Abdallah Laroui, *History of the Maghreb: An Interpretive Essay*, trans. Ralph Manheim (Princeton University Press, 1977), 299–301; and William Gallois, "The Destruction of the Islamic State of Being, Its Replacement in the Being of the State: Algeria, 1830–1847," *Settler Colonial Studies* 8, no. 2 (January 2017): 131–51.

85. "The French Republic," *New York Herald*, December 3, 1850.

86. "Letter from London," *National Era*, December 5, 1850.

87. Sessions, *By Sword and Plow*, 190–93.

88. "France. French Slave Trade in Algeria." *Niles' National Register* 69 (September 1845–March 1846), 65.

89. "The French in Algeria," *New York Times*, March 13, 1855.

90. "The French in Algeria." For American commentaries on laborers imported to Algeria see, for example, "Arrival of the Africa," [Pomeroy, Ohio] *Meigs County Telegraph*, May 12, 1857; "The Emperor Napoleon upon the Free Emigration of Africans," [New Lisbon, Ohio] *Anti-Slavery Bugle*, December 18, 1858. On French plans to import East Asian laborers to cultivate Algerian cotton, see Claire Fredj, "Des coolies pour l'Algérie? L'Afrique du Nord et le travail

engagé (1856–1871)," *Revue d'histoire moderne & contemporaine* 63 (2016): 62–83. American missionaries in Africa interacted with French imperialists mainly in Gabon, which became a French protectorate in 1838 before the American Board of Commissioners for Foreign Missions (ABCFM) established a mission there in 1842. Gabon joined Sierra Leone and Liberia as loci of the ABCFM's West African focus when Africa became a missions field in the 1820s. And the ABCFM decided to focus on Christian conversion of African "Negroes," not Arab-descended "Moors." Emily Conroy-Krutz, *Christian Imperialism: Converting the World in the Early American Republic* (Cornell University Press, 2015), 41–48, 176–78.

91. "Message of the French President," [Washington] *Southern Press*, December 6, 1850. Also see, "A New Phase of the Slave Trade," [Wilmington, NC] *Daily Journal*, May 28, 1858.

92. "Slavery Aggressions," *De Bow's Review* 28 (February 1860): 132–38, esp. 133.

93. "Report on the Slave Trade, to the Southern Convention," *De Bow's Review* 24 (June 1858): 473–91; "Speech of Hon. R. B. Rhett," *Lancaster [SC] Ledger*, July 20, 1859. On arguments to reopen the African slave trade in the late antebellum era, see Manisha Sinha, *Counterrevolution of Slavery: Politics and Ideology in Antebellum South Carolina* (University of North Carolina Press, 2003), 125–52; and Karp, *This Vast Southern Empire*, 141–48.

94. "Importance of the Kansas Struggle," *New Orleans Daily Crescent*, September 14, 1857.

95. *Speech of Senator S. A. Douglas, on the Invasion of States; and His Reply to Mr. Fessenden. Delivered in the Senate of the United States, January 23, 1860* (J. Murphy, 1860), 14.

96. Ewa Atanassow, "Nationhood-Democracy's Final Frontier?," and Jennifer Pitts, "Democracy and Domination, Empire, Slavery, and Democratic Corruption in Tocqueville's Thought," in *Tocqueville and the Frontiers of Democracy*, ed. Ewa Atanassow and Richard Boyd (Cambridge University Press, 2013), 178–201, 243–63, esp. 192–93, 251.

97. On antebellum Americans' faulty memory of earlier frontiersmen's history of irregular or guerrilla tactics against American Indians, see Vandevort, *Indian Wars*, 61.

2. The Civil War as a *Razzia*

1. "Abd-El-Kader," *Richmond Dispatch*, August 25, 1860; "Abd-El-Kader and the United States," *New York Times*, October 20, 1860; Ussama Makdisi, *Faith Misplaced: The Broken Promise of U.S.-Arab Relations: 1820–2001* (PublicAffairs, 2010), 61–62.

2. "Civil War in Syria," "Abd-El-Kader on the State of Turkey," [Washington DC] *National Intelligencer*, August 4, 1860; "Latest News From Europe," [Raleigh] *Weekly Standard*, August 8, 1860; John Kiser, *Commander of the Faithful: The Life and Times of Emir Abd el-Kader (1808–1883)* (Monkfish, 2008), 293–303.

3. Only Berbers of the Algerian Zwawa tribes were originally designated for service in Zouave units. The word *Zouave* was derived from Zwawa, the name of a Kabyle tribe of Northwestern Algeria.

4. "The Zouaves Again," *Alexandria [VA] Gazette*, January 2, 1855.

5. Lew Wallace, *Lew Wallace: An Autobiography* (Harper & Brothers, 1906), 245.

6. Robert Broadwater, *Civil War Special Forces: The Elite and Distinct Fighting Units of the Union and Confederate Armies* (ABC-Clio, 2014), 2.

7. Fitz-James O'Brien, "The Zouaves," quoted in Peter Karsten, *The Military in America: From the Colonial Era to the Present* (Free Press, 1986). Malakoff was the site of a French victory during the Crimean War's Siege of Sevastopol, memorable for a French Zouave raising the French flag atop a Russian redoubt.

8. Wallace, *Lew Wallace*, 270.
9. Wallace, *Lew Wallace*, 270.
10. Don Troiani, Earl Coates, and Michael McAfee, *Don Troiani's Regiments and Uniforms of the Civil War* (Stackpole, 2002), 61–64, 71.
11. Eugene Ware, *The Lyon Campaign in Missouri: Being a History of the First Iowa Infantry* (Crane & Co., 1907), esp. 86.
12. Thomas DeLeon, quoted in Lee Wallace, Jr., "Coppens' Louisiana Zouaves," *Civil War History* 8 (September 1962): 269–82, esp. 272.
13. Adam Goodheart, *1861: The Civil War Awakening* (Vintage, 2012), 194, 287.
14. Earl Hess, *Civil War Infantry Tactics: Training, Combat, and Small-Unit Effectiveness* (Louisiana State University Press, 2015), 69–70.
15. Quoted in Kristie Ross, "Arranging a Doll's House: Refined Women as Union Nurses," in *Divided Houses: Gender and the Civil War*, ed. Catherine Clinton and Nina Silber (Oxford University Press, 1992), 99–113, esp. 106.
16. Quoted in Crystal Feimster, *Southern Horrors: Women and the Politics of Rape and Lynching* (Harvard University Press, 2009), esp. 19.
17. Terry Jones, *Lee's Tigers: The Louisiana Infantry in the Army of Northern Virginia* (Louisiana State University Press, 1987), 62.
18. M. M. McAllen, *Maximilian and Carlota: Europe's Last Empire in Mexico* (Trinity University Press, 2014), 16.
19. "Zouaves Are Coming!" [West Baton Rouge] *Sugar Planter*, April 27, 1861.
20. "National Theater," *Cincinnati Daily Press*, May 30, 1861.
21. "The Arabs," *Cleveland Morning Leader*, March 24, 1864.
22. "Zouaves," *Wilmington Journal*, June 13, 1861.
23. Michael Bonura, *Under the Shadow of Napoleon: French Influence on the American Way of Warfare from the War of 1812 to the Outbreak of WWII* (New York University Press, 2012); William Skelton, *An American Profession of Arms: The Army Officer Corps, 1784–1861* (University Press of Kansas, 1993).
24. Edward Hagerman, *American Civil War and the Origins of Modern Warfare: Ideas, Organization, and Field Command* (Indiana University Press, 1992), 5–13.
25. Bonura, *Under the Shadow of Napoleon*, 80–113; William Martel, *Victory in War: Foundations of Modern Strategy* (Cambridge University Press, 2011), 77.
26. Americans' use of the term *counterinsurgency* emerged during the early 1960s, perhaps coined by President John Kennedy. Gian Gentile, *Wrong Turn: America's Deadly Embrace of Counterinsurgency* (New Press, 2015), 12–13. A recent study that emphasizes the American military's embrace of French counterinsurgency doctrine beginning with the Algerian War of Independence, 1954–62, is Terrence Peterson, *Revolutionary Warfare: How the Algerian War Made Modern Counterinsurgency* (Cornell University Press, 2024).
27. Antoine-Henri de Jomini, *The Art of War*, trans. G. H. Mendell and W. P. Craighill (Legacy Books, 2008), 14, 18; Walter Laqueur, *Guerrilla Warfare: A Historical and Critical Study* (Routledge, 2017), 100–101.
28. Thomas Rid, "Razzia: A Turning Point in Modern Strategy," *Terrorism and Political Violence* 21, no. 4 (2009): 617–35, esp. 618. https://doi.org/10.1080/09546550903153449.
29. *Razzia* was a term derived from the Bedouin word for raid, *ghazwa*.
30. Matthew Moten, *The Delafield Commission and the American Military Profession* (Texas A&M University Press, 2000), 85.
31. James Arnold, *Jeff Davis's Own: Cavalry, Comanches, and the Battle for the Texas Frontier* (Wiley, 2000), 29; Douglas Porch, "Bugeaud, Galliéni, Lyautey: The Development of French

Colonial Warfare," in *Makers of Modern Strategy: from Machiavelli to the Nuclear Age*, ed. Peter Paret (Princeton University Press, 1986), 376–407, esp. 376.

32. Philip Kearny, *Service with French Troops in Africa* (n.p., 1844), 1; Thomas Kearny, *General Philip Kearny: Battle Soldier of Five Wars, Including the Conquest of the West* (G. P. Putnam's Sons, 1937), ix; Bruce Vandevort, *Indian Wars of Canada, Mexico, and the United States, 1812–1900* (Routledge, 2006), 60.

33. K. Jack Bauer, *Mexican War 1846–1848* (University of Nebraska Press, 1992), 223–25; Harwood Hinton and Jerry Thompson, *Courage Above All Things: General John Ellis Wool and the U.S. Military, 1812–1863* (University of Oklahoma Press, 2020), 46–50.

34. Andrew Birtle, *U.S. Army Counterinsurgency and Contingency Operations Doctrine, 1860–1941* (Government Printing Office, 2004), 65.

35. Benjamin Brower, *Desert Named Peace: The Violence of France's Empire in the Algerian Sahara, 1844–1902* (Columbia University Press, 2011), 70–73.

36. Randolph Marcy, *Prairie Traveler: A Hand-book for Overland Expeditions, with Maps, Illustrations, and Itineraries of the Principal Routes Between the Mississippi and the Pacific* (Harper & Brothers, 1859), 183, 203. Marcy cited an 1856 edition of Daumas's *Le Grand Desert*. He misspelled Daumas's name as Dumas.

37. Secretary of War Jefferson Davis to President Franklin Pierce, December 1, 1856, in *Papers of Jefferson Davis*, ed. Lynda Crist and Mary Dix (Louisiana State University Press, 1989), 6:68–69; U.S. Military Academy Commission, *Report . . . to Examine into the Organization, System of Discipline, and Course of Instruction of the United States Military Academy at West Point* (n.p., 1860), 331.

38. Kevin Waite, "Jefferson Davis and Proslavery Visions of Empire in the Far West," *Journal of the Civil War Era* 6, no. 4 (2016): 536–65.

39. Carol Reardon, *With a Sword in One Hand and Jomini in the Other: The Problem of Military Thought in the Civil War North* (University of North Carolina Press, 2012), 26–69.

40. [William Sherman] General Orders No. 62, July 24, 1862, US War Department, *War of the Rebellion: A Compilation of the Official Records of the Union and Confederate Armies* (GPO, 1886) [O.R.], series 1, vol. 17, part 2, 119.

41. "A flying column is seldom used in regular warfare among civilised nations." "Life in a French Kitchen," *Once a Week* 2 (December 1859–June 1860): 197. The formation dated in the modern era to French and Austrian actions against guerrillas in Corsica in the 1730s. A Mexican flying column surprised and captured three hundred Texans in March 1836. Treated as pirates by the Mexican government, the Texans were infamously executed at Goliad. General Zachary Taylor organized an American flying column against Comanche Indians and partisan Mexican forces near Reynosa, Mexico, in September 1846. Charles Calwell, *Small Wars: Their Principles and Practice* (His Majesty's Stationary Office, 1906), 136; Spencer Tucker, *Almanac of American Military History* (ABC-CLIO, 2013), 1:613; Robert Broadwater, *General George H. Thomas: A Biography of the Union's "Rock of Chickamauga"* (McFarland & Company, 2009), 23.

42. Robert Asprey, *War in the Shadows: The Guerrilla in History* (Doubleday & Co., 1975), 1:168. The American military actually experimented with a camel corps for desert warfare, which was successful but short lived. In 1836, a US Army lieutenant, George Crosman, first recommended to the War Department the military usage of camels. In 1855, at the recommendation of Secretary of War Jefferson Davis and on the basis of the French army's usage of camels in the Sahara, Congress approved deployment of several dozen camels as beasts of burden. The camels outperformed horses and mules, but the Civil War ended the experiment. Lewis Lesley, "Purchase and Importation of Camels by the United States Government, 1855–1857," *Southwestern Historical Quarterly* 33, no. 1 (1929):18–33; Thomas Connelly, "American Camel Experiment: A Reappraisal," *Southwestern Historical Quarterly* 69, no. 4 (1966): 442–62.

43. Captain George McClellan, for example, observed the work of Russian Cossack forces in 1855 and recommended their techniques be deployed against American Indians. Eufrosina Dvoichenko-Markov, "Americans in the Crimean War," *Russian Review* 13, no. 2 (1954): 143.

44. "The French in Algeria," *New York Times*, March 13, 1855.

45. James Schneider, "Loose Marble—and the Origins of Operational Art," *Parameters: The US Army War College Quarterly* 19, no. 1 (1989): 92; Raymond Lassarat, *Alexis Godillot 1816–1893* (R. Lassarat, 1984), 24–45.

46. Earl Hess, *Civil War Logistics: A Study of Military Transportation* (Louisiana State University Press, 2017), 171.

47. Alain Cointat, *Les Souliers de la Gloire: Alexis Godillot (1816–1893)* (Presses du Midi, 2006), 123; Montgomery Meigs to W. S. Pennington, August 9, 1861, O.R., series 3, vol. 1, 393; Don Troiani, *Regiments and Uniforms of the Civil War* (Stackpole, 2002), 64. In 1862 a military board recommended that the entire Union army adopt a uniform based on the French chasseur garb, although the recommendation was not adopted.

48. Montgomery Meigs to D. Butterfield, May 11, 1863, O.R., series 1, vol. 25, part 2, 490–91.

49. Abraham Lincoln to Ulysses Grant, April 30, 1864, in Collected Works of Abraham Lincoln.

50. William Sherman, *Sherman's Civil War: Selected Correspondence of William T. Sherman, 1860–1865*, ed. Brooks Simpson and Jean Berlin (University of North Carolina Press, 2014), 703.

51. Samuel Bowman and Richard Irwin, *Sherman and His Campaigns: A Military Biography* (C. B. Richardson, 1865), 235; William Sherman, *Memoirs of General William T. Sherman* (D. Appleton, 1886), 2:194.

52. William Sherman to Henry Halleck, December 24, 1864, O.R., series 1, vol. 44, 799.

53. Erik Ringmar, "Francis Lieber, Terrorism, and the American Way of War," *Perspectives on Terrorism* 3, no. 4 (2009): 52–60; Julian Ku and John Yoo, *Taming Globalization: International Law, the US Constitution, and the New World Order* (Oxford University Press, 2012), 147.

54. Francis Lieber, *Instructions for the Government of Armies of the United States in the Field* [1863] (Government Printing Office, 1898), 7.

55. Lieber, *Instructions*, 10.

56. Recent scholarship has emphasized that the Lieber Code, as an "artifact of Native wars," reflected American settler colonial history. See, for example, Helen Kinsella, "Settler Empire and the United States: Francis Lieber on the Laws of War," *American Political Science Review* 117, no. 2 (2023): 629–42.

57. Lieber, *Instructions*, 9.

58. Lieber, *Instructions*, 7. Neither the Lieber Code nor prior treatises on international law nor the Hague Convention of 1907 provided for protection of the lives or property of "civilians," a term not used in international law until 1949. Jeremy Rabkin, "Anglo-American Dissent from the European Law of War: A History with Contemporary Echoes," *San Diego International Law Journal* 16, no. 1 (2014): 5.

59. Lieber, *Instructions*, 4; Lieber quoted in Aaron Sheehan-Dean, *Calculus of Violence: How Americans Fought the Civil War* (Louisiana State University Press, 2018), 65–66.

60. Quoted in Daniel Sutherland, *American Civil War Guerrillas: Changing the Rules of Warfare* (ABC-CLIO, 2013), 94. Sheehan-Dean argues that the Lieber Code limited the Civil War's death toll. Sheehan-Dean, *Calculus of Violence*, 181.

61. Quoted in Walter Hixson, *American Settler Colonialism: A History* (Palgrave, 2013), 107; "Gen. Rob't E. Lee Again," *Vicksburg Daily Citizen*, July 2, 1863, reprinted in *[Barton VT] Orleans County Monitor*, March 18, 1901.

62. David Clinton, *Tocqueville, Lieber, and Bagehot: Liberalism Confronts the World* (Palgrave Macmillan, 2003), 6.

63. Henry Halleck, *Elements of Military Art and Science* [1846] (D. Appleton, 1863), 321.

64. Thomas Bugeaud, *Practice of War: Being a Translation of a French Military Work Entitled "Maxims, Counsels and Instructions on the Art of War. . . ."* (West and Johnson, 1863), 145. The earlier French version was Bugeaud, *Instructions pratiques du maréchal Bugeaud* (Leveneu, 1854).

65. Antoine-Henri Jomini, *Summary of the Art of War* [1838] (Putnam, 1854), 42.

66. Bugeaud, *Practice of War*, 129.

67. Bugeaud, *Practice of War*, 129, 128.

68. Bugeaud, *Practice of War*, 130–32; Sherman quoted in Thomas Robisch, "General William T. Sherman: Would the Georgia Campaigns of the First Commander of the Modern Era Comply with Current Law of War Standards?" *Emory International Law Review* 9, no. 2 (1995): 470. Both the Lieber Code and Bugeaud's pronouncement of international law forbade the execution of prisoners of war, torture, and usage of poison.

69. Sherman, *Sherman's Civil War*, 279, 311. In September 1863, Sherman wrote Henry Halleck, general-in-chief of the US Army, "We will remove and destroy every obstacle, if need be, take every life, every acre of land, every particle of property, everything that to us seems proper. . . . All who do not aid us are enemies." Sherman, *Memoirs*, 1:367.

70. Quoted in John Marszalek, *Sherman: A Soldier's Passion for Order* (Southern Illinois University Press, 2007), 196.

71. William Sherman to Ulysses Grant, October 4, 1862, O.R., series 1, vol. 17, part 2, 260.

72. Bugeaud quoted in William Gallois, *History of Violence in the Early Algerian Colony* (Palgrave Macmillan, 2013), 124, 125.

73. The leading military theorist of the early nineteenth century, the Prussian Carl von Clausewitz, emphasizing that certain kinds of warfare could be humane, specified that "wars between civilized nations are far less cruel and destructive than wars between savages." Carl von Clausewitz, *On War* [1832], trans. Michael Howard and Peter Paret (Princeton University Press, 1976), 76. Even though the Union military implicitly embraced French counterinsurgency strategy and tactics associated with razzia, the term connoted disreputable warfare in the postwar era. An early history of the Civil War described Lee's Gettysburg campaign as "a gigantic raid, or immense French Algerian-razzia, unworthy of this age of the world." J. Watts de Peyster, *The Decisive Conflicts of the Late Civil War, or Slaveholders' Rebellion: Battles Morally, Territorially, and Militarily Decisive*, 3 vols. (MacDonald and Co., 1867), 1:59.

74. Stuart Miller, *"Benevolent Assimilation": the American Conquest of the Philippines, 1899–1903* (Yale University Press, 1982), 162; Brian Linn, *The U.S. Army and Counterinsurgency in the Philippine War, 1899–1902* (University of North Carolina Press, 1989), 53.

75. Porch, "Bugeaud, Galliéni, Lyautey," 402–405; Clay Mountcastle, *Punitive War: Confederate Guerrillas and Union Reprisals* (University of Kansas Press, 2009), 12–19.

76. Pekka Hämäläinen, "Reconstructing the Great Plains: The Long Struggle for Sovereignty and Dominance in the Heart of the Continent," *Journal of the Civil War Era* 6 (December 2016): 481–509.

77. Grant quoted in Mark Neely, *The Civil War and the Limits of Destruction* (Harvard University Press, 2009), 115.

78. Quoted in Neely, *Civil War*, 112.

79. Lance Janda, "Shutting the Gates of Mercy: The American Origins of Total War, 1860–1880," *Journal of Military History* 59 (January 1995): 7–26, esp. 13; O.R., series1, XLIII, part 1, 698, 917.

80. Robert Utley, *Frontier Regulars: The United States Army and the Indian, 1866–1891* (University of Nebraska Press, 1984), 44–52.

81. Bruce Vandervort, "War and Imperial Expansion," in *Cambridge History of War*, ed. Roger Chickering, Dennis Showalter, and Hans van de Ven (Cambridge University Press, 2012), 4: *War in the Modern World*; Grant quoted in Janda, "Shutting the Gates of Mercy," 23.

82. George Crook, *General George Crook: His Autobiography*, ed. Martin Schmitt (University of Oklahoma Press, 1986), 69, 87; Robert Mackey, *Uncivil War: Irregular Warfare in the Upper South, 1861–1865* (University of Oklahoma Press, 2005), 99–100.

83. Wesley Pirkle, "Major General George Crook's Use of Counterinsurgency Compound Warfare during the Great Sioux War of 1876–77," M.A. thesis, US Army Command and General Staff College, 2008, 12; Utley, *Frontier Regulars*, 54. Until World War I, native peoples who provided military service served in auxiliary units in both the French and US armies, not in regular combat units.

84. David Prochaska, *Making Algeria French: Colonialism in Bône, 1870–1920* (Cambridge University Press, 2004), 10; Adria Lawrence, *Imperial Rule and the Politics of Nationalism: Anti-Colonial Protest in the French Empire* (Cambridge University Press, 2013), 53–54; Marie Post and Régis de Trobriand, *Life and Memoirs of Comte Régis de Trobriand: Major-General in the Army of the United States* (E. P. Dutton & Co., 1910), 417.

85. Paul Wylie, *Blood on the Marias: The Baker Massacre* (University of Oklahoma Press, 2016), 221.

86. Régis de Trobriand, *Military Life in Dakota: The Journal of Philippe Régis de Trobriand* (Alvord Memorial Commission, 1951), 64.

87. Utley, *Frontier Regulars*, 53.

88. De Trobriand, *Military Life in Dakota*, 65. The psychological impact of French forces' assaults on Algerian women was noticed by an American painter, Frederick Bridgman, who painted in North Africa throughout the 1870s and 1880s. He was in Algiers shortly after the suppression of the Kabyle-led Mokrani Revolt of 1871–72. Osman Benchérif, *The Image of Algeria in Anglo-American Writings 1785–1962* (University Press of America, 1997), 130. In an 1890 memoir Bridgman observed that the "Kabyles . . . in whose memory the outrages of the French soldiers are deeply embedded, look with suspicion on foreigners; this race in particular, when in war among themselves or with near neighbors, almost invariably respected the women. The same cannot be said of the French when they conquered the Kabyles." Frederick Bridgman, *Winters in Algeria* (Harper & Brothers, 1890), 67. On rape as a phenomenon of Sherman's irregular war in the Savannah Campaign of 1864, see Lisa Frank, *Civilian War: Confederate Women and Union Soldiers During Sherman's March* (Louisiana State University Press, 2015).

89. Quoted in Douglas Porch, *French Foreign Legion: A Complete History of the Legendary Fighting Force* (Skyhorse, 2010), 81.

90. Jay Luvaas, "The Influence of the German Wars of Unification on the United States," in *On the Road to Total War: The American Civil War and the German Wars of Unification, 1861–1871*, ed. Stig Förster and Jorg Nagler (Cambridge University Press, 2002): 597–620; Manfred Jonas, *The United States and Germany: A Diplomatic History* (Cornell University Press, 1984), 26–34.

91. Quoted in Carl Degler, "American Civil War and German Wars of Unification: The Problem of Comparison," in *On the Road to Total War*, ed. Förster and Nagler, 53–72, at 68.

92. Quoted in Douglas Porch, *Counterinsurgency: Exposing the Myths of the New Way of War* (Cambridge University Press, 2013), 71.

93. A traditional argument for a unique American approach to war focusing on attrition and annihilation is Russell Weigley, *American Way of War: A History of United States Military Strategy and Policy* (Indiana University Press, 1977). Brian Linn, in *Echo of Battle: The Army's War of War*

(Harvard University Press, 2007), disputing Weigley's thesis, argued that counterinsurgency was a part of Americans' adaptive approach to warfare.

94. Michael Geyer and Charles Bright, "Global Violence and Nationalizing Wars in Eurasia and America: The Geopolitics of War in the Mid-Nineteenth Century," *Comparative Studies in Society and History* 38 (October 1996): 619–57, esp. 630.

95. Sherman, *Memoirs*, 2:183.

3. The Limits of Republican Citizenship

1. Donal Hassett, "Reinventing Empire in the Wake of the Great War: Imperial Citizenship and the 'Wilsonian Moment' in Colonial Algeria," *Comparativ: Zeitschrift für Globalgeschichte und Vergleichende Gesellschaftsforschung* 26, no. 6 (2016): 37–55, esp. 43. Khaled was the grandson of the Berber sheikh Abdelkader El Djezairi, who organized Algeria's first resistance to the French occupation. Khaled did not maintain his leadership of the Algerian movement and went into exile in Syria in 1924.

2. Quoted in Saddek Benkada, "La revendication des libertés publiques dans le discours politique du nationalisme algérien et de l'anticolonialisme français (1919–1954)," *Insaniyat* 25–26 (2004): 179–99, esp. 184. The American government apparently gave Khaled's letter to the French government, which kept its existence secret until its publication in 1980. Natalya Vince, *The Algerian War, the Algerian Revolution* (Palgrave, 2020), 24.

3. National Association for the Advancement of Colored People, *Annual Report* (Annual Report, 1920), 66.

4. Jeannette Jones, *In Search of Brightest Africa: Reimagining the Dark Continent in American Culture, 1884–1936* (University of Georgia Press, 2011), 117.

5. Saliha Belmessous, *Assimilation and Empire: Uniformity in French & British Colonies, 1541–1954* (Oxford University Press, 2014), 160–64; Rabah Aissaoui, "'Between Two Worlds': Emir Khaled and the Young Algerians at the Beginning of the Twentieth Century in Algeria," in *Algeria Revisited: History, Culture and Identity*, ed. Rabah Aissaoui and Claire Eldridge (Bloomsbury, 2017), 56–78, esp. 60–63; Michael Goebel, *Anti-Imperial Metropolis: Interwar Paris and the Seeds of Third World Nationalism* (Cambridge University Press, 2015), 151–54; Clarence Contee, "Du Bois, the NAACP, and the Pan-African Congress of 1919," *Journal of Negro History* 57, no. 1 (1972): 13–28; Martin Evans, *Algeria: France's Undeclared War* (Oxford University Press, 2012), 45. Nor did Wilson, as chairman of the Paris Peace Conference, support a declaration of racial equality offered by Japan as an amendment to the Treaty of Versailles. Marilyn Lake and Henry Reynolds, *Drawing the Global Colour Line: White Men's Countries and the International Challenge of Racial Equality* (Cambridge University Press, 2008), 289–302.

6. Eric Foner, *Nothing but Freedom: Emancipation and Its Legacy* (Louisiana State University Press, 2007), 107–49; Carl Degler, *Neither Black nor White: Slavery and Race Relations in Brazil and the United States* (University of Wisconsin Press, 1986). Access to citizenship of Black Civil War soldiers has been contrasted with the disenfranchisement of Black veterans of Brazil's Triple Alliance War, in Vitor Izecksohn, *Slavery and War in the Americas: Race, Citizenship, and State Building in the United States and Brazil, 1861–1870* (University of Virginia Press, 2014).

7. Augustin Bernard, "Rural Colonization in North Africa (Algeria, Tunis, and Morocco)," in American Geographical Society, *Pioneer Settlement: Cooperative Studies by Twenty-Six Authors*, ed. W. L. G. Joerge (Books for Libraries, 1969): 221–35, esp. 226.

8. Kamel Kateb, *Européens, « Indigènes » et Juifs en Algérie (1830–1962). Représentation et réalités des populations* (Institut National d'Etudes Démographiques, 2001), 187; Diana Davis, *Resurrecting the Granary of Rome: Environmental History and French Colonial Expansion in North Africa* (Ohio University Press, 2007), 92.

9. US Census Bureau, "1870 Census: Volume 1. The Statistics of the Population of the United States," accessed April 21, 2025, https://www.census.gov/library/publications/1872/dec/1870a.html.

10. See Oissila Saaidia, *Algérie coloniale. Quand chrétiens et musulmans cohabitent: musulmans et chrétiens: contrôle de l'État (1830–1914)* (CNRS Editions, 2015). As American policymakers in the early twentieth century would forge a category of separate citizenship for territorial peoples, French policymakers did so in integrating Algeria in 1848.

11. Both the French Second (1848–51) and Third (1870–1940) Republics declared the assimilation of Algeria to France (actually both times by Adolphe Crémieux). Crémieux wrote, "In 1848 I was a member of the provisional government, and I used, to a deputation which had come from Algiers, the following words:—'The Republic desires the assimilation of Algeria to France.' In 1870, under the Republic, I carried out this assimilation, so far as it rested with me to do so." Quoted in Frederic Conybeare, "A Study in Jew-Baiting," *National Review* 33 (1899): 783–801, esp. 789.

12. Gregory Downs, *After Appomattox: Military Occupation and the Ends of War* (Harvard University Press, 2015), 113–35, esp. 114.

13. Natalie Ring, *The Problem South: Region, Empire, and the New Liberal State, 1880–1930* (University of Georgia Press, 2012), 82–85.

14. Don Doyle, *Cause of All Nations: An International History of the American Civil War* (Basic, 2015), 299–311; Andrew Zimmerman, "From the Second American Revolution to the First International and Back Again: Marxism, the Popular Front, and the American Civil War," in *The World the Civil War Made*, ed. Gregory Downs and Kate Masur (University of North Carolina Press, 2015): 304–36; Yasmin Khan, *Enlightening the World: The Creation of the Statue of Liberty* (Cornell University Press, 2010), 7, 40–41.

15. William Novak and Stephen Sawyer, "Emancipation and the Creation of Modern Liberal States in America and France," *Journal of the Civil War Era* 3, no. 4 (2013): 467–500.

16. Studies include Lake and Reynolds, *Drawing the Global Colour Line*; James Belich, *Replenishing the Earth: The Settler Revolution and the Rise of the Angloworld* (Oxford University Press, 2011); Jennifer Pitts, *Turn to Empire: The Rise of Imperial Liberalism in Britain and France* (Princeton University Press, 2006); and Belmessous, *Assimilation & Empire*.

17. Robert Lieberman, *Shaping Race Policy: The United States in Comparative Perspective* (Princeton University Press, 2005), 49.

18. Among the few comparisons of the American South and French Algeria, Richard Bensel suggested a parallel between the Union's defeat of the Confederacy and France's "less successful" effort to integrate Algeria: "In [both] cases, the central state relied on settlers or other sponsored groups to represent state interests and neglected or suppressed indigenous groups." Richard Bensel, *Yankee Leviathan: The Origins of Central State Authority in America, 1859–1877* (Cambridge University Press, 1990), 9.

19. Novak and Sawyer, "Emancipation and the Creation"; Serge Gavronsky, *French Liberal Opposition and the American Civil War* (Humanities, 1968); Stève Sainlaude, *France and the American Civil War: A Diplomatic History* (University of North Carolina Press, 2019), 81–178.

20. Agénor comte de Gasparin, *Uprising of a Great People: The United States in 1861*, trans. Mary Booth (Charles Scribner, 1862), 78, 236, 241; Agénor comte de Gasparin, *America Before Europe*, trans. Mary Booth (Charles Scribner, 1862), 219; Doyle, *Cause of All Nations*, 135–38.

21. Quoted in George Blackburn, *French Newspaper Opinion on the American Civil War* (Greenwood, 1997), 135.

22. Barbara Karsky, "Les libéraux français et l'émancipation des esclaves aux États-Unis, 1852–1870," *Revue d'histoire moderne et contemporaine* 21, no. 4 (1974): 575–90, esp. 589.

23. *Le Monde*, April 26, 1865, quoted in Blackburn, *French Newspaper Opinion*, 134.

24. Cluseret quoted in Philip Katz, *From Appomattox to Montmartre: Americans and the Paris Commune* (Harvard University Press, 1998), 11.

25. Melvyn Stokes, "Europeans Interpret the American South of the Civil War Era: How British and French Critics Received *The Birth of a Nation* (1915) and *Gone with the Wind* (1939)," in *The U.S. South and Europe: Transatlantic Relations in the Nineteenth and Twentieth Centuries*, ed. Cornelis van Minnen and Manfred Berg (University of Kentucky Press, 2013): 181–204, esp. 203.

26. Georges Clemenceau, *American Reconstruction 1865–1870*, ed. Fernand Baldensperger, trans. Margaret MacVeagh (Da Capo, 1969), 40. During and after World War I Clemenceau would lead reform measures to promote Algerian participation in local Algerian governance through the 1919 Jonnart Law. Christopher Andrew and Alexander Kanya-Forstner, *Climax of French Imperial Expansion, 1914–1924* (Stanford University Press, 1981), 138–39.

27. An argument for the essentially conservative nature of Reconstruction, without assessing its transnational context, is Michael Benedict, "Preserving the Constitution: The Conservative Basis of Radical Reconstruction," *Journal of American History* 61, no. 1 (1974): 65–90.

28. Stevens declared, "Nothing is so likely to make a man a good citizen as to make him a freeholder." Thaddeus Stevens, *Speech of Hon. T. Stevens, of Pennsylvania, Delivered in the House of Representatives, March 19, 1867: On the Bill (H.R. no. 20) Relative to Damages to Loyal Men, and for Other Purposes* (Republican Congressional Executive Committee, 1867), 4. Clemenceau quoted in Sylvie Brodziak, *Clemenceau* (Presses Universitaires de Vincennes, 2015), 64.

29. Clemenceau, *American Reconstruction*, 62.

30. Clemenceau, *American Reconstruction*, 62.

31. Clemenceau, *American Reconstruction*, 62.

32. For a different view emphasizing the awe with which Clemenceau regarded Reconstruction, see Don Doyle, *Age of Reconstruction: How Lincoln's New Birth of Freedom Remade the World* (Princeton University Press, 2024), 241–59.

33. Doyle, *Cause of All Nations*, 303.

34. Quoted in Davis, *Resurrecting the Granary of Rome*, 49.

35. Quoted in Sandrine Lemaire, Pascal Blanchard, and Nicolas Bancel, "Milestones in Colonial Culture Under the Second Empire (1851–1870)," in *Colonial Culture in France Since the Revolution*, ed. Pascal Blanchard, Sandrine Lemaire, Nicolas Bancel, and Dominic Thomas (Indiana University Press, 2014): 75–89, esp. 86; Michael Brett, "Legislating for Inequality in Algeria: The Senatus-Consulte of 14 July 1865," *Bulletin of the School of Oriental and African Studies*, University of London 51, no. 3 (1988): 440–61, esp. 453–55.

36. J. E. Sartor, *De la Naturalisation en Algérie, sénatus-consulte du 5 juillet 1865 . . . Musulmans, Israélites, Européens* (Retaux frères, 1865), 11–12.

37. Quoted in André Drainville, *History of World Order and Resistance: The Making and Unmaking of Global Subjects* (Routledge, 2013), 94. French policy did not distinguish between the Berber and Arab ethnic groups, both Muslim, but about one-quarter of the native Algerian population were Berbers, centered in mountainous Kabylia and known among French writers for independent thought and action.

38. The French Second Republic also offered citizenship to West Indian slaves and natives in the colony of Senegal. Napoleon III abrogated those rights in Senegal, but they were restored by the Third Republic.

39. Howard Jones, *Blue and Gray Diplomacy: A History of Union and Confederate Foreign Relations* (University of North Carolina Press, 2010), 285–320.

40. Kate Masur, *An Example for All the Land: Emancipation and the Struggle over Equality in Washington, D.C.* (University of North Carolina Press, 2012), 127–73.

41. Quoted in Benjamin Stora, *Algeria, 1830–2000: A Short History*, trans. Jane Marie Todd (Cornell University Press, 2004), 5; Sven Beckert, *Empire of Cotton: A Global History* (Knopf, 2014), 249–50; Richard Roberts, *Two Worlds of Cotton: Colonialism and the Regional Economy in the French Soudan, 1800–1946* (Stanford University Press, 1996), 66–70. In 1860, France imported 93 percent of its cotton from the United States.

42. Raousett-Boulbon quoted in Davis, *Resurrecting the Granary*, 42.

43. Reclus quoted in Jacques Portes, *Fascination and Misgivings: The United States in French Opinion, 1870–1914* (Cambridge University Press, 2000), 134.

44. James Bryce, "British Experience in the Government of Colonies," *Century* 57 (1899): 718–29, esp. 723; Jens-Uwe Guettel, *German Expansionism, Imperial Liberalism, and the United States, 1776–1945* (Cambridge University Press, 2012), 34; Belich, *Replenishing the Earth*, 167.

45. Pierre Charles de Saint-Amant, *Des colonies: particulièrement de la Guyane française, en 1821* (Chez Barrois, 1822), 56, 58; R. N. Coles, "One Hundred Years Ago," *British Chess Magazine* 67 (1947): 94; Malcolm Rohrbough, *Rush to Gold: The French and the California Gold Rush, 1848–1854* (Yale University Press, 2013), 100.

46. Pierre Charles de Saint-Amant, *L'Algérie et les nègres libres des États-Unis* (Chez Tous Les Libraires, 1866), 6. Some support for the US annexation of the Philippines arose among segregationists such as Alabama Senator John Morgan, who advocated for African Americans to emigrate to the new territory so they could remove their unwanted presence from the American homeland and Christianize the Moro people there. Karine Walther, *Sacred Interests: The United States and the Islamic World, 1821–1921* (University of North Carolina, 2015), 165.

47. Alexis de Tocqueville, *Democracy in America*, trans. Henry Reeve, 2 vols. (George Adlard, 1839), 1:358; Guillaume Poussin, *The United States: Its Power and Progress*, trans. Edmund Du Barry (Lippincott, Grambo and Co., 1851), 426; William Gallois, "Genocide in Nineteenth-Century Algeria," *Journal of Genocide Research* 15, no. 1 (2013): 69–88; Jennifer Sessions, *By Sword and Plow: France and the Conquest of Algeria* (Cornell University Press, 2011), 180; Gary Stein, "Indian Removal as Seen by European Travelers in America," *Chronicles of Oklahoma* 51, no. 4 (1973–74): 399–410.

48. Bodichon quoted in Benjamin Brower, *Desert Named Peace: The Violence of France's Empire in the Algerian Sahara, 1844–1902* (Columbia University Press, 2013), 167.

49. Osama Abi-Mershed, *Apostles of Modernity: Saint-Simonians and the Civilizing Mission in Algeria* (Stanford University Press, 2010), 67.

50. See, for example, H. S. Fulkerson, *The Negro as He Was; As He Is; As He Will Be* [1887], in *Anti-Black Thought 1863–1925*, ed. John David Smith, 11 vols. (Garland, 1993), 10:119–237, esp. 174.

51. Saint-Amant, *L'Algérie et les nègres libres*, 7.

52. Michele Mitchell, *Righteous Propagation: African Americans and the Politics of Racial Destiny After Reconstruction* (University of North Carolina Press, 2004), 43–44.

53. Saint-Amant, *L'Algérie et les nègres libres*, 51.

54. Quotation from Robert Stam and Ella Shohat, *Race in Translation: Culture Wars Around the Postcolonial Atlantic* (New York University Press, 2012), 32, describing such favorable treatment of African Americans in Brazil during the twentieth century.

55. On freedpeople's prioritization of suffrage rights see Eric Foner, *Forever Free: The Story of Emancipation and Reconstruction* (Doubleday, 2013), 89–90; Alexander Keyssar, *Right to Vote: The Contested History of Democracy in the United States* (Basic, 2001), 180; Rogers Smith, *Civic Ideals: Conflicting Visions of Citizenship in U.S. History* (Yale University Press, 1997), 212–16.

56. Saint-Amant, *L'Algérie et les nègres libres*, v, 26, 50–51.

57. Roger Botte and Alessandro Stella, *Couleurs de l'esclavage sur les deux rives de la Méditerranée (Moyan ge-XXe siècle)* (Karthala Editions, 2012), 374–75; Jean Baude, *L'Algerie*, 3 vols. (Atheneum, 1841), 3:191.

58. Eric Foner, "Lincoln and Colonization," in *Our Lincoln: New Perspectives on Lincoln and His World*, ed. Eric Foner (W. W. Norton, 2008), 135–66; Mitchell, *Righteous Propagation*, 16–50.

59. Sylvia Jacobs, *African Nexus: Black American Perspectives on the European Partitioning of Africa, 1880–1920* (Greenwood, 1981), 9–13.

60. See Andrew Zimmerman, *Alabama in Africa: Booker T. Washington, the German Empire, and the Globalization of the New South* (Princeton University Press, 2012); and Beckert, *Empire of Cotton*, 340–78.

61. W. E. B. Du Bois, *Select Bibliography of the Negro American . . . Together with the Proceedings of the Tenth Conference for the Study of the Negro Problems, Held at Atlanta University, on May 30, 1905* (Atlanta University Press, 1905), 5. Emphasis in original.

62. Mark Summers, *Dangerous Stir: Fear, Paranoia, and the Making of Reconstruction* (University of North Carolina Press, 2014), 84; Heather Richardson, *Death of Reconstruction: Race, Labor, and Politics in the Post-Civil War North, 1865–1901* (Harvard University Press, 2004), 183.

63. Quentin Deluermoz, *Le crépuscule des révolutions, 1848–1871* (Éditions du Seuil, 2012), 331–54; Georges Haupt, "The Commune as Symbol and Example," in *Aspects of International Socialism, 1871–1914: Essays by Georges Haupt*, trans. Peter Fawcett (Cambridge University Press, 2011), 23–47; Alistair Horne, *Fall of Paris: The Siege and the Commune, 1870–71* (Penguin, 2007), 247–314.

64. The Commune's impact on the Reconstruction politics has been remarked in Nell Painter, *Standing at Armageddon: A Grassroots History of the Progressive Era* (Norton, 2013), 17–24; Richardson, *Death of Reconstruction*, 85–117; Adam Tuchinsky, *Horace Greeley's "New-York Tribune": Civil War-Era Socialism* (Cornell University Press, 2009), 196–219; and more fully in Katz, *From Appomattox to Montmartre*.

65. Stewart Edwards, *The Paris Commune, 1871* (Quadrangle, 1971), 217–19.

66. Linus Brockett, *Paris Under the Commune: Or . . . A Second Reign of Terror* (1871); Benjamin Butler in the *New York Herald*, July 30, 1871; and Edward King, in *The Great South* (1875), quoted in Katz, *From Appomattox to Montmartre*, 72, 94, 116.

67. *New York Tribune* quoted in Tuchinsky, *Horace Greeley's "New-York Tribune,"* 202.

68. "Real Nature of the Coming Struggle," *The Nation*, April 9, 1874, 230–31, esp. 230; Tuchinsky, *Horace Greeley's "New-York Tribune,"* 204.

69. Eric Foner, *Reconstruction: America's Unfinished Revolution, 1863–1877* (Harper and Row, 1988), 586–87; Richardson, *Death of Reconstruction*, 135; quotations from John Park, *Elusive Citizenship: Immigration, Asian Americans, and the Paradox of Civil Rights* (New York University Press, 2004), 189. See also Michael Ross, *Justice of Shattered Dreams: Samuel Freeman Miller and the Supreme Court During the Civil War Era* (Louisiana State University Press, 2003), 189–240.

70. Quotations from Downs, *After Appomattox*, 72, 189, 198.

71. Claude Martin, *La Commune d'Alger (1870–1871)* (Heraklès, 1936); James McDougall, *History of Algeria* (Cambridge University Press, 2017), 79; David Prochaska, *Making Algeria French: Colonialism in Bône, 1870–1920* (Cambridge University Press, 2004), 251.

72. Jamil Abun-Nasr, *History of the Maghrib* (Cambridge University Press, 1971), 248–49.

73. While the American South and French Algeria both experienced increasingly controversial military occupation in the late 1860s, even in 1871, when, owing to the Franco-Prussian War, French troops in North Africa shrank to forty-three thousand, that total, in terms of soldiers per civilian population, constituted seven times the US troop density in the former

Confederacy in 1867. In that year of Radical Reconstruction there were twenty-five thousand Union soldiers policing the region. Downs, *After Appomattox*, 262; Michael Greenhalgh, *Military and Colonial Destruction of the Roman Landscape of North Africa, 1830–1900* (Brill, 2014), 366.

74. Édouard Laboulaye, *Histoire des États-Unis*, 3 vols. (Charpentier, 1870), 1:71–72, 90. Laboulaye first expressed his preference for Algeria to develop based on ideals of private property and respect for individual rights of settlers and native peoples alike in 1855, in *Histoire politique des États-Unis . . . 1620–1789*. For analysis see Stephen Sawyer, "An American Model for French Liberalism: The State of Exception in Édouard Laboulaye's Constitutional Thought," *Journal of Modern History* 85, no. 4 (2013): 739–71. For a comparison of settler societies in the United States to 1795 and in French Algeria to 1848 see Ashley Sanders, "Between Two Fires: The Origins of Settler Colonialism in the United States and French Algeria," (2015), *Library Staff Publications and Research*, Paper 32, accessed April 22, 2025, http://scholarship.claremont.edu/library_staff/32.

75. Novak and Sawyer, "Emancipation and the Creation," 485.

76. David Prochaska, "Political Culture of Settler Colonialism in Algeria: Politics in Bone (1870–1920)," *Revue de l'Occident musulman et de la Méditerranée* 48–49 (1988): 293–311, esp. 295.

77. The Third Republic maintained the 1865 Sénatus-consulte that all Algerian Muslims were French subjects, eligible for French citizenship upon agreeing to live under French personal status laws. But since marriage, family law, and the distribution of inheritance were regulated in Islamic law, until World War I only 2,396 Algerians were willing to put themselves under French imperial law and become French citizens, and Europeans grew increasingly hostile to the idea. Eugene Rogan, *Arabs: A History* (Basic, 2012), 235; Patrick Weil, *How to Be French: Nationality in the Making Since 1789*, trans. Catherine Porter (Duke University Press, 2008), 215–19.

78. Quoted in Mahfoud Bennoune, *Making of Contemporary Algeria, 1830–1987* (Cambridge University Press, 2002), 44.

79. Bertrand Taithe, *Citizenship and Wars: France in Turmoil, 1870–1871* (Routledge, 2001), 87. French troops killed Mokrani on May 5, 1871.

80. Davis, *Resurrecting the Granary*, 93; Rahima Osmane, "Land Expropriation and Assimilation: A Comparative Study of French Policy in Algeria and Federal Indian Policy in the United States during the Nineteenth Century," PhD diss., University of Keele, 1988, 171, 255, 267. The first régimes d'exception, meaning jurisdictions departing from the principle of a single law for all, were the postslavery colonies of Martinique and Guadeloupe. Achille Mbembe, *On the Postcolony* (University of California Press, 2001), 29.

81. The Code de l'indigénat was not homogenous but rather a pattern of discriminatory laws, with nuances shaped by local conditions, that developed across the French Empire. Its origins in Algeria lay in "special infractions" for which Algerians were liable, decreed by Governor-General Bugeaud as early as 1844. Isabelle Merle, "De la « légalisation » de la violence en contexte colonial. Le régime de l'indigénat en question," *Politix* 17 (2004): 137–62, esp. 144.

82. Weil, *How to be French*, 211–12; Wolfgang Schivelbusch, *Culture of Defeat: On National Trauma, Mourning, and Recovery*, trans. Jefferson Chase (Metropolitan, 2001), 73–86, 176–87; David Blight, *Race and Reunion: The Civil War in American Memory* (Belknap, 2002).

83. Rogan, *Arabs*, 235; Aissaoui, "'Between Two Worlds,'" 76.

84. Jean Mélia, *Le triste sort des musulmans indigènes d'Algérie* (1935), quoted in Patrick Weil, "Le statut des musulmans en Algérie colonial: Une nationalité française dénaturée," *Histoire de la Justice* 16 (2005): 95–109, esp. 103.

85. "Multiracial in America: Proud, Diverse and Growing in Numbers," Pew Research Center, June 11, 2015, 23, accessed April 22, 2025, https://www.pewresearch.org/socialtrends/2015/06/11/chapter-1-race-and-multiracial-americans-in-the-u-s-census/; Belmessous, *Assimilation & Empire*, 148–49; Todd Shepard, *Invention of Decolonization: The Algerian War and the Remaking of France*

(Cornell University Press, 2006), 35. Isabelle Merle has noted the similarity of the Code de l'indigénat to segregation laws in Anglophone countries including the United States. Merle, "De la « légalisation » de la violence en contexte colonial," 141.

86. Booker T. Washington, *Future of the American Negro* (Small, Maynard & Co, 1899), 103.
87. Quoted in Aissaoui, "'Between Two Worlds,'" 63.
88. Williams quoted in Blight, *Race and Reunion*, 168.
89. Quoted in Jan Jansen, "Celebrating the 'Nation' in a Colonial Context: 'Bastille Day' and the Contested Public Space in Algeria, 1880–1939," *Journal of Modern History* 85, no. 1 (2013): 36–68, esp. 54.
90. Fiona Barclay, Charlotte Ann Chopin, and Martin Evans, "Introduction: Settler Colonialism and French Algeria," *Settler Colonial Studies* 8, no. 2 (2018): 115–30, https://doi.org/10.1080/2201473X.2016.1273862; Blight, *Race and Reunion*, 222–28.
91. *Plessy v. Ferguson*, 163 U.S. 537 (1896), 550.
92. Emmanuelle Saada, *Empire's Children: Race, Filiation, and Citizenship in the French Colonies* (University of Chicago Press, 2012), 96; Frederick Cooper, "Conditions Analogous to Slavery: Imperialism and Free Labor Ideology in Africa," in *Beyond Slavery: Explorations of Race, Labor, and Citizenship in Postemancipation Societies*, ed. Frederick Cooper, Thomas Holt, and Rebecca Scott (University of North Carolina Press, 2000), 107–49, esp. 108.
93. For example, French planners, although with mixed results, sought to develop long-range railroad networks to integrate Algeria with France and with West Africa and to encourage migration, similar to the US transcontinental railroad system that linked East and West. Prochaska, *Making Algeria French*, 83–111; Sanford Elwitt, *Making of the Third Republic: Class and Politics in France, 1868–1884* (Louisiana State University Press, 1975), 282–90; Raymond Betts, "Immense Dimensions: The Impact of the American West on Late Nineteenth Century European Thought about Expansion," *Western Historical Quarterly* 10, no. 2 (1979): 149–66, esp. 153; Emma Deputy, "Ideologies of Development in French Algeria: Saint-Simonians, Manifest Destiny, and Globalization," in *African Culture and Global Politics: Language, Philosophies, and Expressive Culture in Africa and the Diaspora*, ed. Toyin Falola and Danielle Sanchez (Routledge, 2014), 17–36.
94. Louis Valéry Vignon, *La France dans l'Afrique du nord, Algérie et Tunisie* (Guillaumin et Cie, 1888), 276.
95. William Vaughn, *Schools for All: The Blacks and Public Education in the South, 1865–1877* (University Press of Kentucky, 2015), 19; Edward Clark, *A Bill to Promote Mendicancy: Facts and Figures Showing That the South Does Not Need Federal Aid for Her Schools* (Evening Post, 1886), 8.
96. Quoted in Susan Kollin, *Captivating Westerns: The Middle East in the American West* (University of Nebraska Press, 2015), 56.
97. This was the sense of the novelist Edith Wharton of her visits to Algiers in 1888 and Biskra, on the Sahara's northern edge, in 1914. Stacy Holden, "Desert Nostalgia in Edith Wharton's Wartime Writing," *Edith Wharton Review* 38, no. 2 (2022): 144–66, at 163.
98. Quoted in Kollin, *Captivating Westerns*, 56, 57–58.
99. Quoted in Kollin, *Captivating Westerns*, 57; Ben Vorpahl, *Frederic Remington and the West: With the Eye of the Mind* (University of Texas Press, 1978), 129–30; David Thombs and Stephen Barrett, "The Internet and Firearms Research with Reference to the .43 Spanish Remington Rolling-Block and Its Ammunition," *Journal of the Historical Breechloading Smallarms Association* 4, no. 4 (2012): 13–22; Martin Windrow, *French Foreign Légionnaire 1890–1914* (Bloomsbury, 2011), n.p. Not surprisingly, Remington Arms also sold rifles to the government of France, although this became controversial during the Franco-Prussian War. Alison Efford, "The Arms Scandal of 1870–1872: Immigrant Liberal Republicans and America's Place in the World," in *Reconstruction in*

a Globalizing World, ed. David Prior (Fordham University Press, 2018), 94–120. Frederic Remington and the founder of Remington Arms, Eliphalet Remington, were distant cousins.

100. Kollin, *Captivating Westerns*, 57.

101. Poultney Bigelow, "An Arabian Day and Night," *Harper's New Monthly Magazine* 90 (Dec. 1894): 3–13. Remington's illustrations accompanied Bigelow's article. Gerald Ackerman, *American Orientalists* (ACR Edition, 2010), 167.

102. Aissaoui, "'Between Two Worlds,'" 63. But in contrast to the United States, which demobilized and reduced its military by the mid-1870s, the French Third Republic introduced universal conscription.

103. James Lehning, *To Be a Citizen: The Political Culture of the Early French Third Republic* (Cornell University Press, 2001), 132–53; Shepard, *Invention of Decolonization*, 25–27; Booker T. Washington, "Extracts from an Address in New York City," in *The Booker T. Washington Papers*, ed. Louis Harlan and Raymond Smock, 14 vols. (University of Illinois Press, 1977), 7:116; Jacqueline Moore, *Booker T. Washington, W. E. B. Du Bois, and the Struggle for Racial Uplift* (Rowman & Littlefield, 2003), 3–5. Although French policy in Algeria did not criminalize interracial marriage, as was law in most US states through World War II, miscegenation was "statistically insignificant" and "frowned upon by administrators and settlers." The stereotype of the unapproachable *femme arabe* was popular in French culture. Martin Thomas, *French Empire Between the Wars: Imperialism, Politics and Society* (Manchester University Press, 2005), 68.

104. Tyler Stovall, *White Freedom: The Racial History of an Idea* (Princeton University Press, 2021), 59–95. Stovall notes that opposition to the Paris Commune echoed in the statue's conservative design.

105. Smith, *Civic Ideals*, 371 ff.; *La France nouvelle* was a phrase coined by a liberal journalist, Lucien-Anatole Prévost-Paradol, in a book of that title in 1868. See Mark Hulliung, *Citizens and Citoyens: Republicans and Liberals in America and France* (Harvard University Press, 2002); and Christina Carroll, *Politics of Imperial Memory in France, 1850–1900* (Cornell University Press, 2022).

4. A French Wild West

1. Mark Pottinger, "Buffalo Bill and the Sound of America During the 1889 World's Fair," in *America in the French Imaginary, 1789–1914: Music, Revolution and Race*, ed. Diana Hallman and César Leal (Boydell & Brewer, 2022): 265–95, esp. 295. Emphasis added.

2. Stuart Banner, *Possessing the Pacific: Land, Settlers, and Indigenous People from Australia to Alaska* (Harvard University Press, 2009); James Belich, *Replenishing the Earth: The Settler Revolution and the Rise of the Angloworld, 1783–1939* (Oxford University Press, 2009); David Hamer, *New Towns in the New World: Images and Perceptions of the Nineteenth-Century Urban Frontier* (Columbia University Press, 1990); John Weaver, *The Great Land Rush and the Making of the Modern World, 1650–1900* (McGill Queens University Press, 2006).

3. In a survey of literature on the comparative aspects of American territorial expansion, Michael Adas suggested some similarities of American practice and ideology with other frontier regimes, not only Anglo-American ones. "From Settler Colony to Global Hegemon: Integrating the Exceptionalist Narrative of the American Experience into World History," *American Historical Review* 106 (December 2001): 1692–1720. As studied by Weaver, nineteenth-century frontier settlement patterns have been observed for Spanish and Portuguese colonies, French settlement colonies, the German and Dutch empires, and the Asian territories that Russia conquered and

colonized. Meanwhile, homestead laws emerged in Argentina and, under American control, the Philippines based on the US Homestead Act.

4. An important, non-Anglo-American transnational study is Jens-Uwe Guettel, *German Expansionism, Imperial Liberalism, and the United States, 1776–1945* (Cambridge University Press, 2012).

5. James McDougall, *History of Algeria* (Cambridge University Press, 2017), 58, 103, 107.

6. John Morell, *Algeria: The Topography and History, Political, Social, and Natural, of French Africa* (Nathaniel Cooke, 1854), 348; McDougall, *History of Algeria*, 90; US Department of the Treasury, *Colonial Administration, 1800–1900: Methods of Government and Development Adopted by the Principal Colonizing Nations in Their Control of Tropical and Other Colonies and Dependencies* (Government Printing Office, 1903), 2840; US Census Bureau, *Seventh Census of the United States* (Robert Armstrong, 1853), ix; US Census Bureau, *Twelfth Census of the United States* (United States Census Office, 1901), xviii; Nancy Shoemaker, *American Indian Population Recovery in the Twentieth Century* (University of New Mexico Press, 2000), 4.

7. Fiona Barclay, Charlotte Ann Chopin, and Martin Evans, "Introduction: Settler Colonialism and French Algeria," *Settler Colonial Studies* 8 (2018): 115–30, esp. 129. Some French imperialists as early as 1848 called for European settlers to enjoy the right of *jus soli*, birthplace citizenship, hailing the practice in the United States inherited from English common law. Avner Ofrath, *Colonial Algeria and the Politics of Citizenship* (Bloomsbury, 2023), 36.

8. On the emergence of the concept of liberal empire in the United States and France see William Novak and Stephen Sawyer, "Emancipation, and the Creation of Modern Liberal States in America and France," *Journal of the Civil War Era* 3 (December 2013): 467–500.

9. Robert Young, *Marketing Marianne: French Propaganda in America, 1900–1940* (Rutgers University Press, 2004), 10–11; Ian Lustick, *Unsettled States, Disputed Lands Britain and Ireland, France and Algeria, Israel and the West Bank-Gaza* (Cornell University Press, 2018), 82.

10. Emily Burns, *Transnational Frontiers: The American West in France* (University of Oklahoma Press, 2018), esp. 3, 157–68; Margaret Andersen, *Regeneration Through Empire: French Pronatalists and Colonial Settlement in the Third Republic* (University of Nebraska Press, 2015), 62–82, 206–11.

11. Jessica Lepler, *Many Panics of 1837: People, Politics, and the Creation of a Transatlantic Financial Crisis* (Cambridge University Press, 2013), esp. 214. The Panic of 1837 was caused by sudden uncertainty in the spring of that year about bank credit available for public land purchases. The term *panic* appeared in the late 1850s.

12. For example, a Texan, Volney Howard, sought to minimize the scope of homestead legislation by limiting its availability only to applicants without property; otherwise, he declared in Congress in 1852, it would be a "wilder scheme of socialism than the French socialist ever dreamed of in his wildest visions." Likewise, in 1860 a Southern writer would summarize the Republican Party platform of 1860, in "its Homestead Bill, and the Preamble of the Declaration of Independence," as a blunt espousal of "the whole agrarian, communistic, free love, anarchical and leveling doctrines of Mr. [Horace] Greely, and of [French utopian Charles] Fourier, from whom he borrows." Helene Zahler, *Eastern Workingmen and National Land Policy, 1829–1862* (Greenwood, 1941), 150; "Horace Greeley and His Lost Book," *Southern Literary Messenger* 31 (September 1860), 212–20, esp. 213. For other descriptions of land reform as socialism, see Jamie Bronstein, *Land Reform and Working-Class Experience in Britain and the United States, 1800–1862* (Stanford University Press, 1999), 236–37; and Zahler, *Eastern Workingmen*, 152–53.

13. Quoted in Mark Lause, *Young America: Land, Labor, and the Republican Community* (University of Illinois Press, 2005), 51.

14. Laura Jensen, *Patriots, Settlers, and the Origins of American Social Policy* (Cambridge University Press, 2003), 193.

15. Jennifer Sessions, *By Sword and Plow: France and the Conquest of Algeria* (Cornell University Press, 2011), 267, 292.

16. Benjamin Claude Brower, *Desert Named Peace: The Violence of France's Empire in the Algerian Sahara, 1844–1902* (Columbia University Press, 2009), 42–43; John Ruedy, *Modern Algeria: The Origins and Development of a Nation* (Indiana University Press, 2005), 68–71; Benjamin Stora, *Algeria, 1830–2000: A Short History*, trans. Jane Marie Todd (Cornell University Press, 2004), 5.

17. Alexis de Tocqueville, *Writings on Empire and Slavery*, ed. Jennifer Pitts (Johns Hopkins University Press, 2001), 36.

18. Michel Chevalier, *Society, Manners and Politics in the United States: Being a Series of Letters on North America*, translated from the third Paris edition (Weeks, Jordan & Co., 1839), 37. Emphasis in original.

19. A contrast to Chevalier and Tocqueville is the perspective a half century later of Stanislas Lebourgeois of the French foreign ministry, who, after visiting Algeria in 1880, observed, the "settler *living in the midst of Arabs*, far from his countrymen, was completely isolated and was overcome with boredom, and discouragement was quick to seize him. He had only one idea, [to] leave the country where he lived so hard." Stanislas Lebourgeois, "De la colonisation algérienne par voies ferrées," *Revue de Geographie* 20 (May 1887): 286–92, esp. 287. Emphasis added.

20. Michael Heffernan, "The Parisian Poor and the Colonization of Algeria During the Second Republic," *French History* 3 (December 1989): 377–403, esp. 384, 393; Ted Margadant, *French Peasants in Revolt: The Insurrection of 1851* (Princeton University Press, 1979), 112. On the relationship of the French 1848 revolution and Algeria's incorporation, see Jennifer Sessions, "Colonizing Revolutionary Politics: Algeria and the French Revolution of 1848," *French Politics, Culture & Society* 33 (Spring 2015): 75–100.

21. For American responses to the June Days upheaval, see Carl Guarneri, *Utopian Alternative: Fourierism in Nineteenth-century America* (Cornell University Press, 1994), 337–40; Timothy Roberts, *Distant Revolutions: 1848 and the Challenge to American Exceptionalism* (University of Virginia Press, 2009), 28–31; Richard Rohrs, "American Critics of the French Revolution of 1848," *Journal of the Early Republic* 14 (Autumn 1994): 359–77; and Adam Tuchinsky, *Horace Greeley's "New-York Tribune": Civil War–Era Socialism and the Crisis of Free Labor* (Cornell University Press, 2009), 82–107.

22. G. Reynolds, "The French Struggle for Naval and Colonial Power," *Atlantic Monthly*, November 1863, 626–37, esp. 631.

23. Chevalier, *Society, Manners and Politics*, 144.

24. William Bromwell, *History of Immigration to the United States* [1856] (Applewood, 2010), 140; Sessions, *By Sword and Plow*, 219.

25. Guillaume Poussin, *The United States: Its Power and Progress* [1843], trans. Edmund Du Barry (Lippincott, Grambo and Co., 1851), 480; Jeremy Jennings, "French Visions of America: From Tocqueville to the Civil War," in *America Through European Eyes: British and French Reflections on the New World from the Eighteenth Century to the Present*, ed. Aurelian Craiutu and Jeffrey Isaac (Pennsylvania State University Press, 2009), 161–86, esp. 171–76.

26. Poussin, *The United States*, 481.

27. Sessions, *By Sword and Plow*, 230, 231.

28. Annuaire des Deux Mondes: Histoire Générale des Divers États 9 (1858–1859), 781.

29. Rahima Osmane, "Land Expropriation and Assimilation: A Comparative Study of French Policy in Algeria and Federal Indian Policy in the United States During the Nineteenth Century," PhD diss., University of Keele, 1988, esp. 170, 264; Diana Davis, *Resurrecting the Granary*

of Rome: Environmental History and French Colonial Expansion in North Africa (Ohio University Press, 2007), 48, 94. The English philosopher John Locke's view of uncultivated land as "waste" provided an early view of the rationale for colonization designed to encourage "improvement of Pasturage, Tillage, or Planting." John Locke, Two Treatises of Government (1698), quoted in David Armitage, "John Locke: Theorist of Empire?," in Empire and Modern Political Thought, ed. Sankar Muthu (Cambridge University Press, 2012), 84–111, esp. 107.

30. Davis, Resurrecting the Granary of Rome, 49–50, 85.

31. Osmane, "Land Expropriation and Assimilation," 171; Heffernan, "The Parisian Poor," 384.

32. Osmane, "Land Expropriation and Assimilation," 86–89. Prospective settlers had to possess at least 1,200 francs. In the 1820s the Australian colonial government had made grants of free land and free convicts to wealthy capitalists, although, while it was expected that they would develop agriculture, this was not a requirement for them to obtain title. Belich, Replenishing the Earth, 263–68.

33. Quoted in William Smith, Bonapartes: History of a Dynasty (Bloomsbury, 2007), 138.

34. Davis, Resurrecting the Granary of Rome, 84–85; Osama Abi-Mershed, Apostles of Modernity: Saint-Simonians and the Civilizing Mission in Algeria (Stanford University Press, 2010), 33.

35. Sandrine Lemaire, Pascal Blanchard, and Nicolas Bancel, "Milestones in Colonial Culture Under the Second Empire (1851–1870)," in Colonial Culture in France Since the Revolution, ed. Pascal Blanchard, Sandrine Lemaire, Nicolas Bancel, and Dominic Thomas (Indiana University Press, 2013), 75–89, esp. 86.

36. Napoléon's phrase is from his letter to Governor General of Algeria Marshal Pélissier, February 6, 1863, quoted in "Louis Napoleon as a Model for the South," De Bow's New Orleans Monthly Review 8 (January 1870): 1–12, esp. 7.

37. Alexis de Tocqueville, Democracy in America, trans. Henry Reeve, 2 vols. (George Adlard, 1839), I:358. See also Tocqueville, Writings on Empire and Slavery, xiv; Poussin, The United States, 426; and Gary Stein, "Indian Removal as Seen by European Travelers in America," Chronicles of Oklahoma 51 (Winter 1973–74): 399–410.

38. William Gallois, "Genocide in Nineteenth-Century Algeria," Journal of Genocide Research 15 (February 2013): 69–88, esp. 72; Jennifer Pitts, Turn to Empire: The Rise of Imperial Liberalism in Britain and France (Princeton University Press, 2006), 185–88, 320–22, esp. 322.

39. Whereas proslavery Americans had largely rejected land reform measures on account of their dangerous resemblance to French "socialist" doctrine, Bodichon's arguments gained favor among Southern spokesmen, who in the 1850s cited his observations about the inevitability of race war in mixed race societies in calling for permanent racial separation in the US western territories. See the speech of Congressman Lemuel Evans of Texas, "Stability of American Institutions," Appendix to the Congressional Globe, 34th Congress 3d Session, Feb. 4, 1857, 230; and Reginald Horsman, Race and Manifest Destiny: The Origins of American Racial Anglo-Saxonism (Harvard University Press, 2009), 275–76.

40. Osmane, "Land Expropriation and Assimilation," 82–84, esp. 84.

41. Banner, Possessing the Pacific, 2, 26; Andrew Armitage, Comparing the Policy of Aboriginal Assimilation: Australia, Canada, and New Zealand (UBC, 1995), 14–16, 199–200.

42. Banner, Possessing the Pacific, 176; Stuart Banner, How the Indians Lost Their Land: Law and Power on the Frontier (Harvard University Press, 2007), 113–249; US Serial Set, Number 4015, 56th Congress, 1st Session, Pages 678 and 679, in US Library of Congress, "Indian Land Cessions in the United States, 1784 to 1894," accessed April 22, 2025, https://www.loc.gov/collections/century-of-lawmaking/articles-and-essays/century-presentations/indian-land-cessions/; Leonard Sadosky, Revolutionary Negotiations: Indians, Empires, and Diplomats in the Founding of America (University of Virginia Press, 2010), 128–38.

43. Robert Rydell and Rob Kroes, *Buffalo Bill in Bologna: The Americanization of the World, 1869–1922* (University of Chicago Press, 2012), 109–10.

44. David Wrobel, *Global West: American Frontier: Travel, Empire, and Exceptionalism from Manifest Destiny to the Great Depression* (University of New Mexico Press, 2014), 36–37; Burns, *Transnational Frontiers*, 12, 67. Napoléon was imprisoned in France during Catlin's exhibition of the Iowa and Ojibwe but likely had access to published accounts of their performances like those of George Sand, who emphasized the American Indians' exploitation and near extinction. *L'Illustration*, a popular pro-colonial newspaper founded in 1843 that offered French people romantic images of Algerians, also published illustrations of the Indians. Frédéric Maguet, "Des Indiens de papier," *Gradhiva* 3 (2006), http://journals.openedition.org/gradhiva/225; Sessions, *By Sword and Plow*, 222–23.

45. "Correspondence," *Littell's Living Age* 18 (July 22, 1848): 179–91, esp. 180.

46. On this concept see Margaret Mujamdar, "Exceptionalism and Universalism: The Uneasy Alliance in the French-Speaking World," in *French Exception*, ed. Emmanuel Godin and Tony Chafer (Berghahn, 2005), 16–29; and Alice Conklin, *Mission to Civilize: The Republican Idea of Empire in France and West Africa, 1895–1930* (Stanford University Press, 1997).

47. John Bigelow to William Seward, March 10, 1865, no. 52, in US Department of State, *Papers Relating to Foreign Affairs . . . Part III* (Government Printing Office, 1866), 376–77. On Franco-American diplomatic relations during the Civil War see Lynn Case and Warren Spencer, *The United States and France: Civil War Diplomacy* (University of Pennsylvania Press, 1970); and Stève Sainlaude, *France and the American Civil War: A Diplomatic History*, trans. Jessica Edwards (University of North Carolina Press, 2019).

48. "The Last Imperial Plan," *Littell's Living Age* 76 (January 1863), 525–27, esp. 526. Reflecting French ambition for Algeria to become a destination for large numbers of European immigrants, few advocates of Algeria's conquest compared the situation to British India, though the cases were similar in regard to a European minority settling among and attempting to exert control over a large Indigenous majority. And regarding French scrutiny of irrigation in British India, see footnote 82.

49. On the eve of the French arrival in Algiers, for example, the American Board of Commissioners for Foreign Missions representative Jeremiah Evarts pointed out the Cherokees' similarity to other weak but nonetheless sovereign communities in the world, including China, Switzerland, and Greece, among others. Evarts, anticipating Louis Napoléon, argued that the United States would be "stained" by the drastic measure of removal, earning international disdain and violating the law of nations. *Essays on the Present Crisis in the Condition of the American Indians* (Perkins & Marvin, 1829), esp. 4, 8, 10, 21, 26, 27, 92.

50. "The Last Imperial Plan," 526.

51. Merle Curti and Kendall Birr, "The Immigrant and the American Image in Europe, 1860–1914," *Mississippi Valley Historical Review* 37 (September 1950): 203–30, esp. 204; Folke Dovring, "European Reactions to the Homestead Act," *Journal of Economic History* 22 (December 1962): 461–72, esp. 470. New York Congressman Gerrit Smith introduced the phrase "land for the landless" in a speech for a homestead bill, February 21, 1854. *Gerrit Smith on Land Monopoly with Introduction by Wm. Lloyd Garrison the Younger* (Public Pub. Co., 1906), 19. The phrase grew in popularity, though its radical "agrarian" implications remained a topic of debate. As late as 1861 the State Agricultural Society of Michigan felt it necessary to declare "land for the landless" was not "proletarian radicalism." *Transactions of the State Agricultural Society of Michigan* 11 (1861): 64.

52. Richard White, *"It's Your Misfortune and None of My Own": A New History of the American West* (University of Oklahoma Press, 1991), 143–47. For Europeans' contemplation of

the significance of American railroads for territorial expansion see Raymond Betts, "Immense Dimensions: The Impact of the American West on Late Nineteenth-Century European Thought About Expansion," *Western Historical Quarterly* 10 (April 1979): 149–66; *Papers Relating to Foreign Affairs . . . First Session of the Thirty-Eighth Congress* (Government Printing Office, 1864), Part II, 1399–1400.

53. Élisée Reclus, "La crise de l'émigration Allemande," *Revue du monde colonial, asiatique et américain; organe politique des deux-mondes* 7 (1862): 397–401, esp. 399, 397.

54. *Papers Relating to Foreign Affairs . . . First Session Thirty-Eighth Congress* (Government Printing Office, 1864), Part II, 1319.

55. *Papers Relating to Foreign Affairs . . . Second Session Thirty-Ninth Congress* (Government Printing Office, 1867), Part I, 288.

56. Dovring, "European Reactions to the Homestead Act," 463–44.

57. Maurice Wahl, *L'Algérie* (F. Alcan, 1897), esp. 335.

58. Davis, *Resurrecting the Granary of Rome*, 95–96. At this time the state held about twice as much land in Algeria as settlers did.

59. Warnier quoted in Brower, *Desert Named Peace*, 24.

60. Mahfoud Bennoune, *The Making of Contemporary Algeria, 1830–1987* (Cambridge University Press, 2002), 47; Osmane, "Land Expropriation and Assimilation," 266.

61. Osmane, "Land Expropriation and Assimilation," 176.

62. Charles-Robert Ageron, *Les Algériens musulmanes et la France (1871–1919)*, 2 vols. (Presses Universitaires de France, 1968), esp. I:78.

63. Paul Leroy-Beaulieu, "La colonisation comparée en Algérie et aux Etats-Unis," *L'economiste français* 3 (September 11, 1875), 324–26, esp. 326.

64. Wahl, *L'Algérie*, 335; "L'Algérie," *Scottish Geographical Magazine* 14 (1898): 214–15.

65. Jean-Jules Clamageran, *L'Algérie* (G. Baillière et cie, 1883), 562; "Senators of the Third Republic: Clamageran Jean-Jules," website of the French Senate, accessed April 22, 2025, http://www.senat.fr/senateur-3eme-republique/clamageran_jean_jules1455r3.html.

66. Jules Duval, *L'Algérie et les colonies françaises* (Librairie Guillaumin, 1877), 51.

67. Davis, *Resurrecting the Granary of Rome*, 92.

68. Two such writers were Patrice de MacMahon, governor general of Algeria, 1864–70, and future president of the republic; and Paul Leroy-Beaulieu. In a letter to the French Senate from Algeria, MacMahon cited the challenge of an Algerian "population of 2,500,000 inhabitants of a proud, energetic, [and] militant race" as testimony to the grit of European settlers to overcome great odds, unlike Euro-American settlers, who, "on arrival in America . . . found a territory of immense expanse, inhabited by a population, which . . . was insignificant." Patrice de MacMahon, "Discours au Sénat du duc de Magenta sur une pétition relative à la constitution de l'Algérie" (1870), quoted in Ashley Sanders, "Between Two Fires: The Origins of Settler Colonialism in the United States and French Algeria" (2015), *Library Staff Publications and Research*, Paper 32, accessed April 22, 2025, http://scholarship.claremont.edu/library_staff/32. Meanwhile, Leroy-Beaulieu, keen to explode the myth of the disappearing Arab in support of his argument for assimilating Algerians into French colonial society, used French census data from 1872 and 1881 to report that over that time the Arab population increased by a third, to 2.85 million. Paul Leroy-Beaulieu, *L'Algérie et la Tunisie* (Librairie Guillaumin, 1887), 65.

69. Duval, *L'Algérie*, 48.

70. Émile Levasseur, "Rapport Sur le Concours Pour Le Prix Léon Faucher," in Académie des sciences morales et politiques, *Séances et travaux de l'Académie des sciences morales et politiques, compte rendu* 92 (1870): 315–57, esp. 351–52.

71. Émile Levasseur, *La question de l'or* (Librairie de Guillamen et cie, 1858).

72. Europeans comprised 10 percent of the Algeria population in 1880. David Prochaska, *Making Algeria French: Colonialism in Bône, 1870–1920* (Cambridge University Press, 2004), 144; Bouda Etemad, *Possessing the World: Taking the Measurements of Colonisation from the 18th to the 20th Century* (Berghahn, 2007), 158.

73. Duval, *L'Algérie*, 51.

74. Jean-Jules Clamageran, *L'Algérie: Impressions de voyage 17. 3.– 4. 6. 1873 suivies d'une étude sur les institutions kabyles et la colonisation* (Baillière, 1874), 270.

75. Leroy-Beaulieu, "La colonisation," 326.

76. Leroy-Beaulieu, "La colonisation," 325.

77. [Gouvernement General de l'Algerie], *Coup d'oeil sur l'histoire de la colinisation en algérie* (A. Bouyer, 1878), 25. Emphasis added.

78. Leroy-Beaulieu, "La colonisation," 326.

79. Leroy-Beaulieu, *L'Algérie et la Tunisie*, 65.

80. James Lehning, *To Be a Citizen: The Political Culture of the Early French Third Republic* (Cornell University Press, 2001), 132–44; Todd Shepard, *Invention of Decolonization: The Algerian War and the Remaking of France* (Cornell University Press, 2008), 25–27. A decree of Louis Napoléon, the Sénatus consulte of 1865 and reiterated in the Code de l'indigénat of 1881, offered citizenship to Algerian men who renounced rights and responsibilities under Muslim law. Only some 1,300 men enrolled in this process by 1901, which amounted to apostasy.

81. Osmane, "Land Expropriation and Assimilation," 171, 271; Richard White, "Contested Terrain: The Business of Land in the American West," in *Land in the American West: Private Claims and the Common Good*, ed. William Robbins and James Foster (University of Washington Press, 2011), 190–206. For discussion of opposition to John Wesley Powell's attempt in 1878 to organize the West into democratically run "zones" for mining, grazing, logging, and agriculture, consistent with the vision of the Homestead Act, which prioritized the role of small landowners, see White, *It's Your Misfortune*, 150–54.

82. Brock Cutler, "Imperial Thirst: Water and Colonial Administration in Algeria, 1840–1880," *Review of Middle East Studies* 44 (Winter 2010): 167–75; Maurits Ertsen, "Colonial Irrigation: Myths of Emptiness," *Landscape Research* 31 (March 2006): 147–67; Timothy Rickard, "The Great Plains as Part of an Irrigated Western Empire, 1890–1914," in *Great Plains: Environment and Culture*, ed. Brian Blouet and Frederick Luebke (University of Nebraska Press, 1979), 81–98, esp. 88; Donald Worster, *Rivers of Empire: Water, Aridity, and the Growth of the American West* (Oxford University Press, 1985), 143–56. In the nineteenth century, European, Australian, and American hydraulic engineers and geologists generally held British India in highest regard for the efficiency of the government-organized irrigation networks of the Ganges and Indus river systems. However, in the 1890s American newspapers suddenly carried dozens of accounts of French engineers "reclaiming the Sahara" via installation of artesian wells, their value magnified by the extension of railroads connecting the desert and the coast. A US Navy engineer had first alerted American audiences to this French feat in 1880. Seaton Schroeder, USN, "Artesian Wells and the Great Sahara," *Popular Science Monthly* 16 (February 1880): 530–39.

83. Conklin, *Mission to Civilize*, 22.

84. Adolphe Duponchel, *Le chemin de fer trans-saharien. Jonction coloniale entre l'Algérie et le Soudan. Études préliminaires du projet et rapport de mission avec cartes générale et géologie* (Boehm & Fils, 1878); Douglas Porch, *Conquest of the Sahara* (Macmillan, 2005), 85.

85. Lebourgeois, "De la colonisation algérienne par voies ferrées," 288.

86. Louis Gueydon, governor general of Algeria, to the president of France, in *Situation de l'Algerie*, 1872, Gouvernment general d l'Algerie, Correspondance politique generale, Fonds due Gueydon, Immigration alsacienne et lorraine (1871–1873), ANOM; Wahl, *L'Algérie*, esp. 336;

Edward Bridges, "Algerian Colonisation," *St. James's Magazine and United Empire Review* 36 (1875): 488–97; Davis, *Resurrecting the Granary of Rome*, 93.

87. Quoted in Wolfgang Schivelbusch, *Culture of Defeat: On National Trauma, Mourning, and Recovery* (Metropolitan, 2003), 147.

88. Quoted in Alice Conklin, Sarah Fishman, and Robert Zaretsky, *France and Its Empire Since 1870* (Oxford University Press, 2011), 67.

89. John Irwin White, *Git Along, Little Dogies: Songs and Songmakers of the American West* (University of Illinois Press, 1975), 161–75.

90. Robert Wells, *Life Flows On in Endless Song: Folk Songs and American History* (University of Illinois Press, 2009), 132–33; White, *Git Along, Little Dogies*, 169–75. Songs praising the virtues of homesteading, and parodies of those songs emphasizing homesteading's bleakness, were common. Wrobel, *Global West*, 156.

91. Walter Ebeling, *Fruited Plain: The Story of American Agriculture* (University of California Press, 1980), 171.

92. Susan Matt, "You Can't Go Home Again: Homesickness and Nostalgia in U.S. History," *Journal of American History* 94 (September 2007): 469–97, esp. 485–91; Thomas Dodman, *What Nostalgia Was: War, Empire, and the Time of a Deadly Emotion* (University of Chicago Press, 2018), 4, 186–89; John Strachan, "Between History, Memory, and Mythology: The Algerian Education of Albert Camus," in *France's Lost Empires: Fragmentation, Nostalgia, and la Fracture Coloniale*, ed. Kate Marsh and Nicola Frith (Rowman & Littlefield, 2010), 55–68.

93. Barclay, Chopin, and Evans, "Introduction: Settler Colonialism and French Algeria," 116. In an 1898 retrospective, the French historian and geographer Henri Busson characterized a "5th period" of Algeria's colonial agricultural development, the post-1871 "return to the concession regime" as "inspired by the American law of 'Homestead.'" Henri Busson, "Le développement géographique de la colonisation agricole en Algérie," *Annales de géographie* 31 (January 1898): 34–54, esp. 35. It is interesting to compare American and French writers' images of deserts as both hostile places and opportunities for settlement, as shown in Patricia Limerick, *Desert Passages: Encounters with American Deserts* (University of New Mexico Press, 1985); Henry Nash Smith, *Virgin Land: The American West as Symbol and Myth* (Vintage, 1950); and Davis, *Resurrecting the Granary of Rome*.

94. For comparisons of the frontier's role in renewing the nation or empire see Elizabeth Furniss, "Imagining the Frontier: Comparative Aspects from Canada and Australia," in *Dislocating the Frontier: Essaying the Mystique of the Outback*, ed. Deborah Rose and Richard Davis (Australian National University, 2006), 23–46; and Wrobel, *Global West*.

5. Algeria, Puerto Rico, and the Philippines

1. González was deemed a public charge because she was pregnant and unmarried when she arrived. The Supreme Court misspelled her surname. Christina Burnett, "'They say I am not an American . . .': The Noncitizen National and the Law of American Empire," *Virginia Journal of International Law* 48 (2007–2008), 659–718, at 660.

2. Paul Kramer, "Empires, Exceptions, and Anglo-Saxons: Race and Rule Between the British and U.S. Empires, 1880–1910," in *The American Colonial State in the Philippines: Global Perspectives*, ed. Julian Go and Anne Foster (Duke University Press, 2003): 43–91; Mark-William Palen, *"Conspiracy" of Free Trade: The Anglo-American Struggle over Empire and Economic Globalisation, 1846–1896* (Cambridge University Press, 2016); Stephen Tuffnell, "Anglo-American

Inter-Imperialism: US Expansion and the British World, c.1865–1914," *Britain and the World* 7, no. 2 (2014): 174–95; Karine Walther, *Sacred Interests: The United States and the Islamic World, 1821–1921* (University of North Carolina Press, 2015), 170–71. In a study of American imperial history in global context, A. G. Hopkins writes that its relationship to French imperial policy has been, surprisingly, "largely ignored." A. G. Hopkins, *American Empire: A Global History* (Princeton University Press, 2018), 510.

3. Julian Go, "The Provinciality of American Empire: 'Liberal Exceptionalism' and U.S. Colonial Rule, 1898–1912," *Comparative Studies in Society and History* 49, no. 1 (2007): 74–108; Fabian Hilfrich, *Debating American Exceptionalism: Empire and Democracy in the Wake of the Spanish-American War* (Springer, 2012), 19–22.

4. Kenneth Pomeranz, "Empire & 'Civilizing' Missions, Past & Present," *Daedalus* 134, no. 2 (2005): 34–45.

5. Efrén Rivera Ramos, "Deconstructing Colonialism: The "Unincorporated Territory as a Category of Domination," in *Foreign in a Domestic Sense: Puerto Rico, American Expansion, and the Constitution*, ed. Christina Duffy Burnett and Burke Marshall (Duke University Press, 2001), 104–17, at 107. See also José Cabranes, "Citizenship and the American Empire: Notes on the Legislative History of the United States Citizenship of Puerto Ricans," *University of Pennsylvania Law Review* 127 (December 1978), 391–492; Julian Go and Anne Foster, eds., *The American Colonial State in the Philippines: Global Perspectives* (Duke University Press, 2003); James Edward Kerr, *The Insular Cases: The Role of the Judiciary in American Expansionism* (Kennikat, 1982); and Stuart Miller, *"Benevolent Assimilation": The American Conquest of the Philippines, 1899–1903* (Yale University Press,1982). There is a scholarly consensus that the first Insular Case was *De Lima v. Bidwell*, 182 U.S. 1 (1901), but there is some disagreement over the last. Originally, the Insular Cases were only those decided in 1901. US Supreme Court, *Insular Cases: Comprising the Records, Briefs, and Arguments of Counsel in the Insular Cases of the October Term, 1900, in the Supreme Court of the United States*, compiled by Albert Howe (Government Printing Office, 1901). Recently scholars and jurists have considered *Balzac v. Porto Rico*, 258 U.S. 298 (1922), an Insular Case for affirming the distinction between incorporated and unincorporated territories. Christina Duffy Burnett, "A Note on the Insular Cases," in *Foreign in a Domestic Sense*, ed. Burnett and Marshall, 389–92; Juan Torruella, "The Insular Cases: The Establishment of a Regime of Political Apartheid," *University of Pennsylvania Journal of International Law* 29 (2007): 284–320.

6. Andrew Priest, *Designs on Empire: America's Rise to Power in the Age of European Imperialism* (Columbia University Press, 2021), 56–57; Robert Young, *Marketing Marianne: French Propaganda in America, 1900–1940* (Rutgers University Press, 2004), 9. Jusserand was the French ambassador to the United States from 1903 to 1925.

7. Andrew Hess, "Forgotten Frontier: The Ottoman North African Provinces During the Eighteenth Century," in *Studies in Eighteenth Century Islamic History*, ed. Thomas Naff and Roger Owen (Southern Illinois University Press, 1977), 74–87.

8. Sophie Roberts, *Citizenship and Antisemitism in French Colonial Algeria, 1870–1962* (Cambridge University Press, 2017), 9–11; Patricia Lorcin, *Imperial Identities: Stereotyping, Prejudice and Race in Colonial Algeria* (I. B. Tauris, 1999), 171–95, quoted at 175.

9. Theodore Roosevelt, *Winning of the West*, 4 vols.(G. P. Putnam's Sons, 1889–96), 3:175.

10. Theodore Roosevelt, *Public Papers of Theodore Roosevelt, Governor, 1899*, 2 vols. (Brandow, 1899), 1:267; Theodore Roosevelt, "Expansion and Peace, Published in the 'Independent,' December 21, 1899," in Theodore Roosevelt, *Works of Theodore Roosevelt: The Strenuous Life* (P. F. Collier, 1901), 23–36, at 29, 30, 31. As president, Roosevelt reiterated his admiration of France's civilizing impact in Algeria, a basis for his support at the Algeciras conference in 1906

of an impending French protectorate over Morocco, whose self-government he considered an "abomination." Roosevelt quoted in Walther, *Sacred Interests*, 153.

11. Treaty of Peace Between the United States and Spain, US Congress, 55th Cong., 3d sess., Senate Doc. No. 62, Part 1 (Government Printing Office, 1899), 5–11.

12. Abbott Lawrence Lowell, "The Status of Our New Possessions: A Third View," *Harvard Law Review* 13 (November 1899): 155–76, quoted at 76. Provisions against bills of attainder, ex post facto laws, and the granting of titles of nobility and the provision requiring periodic publication of usage of public money were universal restrictions on Congress.

13. Lowell quoted in Thomas Bender, *Nation Among Nations: America's Place in World History* (Hill and Wang, 2006), 222.

14. *Nation*, December 12, 1895, cited in Henry Blumenthal, *France and the United States: Their Diplomatic Relations, 1789–1914* [1959] (University of North Carolina Press, 2012), 158; William Graham Sumner, *Conquest of the United States by Spain* (1898), cited in Hilfrich, *Debating American Exceptionalism*, 169.

15. Andrew Carnegie, "Americanism versus Imperialism," *North American Review* 168 (January 1899): 1–13, at 7.

16. Cited in Kramer, "Empires, Exceptions, and Anglo-Saxons," 64.

17. George Vest, "Annexation from a Legal Point of View," in William Jennings Bryan et al., *Republic or Empire? The Philippines Question* (Independence Company, 1899), 129–48, at 135.

18. Mark Twain, "To the Person Sitting in Darkness," *North American Review* 172 (February 1901): 161–76.

19. Twain, "To the Person Sitting in Darkness," 169, 173–74.

20. "Some European Colonies," *Washington Sentinel*, April 7, 1900; Rudolph Winnacker, "Elections in Algeria and the French Colonies under the Third Republic," *American Political Science Review* 32 (April 1938): 261–77, esp. 261–62.

21. Carman Fitz Randolph, *Law and Policy of Annexation: With Special Reference to the Philippines, Together with Observations on the Status of Cuba* (Longmans, Green, 1901), 44, 21; Michael Cullinane, *Liberty and American Anti-Imperialism: 1898–1909* (Palgrave Macmillan, 2012), 99; Lanny Thompson, "Imperial Republic: A Comparison of the Insular Territories under U.S. Dominion After 1898," *Pacific Historical Review* 71, no. 4 (2002): 535–74, at 552.

22. "Papers on Current Topics," *San Francisco Call*, April 2, 1901; "Colonial Governments of To-Day," *Minneapolis Journal*, April 2, 1901. After World War I, De Caix developed French policy in Syria and became France's representative to the League of Nations' Permanent Mandates Commission.

23. Thomas Paterson, *American Imperialism and Anti-Imperialism* (Crowell, 1973), 63; "White Man's Burden by Rudyard Kipling," *San Francisco Call*, February 5, 1899; "White Man's Burden," *San Francisco Call*, February 6, 1899.

24. Bonnie Miller, "Image-Makers' Arsenal in an Age of War and Empire, 1898–1899: A Cartoon Essay, Featuring the Work of Charles Bartholomew (of the 'Minneapolis Journal') and Albert Wilbur Steele (of the 'Denver Post')," *Journal of American Studies* 45 (February 2011): 53–75, *Minneapolis Journal* quoted at 67–68.

25. The so-called Teller Amendment to a congressional resolution, signed by President McKinley on April 20, 1898, pledged that the United States would not annex Cuba.

26. Miller, "Image-Makers' Arsenal," 69–70.

27. Quotations from Cabranes, "Citizenship and the American Empire," 431, 432.

28. Virginia Thompson and Richard Adloff, "French Economic Policy in Tropical Africa," in *Colonialism in Africa 1870–1960*, ed. L. H. Gann, Peter Duignan, and Victor Turner (Cambridge University Press, 1969), 127–64.

29. "Papers on Current Topics," *San Francisco Call*, April 2, 1901; "Colonial Governments of To-Day," *Minneapolis Journal*, April 2, 1901.

30. Edward Cavanagh and Lorenzo Veracini, eds., *Routledge Handbook of the History of Settler Colonialism* (Routledge, 2016); Thompson, "Imperial Republic," 537, 555.

31. "Papers on Current Topics," *San Francisco Call*, April 2, 1901; "Colonial Governments of To-Day," *Minneapolis Journal*, April 2, 1901.

32. Osama Abi-Mershed, *Apostles of Modernity: Saint-Simonians and the Civilizing Mission in Algeria* (Stanford University Press, 2010), 1–16, 159–88; James Lehning, *To Be a Citizen: The Political Culture of the Early French Third Republic* (Cornell University Press, 2001), 129–54. De Caix's principal work advocating the association, not assimilation, of North Africans to France was *Arabes et kabyles*, which appeared in 1891.

33. Regarding how (but not whether) Algeria should be colonized, a debate among French colonialists that spanned the Third Republic, Paul Leroy-Beaulieu, a writer keen to understand the French regime through comparisons to other empires, wrote this in *Algerie et Tunisie* (Librairie Guillaumin, 1887), 76:

Should Algeria be regarded as a colony of exploitation, such as the East Indies, or as a[settler] colony such as Australia and Canada? It is an exception, it must be a hybrid colony and form a class apart. If one respects . . . the natives, [and does] not bring any trouble to their . . . enjoyment of the land . . . one could not draw from the country all the resources that it contains, [and] we would not assure French Africa the future to which it can reach. . . . If we wanted to substitute the Europeans for indigenes, we would deprive ourselves of the precious help that a population of three million already half-civilized inhabitants can offer; we would exasperate the Arabs.

This is to say that, different from Robert De Caix, Leroy-Beaulieu advocated colonized peoples' cultural assimilation through exposure to French institutions. On this debate, see Raymond Betts, *Assimilation and Association in French Colonial Theory, 1890–1914* (University of Nebraska Press, 2005).

34. Gerhard Peters and John Woolley, "Republican Party Platform of 1900," The American Presidency Project, accessed April 24, 2025, https://www.presidency.ucsb.edu/node/273319.

35. United States Philippine Commission, *Report of the Philippine Commission to the President*, 2 vols. (Government Printing Office, 1900–01), 1:5. Emphasis added. The commission described the Louisiana Territory as the best governance model for the Philippines, at 1:106–12.

36. Henry Carroll, *Report on the Island of Porto Rico; Its Population, Civil Government, Commerce, Industries, Productions, Roads, Tariff, and Currency, with Recommendations* (Government Printing Office, 1899), 65.

37. *Springfield [Mass.] Republican*, January 11, 1901, cited in Miller, "Benevolent Assimilation," 156–57.

38. Andrew Birtle, *U.S. Army Counterinsurgency and Contingency Operations Doctrine 1860–1941* (Center of Military History, 2009), 32–35, 128. On American troops' comparisons of war in the Philippines and on the western frontier, see Walter Williams, "United States Indian Policy and the Debate over Philippine Annexation: Implications for the Origins of American Imperialism," *Journal of American History* 66 (March 1980): 810–31; and Katharine Bjork, *Prairie Imperialists: The Indian Country Origins of American Empire* (University of Pennsylvania Press, 2018).

39. Will Smiley, "Lawless Wars of Empire? International Law of War in the Philippines, 1898–1903," *Law and History* 36, no. 3 (2018): 511–50, Young quoted at 527.

40. Douglas Porch, "Bugeaud, Gallieni, Lyautey: The Development of French Colonial Warfare," in *Makers of Modern Strategy from Machiavelli to the Nuclear Age*, ed. Peter Paret, Gordon Craig, and Felix Gilbert (Princeton University Press, 1986), 376–407, esp. 390.

41. Hubert Lyautey, "Du rôle colonial de l'Armée," *Revue des deux mondes* 157, no. 2 (1900): 308–28; Edith Wharton, *In Morocco* (MacMillan, 1920), 218.

42. Cambon quoted in William Guéraiche, "Regards français sur la colonisation américaine aux Philippines. (1898–1916)," *Guerres mondiales et conflits contemporains* 209 (January 2003): 103–17, at 107.

43. *Downes v. Bidwell*, 182 U.S. 244, 341–2 (1901).

44. *Downes v. Bidwell*, 286.

45. Burnett, "'They Say I Am Not an American . . .'," 662. See also *Foreign in a Domestic Sense*, ed. Burnett and Marshall.

46. *United States v. Tartar Chemical Company*, 127 Fed. Rep., 944; T. D. 24947, US Treasury Decisions 7 (Jan.–Jun., 1904), 119.

47. *United States v. Tartar Chemical Company*, 121.

48. US Department of the Treasury, *Colonial Administration, 1800–1900* (Government Printing Office, 1901), 1204, 1210, 1403–05.

49. *United States v. Tartar Chemical Company*, 119–21; "Algeria and Porto Rico Receive Treaty," *Washington Times*, August 31, 1902.

50. *Faber v. United States*, 221 U.S. 649, 653 (1911).

51. "To Benefit Porto Ricans," *New York Tribune*, September 7, 1902; "Porto Rico Taken In," *Topeka State Journal*, September 6, 1902; "French Reciprocity Treaty," *New York Sun*, September 1, 1902.

52. Cabranes, "Citizenship and the American Empire," *Downes v. Bidwell* quoted at 438; *DeLima v. Bidwell*, 182, 219 U.S. 1 (1901).

53. Foraker quoted in Cabranes, "Citizenship and the American Empire," 428.

54. *Brief of Argument for Plaintiffs in Error [De Lima], in the Insular Cases: Comprising the Records, Briefs, and Arguments of Counsel in the Insular Cases of the October Term, 1900, in the Supreme Court of the United States, Including the Appendixes Thereto* (Government Printing Office, 1901), 555.

55. Kerr, *The Insular Cases*, 85–86; Bruce Kimball, *Inception of Modern Professional Education: C. C. Langdell, 1826–1906* (University of North Carolina, 2009), 317–19.

56. Coudert did not seek to completely dissociate American imperial law from its British counterpart. Elsewhere in his *De Lima* brief he asserted that the Northwest Territory, Louisiana, California, and Alaska "are colonies just as much as Canada, New Zealand, or Australia are colonies of Great Britain." He made the point to show, awkwardly, that American overseas "colonial" expansion was not itself novel in American history, although denial of "fundamental rights" to the new territories' inhabitants would be. *Brief of Argument for Plaintiffs in Error [De Lima]*, 556, 565–66.

57. *Act Temporarily to Provide for the Administration of the Affairs of Civil Government in the Philippine Islands, and for Other Purposes*, 32 Stat. 691 (1902).

58. Sam Erman, "Meanings of Citizenship in the U.S. Empire: Puerto Rico, Isabel Gonzalez, and the Supreme Court, 1898 to 1905," *Journal of American Ethnic History* 27 (Summer 2008), 5–33; Sam Erman, "Citizens of Empire: Puerto Rico, Status, and Constitutional Change," *California Law Review* 102 (October 2014), 1181–1241.

59. Frederic Coudert, "Reminiscences of Frederic Rene Coudert," unpublished manuscript, Columbia University Oral History Collection, 3–4, 10–11, 25, 51; "Fred'c R. Coudert Passed Away," *Elmira [NY] Summary*, December 26, 1903; *Ponce v. Roman Catholic Church*, 210 U.S. 296 (1908); *Santos v. Roman Catholic Church*, 212 U.S. 463 (1909); José Julián Alvarez-González, "Overseas Possessions of the United States and Religious Liberty," in *Religion and American Law: An Encyclopedia*, ed. Paul Finkelman (Routledge, 2003), 350; William Fortescue, *Third Republic in France, 1870–1940*:

Conflicts and Continuities (Routledge, 2017), 75. Combes's ministry was in power from 1902 to 1905.

60. *Dred Scott v. Sandford*, 60 U.S. 393 (1857), overturned by the Fourteenth Amendment; *Elk v. Wilkins*, 112 U.S. 94 (1884), overturned by the Dawes Act of 1887.

61. Brief for Petitioner-Appellant in *Gonzales v. Williams* 192 U.S. 1 (1904), reprinted in *Brief Making and the Use of Law Books*, ed. Nathan Abbott (West, 1906), quotation at 64.

62. Coudert was similarly cavalier in describing Native Americans facing European settlement: "The Nomad tribes of America presented indeed a problem, but only a passing one. . . . North America could not for mere sentimental reasons remain as a game preserve forever, in order that a few hundred thousand red-skinned hunters might indulge their taste for the chase and gain subsistence thereby as they had done in the past." Frederic Coudert Jr., "Our New Peoples: Citizens, Subjects, Nationals or Aliens," *Columbia Law Review* 3 (January 1903), 13–32, quoted at 13, 31.

63. Arab naturalization to French citizenship before World War I was not as easy to achieve as Coudert declared, however, even among the few Arabs who sought it. Saliha Belmessous, *Assimilation & Empire: Uniformity in French and British Colonies, 1541–1954* (Oxford University Press, 2013), 148–49; Todd Shepard, *Invention of Decolonization: The Algerian War and the Remaking of France* (Cornell University Press, 2006), 35.

64. *Gonzales v. Williams*, 192 U.S. 1, 9 (1904). Actually, for González herself, the point had become moot since after her detention she had married a citizen and thus was allowed to enter the United States.

65. Brief filed by Federico Degetau y Gonzalez as Amicus Curiae Supporting Appellant, quoted in Burnett, "'They Say I Am Not an American . . . ,'" 701, 704.

66. *Indianapolis News*, quoted in "United States Supreme Court," *Lincoln [NE] Commoner*, January 15, 1904; "Queer Status," *Aberdeen [WA] Herald*, January 21, 1904; "Porto Ricans Are Not Aliens-Quaere: Are They Citizens?" *Virginia Law Register* (1904), quoted in Burnett, "'They Say I Am Not an American . . . ,'" 708; "Every Encroachment Important," *Lincoln [NE] Commoner*, September 30, 1904.

67. Frank Castigliola, *France and the United States: The Cold Alliance Since World War II* (Twayne, 1992), 6.

68. Elizabeth Cobbs Hoffman, *American Umpire* (Harvard University Press, 2013); Fareed Zakaria, *From Wealth to Power: The Unusual Origins of America's World Role* (Princeton University Press, 1999). The phrase is from Kramer, "Empires, Exceptions, and Anglo-Saxons," 45.

69. See Margaret Cook Andersen, *Regeneration Through Empire: French Pronatalists and Colonial Settlement in the Third Republic* (University of Nebraska Press, 2015).

6. Algeria's Ambiguities Among American Pan-Africanists

1. Frantz Fanon, *Wretched of the Earth* (Grove, 1963), 93.

2. Samir Meghelli, "From Harlem to Algiers: Transnational Solidarities Between the African American Freedom Movement and Algeria, 1962–1978," in *Black Routes to Islam*, ed. Manning Marable and Hishaam Aidi (Palgrave Macmillan, 2009), 99–119, at 105, https://doi.org/10.1057/9780230623743_7.

3. Bobby Seale, *Seize the Time: The Story of the Black Panther Party and Huey P. Newton* (Black Classic, 1991), 25–34.

4. Henry Blumenthal, *France and the United States: Their Diplomatic Relations, 1789–1914* (University of North Carolina Press, 2012), 147, 158; Jean-Baptiste Duroselle, *France and the United States from the Beginnings to the Present Day* (University of Chicago Press, 1978), 81.

5. Mark Bennitt and Frank Stockbridge, *History of the Louisiana Purchase Exposition . . . from Official Sources* (Universal Exposition, 1905), 585, https://catalog.hathitrust.org/Record/001511566.

6. Bennitt and Stockbridge, *History of the Louisiana Purchase Exposition*, 249.

7. Norman Bolotin, *Chicago's Grand Midway: A Walk Around the World at the Columbian Exposition* (University of Illinois Press, 2017), 83–91.

8. Wisconsin Historical Society, J. Ollmann Lith Co., Singer Advertising Card—Algerian Man, Image ID: 57274, https://www.wisconsinhistory.org/Records/Image/IM57274; Mona Domosh, *American Commodities in an Age of Empire* (Routledge, 2006), 63–94.

9. Blumenthal, *France and the United States*, 194–95.

10. Robert Young, *Marketing Marianne: French Propaganda in America, 1900–1940* (New Brunswick: Rutgers University Press, 2004), 3.

11. Elisabetta Bini, "Drawing a Global Color Line: 'The American Negro Exhibit' at the 1900 Paris Exposition," in *Moving Bodies, Displaying Nations. National Cultures, Race and Gender in World Expositions 19th to 21st Century*, ed. Guido Abbattista (EUT Edizioni Università di Trieste, 2014), 39–65, at 43, 45, https://www.openstarts.units.it/bitstream/10077/10423/1/bini.pdf.

12. Eugene Provenzo, Jr., *W. E. B. DuBois's Exhibit of American Negroes: African Americans at the Beginning of the Twentieth Century* (Rowman & Littlefield, 2013), 7. By the early twentieth century, postcards showing lynchings of African Americans circulated in the United States. While civil rights activists like Ida B. Wells displayed them to arouse opposition to racist violence, they also functioned simply as alluring, cheap means of long-distance correspondence, somewhat similar to the postcards that circulated in the French Empire of beheaded native peoples.

13. Bini, "Drawing a Global Color Line," 48.

14. Bini, "Drawing a Global Color Line," 47–48. See also Andrew Zimmerman, *Alabama in Africa: Booker T. Washington, the German Empire, and the Globalization of the New South* (Princeton University Press, 2010).

15. Benjamin Woodward, "The Exposition of 1900," *North American Review* 170 (1900): 472–79, at 473, http://www.jstor.org/stable/25104981.

16. Zeynep Çelik, *Displaying the Orient: Architecture of Islam at Nineteenth-century World's Fairs* (University of California Press, 1992), 7–8, 90–93, 129–30.

17. W. E. B. Du Bois, "To the Nations of the World" [1900], BlackPast.org, accessed on April 26, 2025, https://www.blackpast.org/african-american-history/1900-w-e-b-du-bois-nations-world.

18. W. E. B. Du Bois, *Darkwater: Voices from Within the Veil* (Harcourt, Brace and Howe, 1920), 73, 74.

19. Richard Fogarty, *Race and War in France: Colonial Subjects in the French Army, 1914–1918* (Johns Hopkins University Press, 2008), 284.

20. Tyler Stovall, *Paris Noir: African Americans in the City of Light* (Houghton Mifflin, 1996), 4–8, 11. Britain initially deployed Indian troops in France, but redeployed them all to the Middle East after 1915. Fogarty, *Race and War in France*, 8.

21. "Colonial Military Participation in Europe (Africa)," *International Encyclopedia of the First World War*, accessed April 26, 2025, https://encyclopedia.1914-1918-online.net/article/colonial_military_participation_in_europe_africa; Jamil Abun-Nasr, *History of the Maghrib* (Cambridge University Press, 1971), 317.

22. Dick van Galen Last and Ralf Futselaar, *Black Shame: African Soldiers in Europe, 1914–1922*, trans. Marjolijn de Jager (Bloomsbury, 2016).

23. Harry Worley and Clarence Contee, "The Worley Report on the Pan-African Congress of 1919," *Journal of Negro History* 55 no. 2 (1970): 140–43, at 142.

24. Young, *Marketing Marianne*, 48–60. Like Allied propaganda, German propaganda dropped over African American troops reminded them about Jim Crow segregation and lynching in the American South and omitted any reference to racism of the French colonial empire. Tyler Stovall, *Paris Noir: African Americans in the City of Light* (Houghton Mifflin, 1996), 13.

25. Emmett Scott, *Scott's Official History of the American Negro in the World War* [1919] (Arno, 1969), 443; Stovall, *Paris Noir*, 18.

26. Galen Last and Futselaar, *Black Shame*, 1, 85, 86; W. E. B. Du Bois, "An Essay Toward a History of the Black Man in the Great War," *The Crisis* (June 1919): 63–87, esp. 87.

27. Scott, *Scott's Official History*, 117, emphasis added.

28. Scott, *Scott's Official History*, 118, emphases in original; quoted in Fogarty, *Race and War in France*, 243.

29. Tyler Stovall, "National Identity and Shifting Imperial Frontiers: Whiteness and the Exclusion of Colonial Labor After World War I," *Representations* 84 (November 2003): 52–72, esp. 56–60; Jamil Abun-Nasr, *History of the Maghrib* (Cambridge University Press, 1971), 319.

30. Tyler Stovall, *White Freedom: The Racial History of an Idea* (Princeton University Press, 2021), 208; Miriam Lowi, *Oil Wealth and the Poverty of Politics: Algeria Compared* (Cambridge University Press, 2009), 55.

31. Scott, *Scott's Official History*, 118, 443. Emphases in original.

32. Chad Williams, "Mobilized Diaspora: The First World War and Black Soldiers as New Negroes," in *Escape from New York: The New Negro Renaissance beyond Harlem*, ed. Davarian Baldwin and Minkah Makalani (University of Minnesota Press, 2013), 247–70, esp. 257; *Encyclopedia of American Race Riots*, ed. James Upton and Walter Rucker, 2 vols. (ABC-CLIO, 2007), 2:662.

33. *Chicago Defender*, August 2, 1919.

34. In 1922 UNIA shrewdly but unsuccessfully petitioned the League of Nations that it administer Germany's former African colonies. Sarah Dunstan, *Race, Rights and Reform: Black Activism in the French Empire and the United States from World War I to the Cold War* (Cambridge University Press, 2021), 39.

35. Mounir Laraba, "A Comparative Study of Nationalist Expressions of the Algerian Community Under French Domination (1919–1954) and the Black Community in the United States of America During the 1960s (1960–1970)," PhD diss., University of Keele, 1988, 113–14. In 1920 the first UNIA convention named Garvey provisional president of Africa, though it neglected to consult residents of Africa.

36. Marcus Garvey, "Who and What Is a Negro," in *Philosophy and Opinions of Marcus Garvey: Or, Africa for the Africans*, ed. Amy Garvey [1923] (Routledge, 2006), part 2, 18–21.

37. Mark Anderson, *From Boas to Black Power: Racism, Liberalism, and American Anthropology* (Stanford University Press, 2019), 19 ff. Wissler, Boas's protégé, was curator of anthropology at the American Museum of Natural History.

38. US Department of State, *Colored Troops in the French Army* [1921], Project Gutenberg, accessed on April 26, 2025, https://www.gutenberg.org/files/58437/58437-h/58437-h.htm.

39. Garvey, "Who and What Is a Negro." Representative of early pan-Africanists, Garvey elsewhere rhetorically embraced Ethiopia; UNIA's official anthem, "Ethiopia, Thou Land of Our Fathers," saluted the northeast African country, and Garvey occasionally used Ethiopia, not colonized, but the ancient nexus of Christianity and the African country invaded by Fascist Italy in 1935, as a synonym for the whole African continent. Robert Weisbord, "Black America and the Italian-Ethiopian Crisis: An Episode in Pan-Negroism," *The Historian* 34 (February 1972): 230–41, at 231; Jeannette Jones, *In Search of Brightest Africa: Reimagining the Dark Continent in American*

Culture, 1884–1936 (University of Georgia Press, 2011), 114, 127–28; Matthew Delmont, *Half American: The Epic Story of African Americans Fighting World War II at Home and Abroad* (Penguin Books, 2022), 16; James Meriwether, *Proudly We Can Be Africans: Black Americans and Africa, 1935–1961* (University of North Carolina Press, 2002), 145; Dunstan, *Race, Rights and Reform*, 129–30.

40. Messali Hadj, "Fight Against French Imperialism!" [1928], in Jacques Simon, *Messali Hadj par les textes*, ed. Jacques Simon [2000], trans. Mitch Abidor, https://www.marxists.org/archive/messali-hadj/1928/fight-french.htm. Morocco became a French protectorate in 1912, and Syria became a French mandate state in 1923.

41. Jacques Simon, *Messali Hadj invente la nation algérienne* (Editions L'Harmattan, 2018), 35.

42. Richard Turner, *Islam in the African-American Experience* (Indiana University Press, 2003), 87–88; Michael Goebel, *Anti-Imperial Metropolis: Interwar Paris and the Seeds of Third World Nationalism* (Cambridge University Press, 2015), 283.

43. Dunstan, *Race, Rights and Reform*, 46.

44. Matthew Guterl, *Josephine Baker and the Rainbow Tribe* (Harvard University Press, 2014), 232; Mary Dudziak, "Josephine Baker, Racial Protest, and the Cold War," *Journal of American History* 81 (1994): 543–70, https://www.jstor.org/stable/pdf/2081171.pdf; Bennetta Jules-Rosette, *Josephine Baker in Art and Life: The Icon and the Image* (University of Illinois Press, 2007), 194.

45. Cheryl Wall, *Women of the Harlem Renaissance* (Indiana University Press, 1995), 48.

46. Marcus Garvey also visited Paris, but his interest in pan-Africanism began while in residence in London in 1914.

47. Jessie Fauset, "Dark Algiers the White, Part I," *The Crisis* (April 1925): 255–58, esp. 255.

48. Fauset, "Dark Algiers the White, Part I," 258; Fauset, "Dark Algiers the White, Part II," *The Crisis* (May 1925), 16–20, esp. 16. See also Claire Garcia, "'For a Few Days We Would Be Residents in Africa': Jessie Redmon Fauset's 'Dark Algiers the White,'" *Ethnic Studies Review* 30 (2007): 103–14.

49. Wall, *Women of the Harlem Renaissance*, 38.

50. Fauset, "Dark Algiers, the White, Part I," 256, 258; "Dark Algiers, the White, Part II," 16.

51. Charlotte Rich, "Fictions of Colonial Anxiety: Edith Wharton's 'The Seed of the Faith' and 'A Bottle of Perrier,'" *Journal of the Short Story in English* 43 (Fall 2004): 59–74.

52. Quoted in Michel Fabre, *From Harlem to Paris: Black American Writers in France, 1840–1980* (University of Illinois Press, 1993), 119; Valeria Popp, "Where Confusion Is: Transnationalism in the Fiction of Jessie Redmon Fauset," *African American Review* 43 (Spring 2009): 131–44.

53. Goebel, *Anti-Imperial Metropolis*, 266; Dunstan, *Race, Rights and Reform*, 102–03; Tyler Stovall, *Transnational France: The Modern History of a Universal Nation* (Routledge, 2022), 305; Reiland Rabaka, *The Negritude Movement: W. E. B. Du Bois, Leon Damas, Aime Cesaire, Leopold Senghor, Frantz Fanon, and the Evolution of an Insurgent Idea* (Lexington Books, 2015), 75–76.

54. Jones, *In Search of Brightest Africa*, 119.

55. Spencer Tucker, "Ferhat Abbas and the Algerian Manifesto of 1943," *Proceedings of the Meeting of the French Colonial Historical Society* 4 (1979): 221–32, at 222.

56. Ferhat Abbas, "En Marge du Nationalisme: La France c'est Moi!" (1936), quoted in Salah el Din el Zein el Tayeb, "Europeanized Algerians and the Emancipation of Algeria," *Middle Eastern Studies* 22 (April 1986): 206–35, at 212.

57. Benjamin Stora, *Ferhat Abbas, une utopie algérienne* (Denoël, 1995), 17, 26, 44.

58. In Switzerland Messali renamed the ENA the Parti du peuple algérien (PPA) with headquarters in Algeria, reiterating a pan-Arab and Islamic orientation while renouncing ties to the French Communist Party, which opposed Algerian independence as an obstacle to workers' rights in France. Elaine Mokhtefi, *Algiers: Third World Capital* (Verso, 2018), 7, 26.

59. Natalya Vince, *The Algerian War, the Algerian Revolution* (Palgrave, 2020), 30.

60. William Middleton, "Pan-Africanism: A Historical Analysis and Critique," *Black Scholar* 1 (January–February 1970), 58–64, at 62; *Circle for Peace and Foreign Relations: About Pan-African Congresses Bulletin 1, 1927*, W. E. B. Du Bois Papers (MS 312), Special Collections and University Archives, University of Massachusetts Amherst Libraries. Reference was made to "French Africa," or French Equatorial Africa, for which the congress advocated "further development" of "native education" and "an extension of political rights for a larger number of natives." Pan African Congress, "Pan African Congress Resolutions [fragment], 1927?," W. E. B. Du Bois Papers (MS 312), Special Collections and University Archives, University of Massachusetts Amherst Libraries.

61. On the other hand, fear of Nazism also reinvigorated African American newspapers' defense of the liberal French Empire in the 1930s. For example, "What Would Germany Do to Us If She Wins?" *(Baltimore) Afro-American*, September 23, 1939.

62. Hugh Mulzac, *A Star to Steer By* (International, 1965), 140, 141. Emphases in original.

63. Quoted in Delmont, *Half American*, 181.

64. Mulzac, *A Star to Steer By*, 194–97.

65. Vince, *The Algerian War*, 44.

66. Christine Levisse-Touzé, *Du capitaine de Hautecloque au général Leclerc* (Editions Complexe, 2000), 243; Mike Thomson, "Paris Liberation Made 'Whites Only,'" *BBC News*, April 6, 2009, http://news.bbc.co.uk/2/hi/europe/7984436.stm; Jean Smith, *Liberation of Paris: How Eisenhower, de Gaulle, and von Choltitz Saved the City of Light* (Simon & Schuster, 2019), 55. Algerian soldiers were attached to the French 2nd Armored Division.

67. Lowi, *Oil Wealth and the Poverty of Politics*, 55.

68. Tucker, "Ferhat Abbas," 223; "Atlantic Charter," Yale Law School Avalon Project, accessed April 26, 2025, https://avalon.law.yale.edu/wwii/atlantic.asp.

69. Tucker, "Ferhat Abbas," 225; Jennifer Johnson, *Battle for Algeria: Sovereignty, Health Care, and Humanitarianism* (University of Pennsylvania Press, 2016), 26.

70. Archie Roosevelt, *For Lust of Knowing: Memoirs of an Intelligence Officer* (Little Brown & Co., 1988), 91.

71. "De Gaulle Frees North Africans," *Chicago Defender*, January 8, 1944.

72. Hakim Adi and Marika Sherwood, *The 1945 Manchester Pan-African Congress Revisited* (New Beacon, 1995), 72.

73. "French Troops Move into Action in Two Colonial Possessions," *Washington Evening Star*, May 24, 1945.

74. Abun-Nasr, *History of the Maghrib*, 325.

75. Ian Lustick, *Unsettled States, Disputed Lands: Britain and Ireland, France and Algeria, Israel and the West Bank-Gaza* (Cornell University Press, 2018), 90, 96.

76. John Kennedy, "Algeria Speech," July 2, 1957, Papers of John F. Kennedy, Pre-Presidential Papers, Senate Files, Box 784, John F. Kennedy Presidential Library.

77. For example, "French Atrocities in Algeria Cause Great Alarm," *(Kansas City) The Call*, May 10, 1957; John Munro, *Anticolonial Front: The African American Freedom Struggle and Global Decolonisation, 1945–1960* (Cambridge University Press, 2017), 265; Frank Castigliola, *France and the United States: The Cold Alliance since World War II* (Twayne, 1992), 116; Martin Thomas, "Defending a Lost Cause? France and the United States Vision of Imperial Rule in French North Africa," *Diplomatic History* 26, no. 2 (2002): 215–47, at 224, https://doi.org/10.1111/1467-7709.00308. In 1946 the French Embassy's Information Service published an interview with Abbas in which he affirmed French sovereignty in Algeria; in response to a question about whether Algeria was more "occidental" or "oriental," Abbas responded, "The Libya desert is a much greater obstacle than the Mediterranean." France Ambassade (US) Service de presse et d'information, *News from France*, June 20, 1946.

78. Mokhtefi, *Algiers*, 25; Matthew Connelly, *Diplomatic Revolution: Algeria's Fight for Independence and the Origins of the Post-Cold War Era* (Oxford University Press, 2002), 119–41.

79. Quoted in Benjamin Stora, "La différenciation entre le F.L.N. et le courant messaliste (été 1954-décembre 1955)," *Cahiers de la Méditerranée* 26, no. 1 (1983): 15–82, at 24, https://doi.org/10.3406/camed.1983.937.

80. Martin Schain, "French Immigration Policy in Comparative Perspective," in *End of the French Exception? Decline and Revival of the 'French Model'*, ed. Tony Chafer and Emmanuel Godin (Palgrave Macmillan, 2010): 125–52, esp. 131.

81. W. E. B. Du Bois, *Autobiography of W. E. B. Du Bois* (Oxford University Press, 2007), 9.

82. James Campbell, *Exiled in Paris: Richard Wright, James Baldwin, Samuel Beckett, and Others on the Left Bank* (University of California Press, 2003), 187, 198; Tyler Stovall, "Fire This Time: Black American Expatriates and the Algerian War," *Yale French Studies* 98 (2000): 182–200, at 191; Munro, *Anticolonial Front*, 227. Wright became a French citizen in 1947.

83. James Baldwin, *Notes of a Native Son* [1955] (Beacon, 1972), 123.

84. Baldwin, *Notes of a Native Son*, 134.

85. James Baldwin, *No Name in the Street* [1972] (Vintage, 2007), 41.

86. William Gardner Smith, *Last of the Conquerors* (Farrar, Strauss, 1948).

87. Smith quoted in Stovall, *Paris Noir*, 254.

88. William Gardner Smith, *The Stone Face* [1963] (New York Review Books, 2021). Belgian partisans helped to assassinate Patrice Lumumba, the first prime minister of the Congo after its independence in 1960. *The Stone Face* was the only depiction of the 1961 massacre in literature until Didier Daeninckx's novel *Meurtes Pour Mémoire* appeared in 1984. The French government acknowledged the massacre in 1998.

89. Likewise, Josephine Baker returned to the United States as a civil rights activist. Drawing on her fame, she refused to perform in facilities not open to people of color, causing some to desegregate. However, she persisted in hailing France as an egalitarian society as a trope for condemning American conditions. In a speech at Fisk University in 1951, she even advised students to go to France or North Africa to experience life without prejudice. Phyllis Rose, *Jazz Cleopatra: Josephine Baker in Her Time* (Doubleday, 1989), 209–10.

90. Lawrence Howard, "The United States and Africa: Trade and Investment," in *Africa Seen by American Negroes*, ed. Sterling Brown (Presence Africaine, 1958), 279–301, at 290.

91. Du Bois accepted Ghanaian President Kwame Nkrumah's invitation to him and his wife, Shirley, in order to compose an "Encyclopedia Africana" about the African diaspora. Du Bois died in Accra July 27, 1963.

92. Quoted in Munro, *Anticolonial Front*, 120.

93. Quoted in Mimi Edmunds, "1960s: Making Connections," in *No Easy Victories: African Liberation and American Activists over a Half-Century, 1950–2000*, ed. William Minter, Gail Hovey, and Charles E. Cobb Jr. (Africa World Press, 2008), 83–112, esp. 94.

94. Quoted in Munro, *Anticolonial Front*, 153.

95. Quoted in Meghelli, "From Harlem to Algiers," 100.

96. Ashraf Rushdy, *Neo-Slave Narratives: Studies in the Social Logic of a Literary Form* (Oxford University Press, 1999), 46.

97. King quoted in Meghelli, "From Harlem to Algiers," 103.

98. "Battle of Algiers a Most Remarkable Film," *[Washington, DC] American Eagle*, March 26, 1968, Illinois Digital Newspaper Collections, accessed April 26, 2025, https://idnc.library.illinois.edu/?a=d&d=AUE19680326.2.33; "Algiers: The Reality Recreated," *New York Times*, October 1, 1967.

99. "A New Theater's Gift: Violent 'Battle of Algiers,'" *Chicago Tribune*, May 30, 1968. In the early years of the US Global War on Terror, some historians and even military practitioners

reconsidered the film for its value in expressing the moral calculations made by both revolutionary and counterinsurgent protagonists. Hugh Roberts, "The Image of the French Army in the Cinematic Representation of the Algerian War: The Revolutionary Politics of *The Battle of Algiers*," in *The Algerian War and the French Army, 1954–62: Experiences, Images, Testimonies*, ed. Martin Alexander, Martin Evans, and J. F. V. Keiger (Palgrave, 2002): 152–63; "The World: Film Studies; What Does the Pentagon See in 'Battle of Algiers'?" *New York Times*, September 7, 2003.

100. Malcolm X, *Malcolm X Speaks: Selected Speeches and Statements*, ed. George Breitman (Pennsylvania State University Press, 1989), 212.

101. Malcolm X quoted in Meghelli, "From Harlem to Algiers," 103.

102. Quoted in Mokhtefi, *Algiers*, 90. Fanon's insight was to critique race ("negritude") as an ultimately limited form of transnational identity among colonized peoples. Fanon, *Wretched of the Earth*, 212–16.

103. Quoted in Meghelli, "From Harlem to Algiers," 102; Mokhtefi, *Algiers*, 90–94.

104. Other prominent pan-Africanists at the time such as Stokely Carmichael, who attended the festival after joining the exiled former Ghanian leader Nkruma in Guinea, rejected Fanon's and the BPP's disavowal of racial essentialism. Sean Malloy, *Out of Oakland: Black Panther Party Internationalism During the Cold War* (Cornell University Press, 2017), 147.

105. Vince, *The Algerian War*, 158.

106. Jeffrey Byrne, *Mecca of Revolution: Algeria, Decolonization, and the Third World Order* (Oxford University Press, 2016), 108, 175.

107. The collapse of oil prices in the mid-1980s helped the emergence of the Islamic Salvation Front party (FIS). Fearing an FIS goal to turn Algeria into an Islamic republic, the Algerian military and secular elites banned the FIS in 1992, triggering a ten-year civil war. See James McDougall, *History of Algeria* (Cambridge University Press, 2017), 286–325.

108. Quoted in Meghelli, "From Harlem to Algiers," 114.

109. Malloy, *Out of Oakland*, 203–7. The Cleavers returned to the United States in 1975. Cleaver ran for the US Senate as a Republican in 1986.

110. Tension within the BPP was also the product of repressive measures by the US government and conflicting priorities between domestic "survival" versus transimperial solidarity. Malloy, *Out of Oakland*, 148–49.

Epilogue

1. Imperialism as the central phenomenon of United States history is the broad argument of *Crossing Empires: Taking U.S. History into Transimperial Terrain*, ed. Kristin Hoganson and Jay Sexton (Duke University Press, 2020). A French counterpart is *French Civilization and Its Discontents: Nationalism, Colonialism, Race*, ed. Tyler Stovall and Georges Van Den Abbeele (Lexington, 2003).

2. This term is modeled after what David Armitage called "cis-Atlantic" places, the history of which is a form of "Atlantic" history. David Armitage, "Three Concepts of Atlantic History," in *The British Atlantic World, 1500–1800*, ed. David Armitage and Michael Braddick (Palgrave, 2002): 11–27, esp. 22.

3. Ian Tyrrell, "Empire in American History," in *Colonial Crucible: Empire in the Making of the Modern American State*, ed. Alfred McCloy and Francisco Scarano (University of Wisconsin Press, 2009), 541–56, at 544.

4. Matthew Elliott, Vote Leave, http://www.voteleavetakecontrol.org; "Not All Cultures Equally Valid, Says Kemi Badenoch," BBC, last modified September 28, 2024, https://www.bbc

.com/news/articles/cg56zlge8g5o; Katherine Kondor and Mark Littler, "Invented Nostalgia: The Search for Identity Among the Hungarian Far-Right," in *Nostalgia and Hope: Intersections Between Politics of Culture, Welfare, and Migration in Europe*, ed. Cristian Norocel, Anders Hellström, and Martin Jørgensen (Springer, 2020): 119–34, https://doi.org/10.1007/978-3-030-41694-2_8; Jules Fediunin, "Conceptualizing Nativism in Authoritarian Russia: From Nationalist Ideology to Antimigrant Riots," *Nationalities Papers* (August 14, 2023): 1–27, https://doi.org/10.1017/nps.2023.60.

5. John Veugelers, *Empire's Legacy: Roots of a Far-Right Affinity in Contemporary France* (Oxford University Press, 2019), 180, 183. This discussion elides the difference between "imperial nostalgia" and "colonial nostalgia" that Patricia Lorcin has delineated and here alludes to a sense of both "decline in international stature" and "loss of sociocultural standing." Patricia Lorcin, "Nostalgias for Empire," *History and Theory* 57, no. 2 (2018): 269–85.

6. John Campbell, *American Discontent: The Rise of Donald Trump and Decline of the Golden Age* (Oxford University Press, 2018): 20, https://doi.org/10.1093/oso/9780190872434.003.0002.

7. "Trump's Dark 'I Am Your Retribution' Pledge—and How GOP Enabled It," *Washington Post*, March 6, 2023; Donald Pease, "Preemptive Impunity: The Constituent Power of Trump's Make America Great Again Movement," *boundary 2* 50, no. 1 (2023): 13–67, esp. 28, https://doi.org/10.1215/01903659-10192102. Trump defeated his opponent, Vice President Kamala Harris, by 1.6 percent in the popular vote and 312 to 226 in the Electoral College.

8. "Le Pen Leads Poll Ahead of France's 2027 Presidential Election," *Bloomberg*, September 12, 2024, https://www.bloomberg.com/news/articles/2024-09-12/le-pen-leads-poll-ahead-of-france-s-2027-presidential-election?embedded-checkout=true; Jacques Paugam, "Marine Le Pen se dit victime d'« une chasse aux sorcières »," *Les Echos*, April 6, 2025, https://www.lesechos.fr/politique-societe/politique/marine-le-pen-sestime-victime-dune-chasse-aux-sorcieres-2158267. A decision on Le Pen's appeal was expected in summer 2026.

9. "Le Pen Calls Embezzlement Conviction a 'Witch Hunt,'" BBC News, April 6, 2025, accessed on April 29, 2025, https://www.bbc.com/news/articles/c8dg90l7ymlo.

10. Marine Le Pen, *Pour que vive la France* (Grancher Éditions, 2012), 18.

11. Nabila Ramdani, "France's New Far-Right Firebrand," *FP*, December 8, 2021, https://foreignpolicy.com/2021/12/08/france-zemmour-lepen-macron-far-right-election. In 2019 the National Front (FN) was renamed the National Rally (RN).

12. "Comment: Trump's Victory Paves Way for Far-Right win in France," *The Connexion*, last modified November 19, 2024, https://www.connexionfrance.com/magazine/comment-trumps-victory-paves-way-for-far-right-win-in-france/690037.

13. Milo Beckman, "Religion and Education Explain the White Vote," FiveThirtyEight, last modified September 23, 2016, https://fivethirtyeight.com/features/religion-and-education-explain-the-white-vote; William Galston, "Donald Trump and the College Degree Divide," *Wall Street Journal*, November 12, 2024, https://www.wsj.com/opinion/donald-trump-and-the-college-degree-divide-education-level-voting-patterns-political-parties-c26c4b02; "5 Charts Showing Where France's National Front Draws Its Support," Pew Research Center, last modified April 21, 2017, https://www.pewresearch.org/short-reads/2017/04/21/5-charts-showing-where-frances-national-front-draws-its-support; Félicien Faury, "French Far-Right: Could Early School Troubles of Some National Rally Voters Explain the Party's Appeal?" *The Conversation*, accessed on April 29, 2025, https://theconversation.com/french-far-right-could-early-school-troubles-of-some-national-rally-voters-explain-the-partys-appeal-232336.

14. President Trump coupled defense of American heritage symbols with blunt criticism of the more recent American war in Iraq, blaming President George W. Bush and President Barack Obama for blundering both entrance into and exiting out of Operation Iraqi Freedom.

The novelty of his approach gained support among older American military veterans for whom Trump's criticism of American global engagements was ironically consistent with his call to regain the world's respect for the United States. "Veterans, Feeling Abandoned, Stand by Donald Trump," *New York Times*, November 2, 2016.

15. William Dunning, *Reconstruction, Political and Economic, 1865–1877* (Harpers, 1907), xv.

16. Donald Davidson et al., *I'll Take My Stand: The South and the Agrarian Tradition* (Louisiana State University Press, 2006), lxi.

17. Euan Hague, Heidi Beirich, and Edward Sebesta, *Neo-Confederacy: A Critical Introduction* (University of Texas Press, 2008), 7, 29.

18. Mildred Rutherford, *Four Addresses* (Mildred Rutherford Historical Circle, 1916), 38, 67; Karen Cox, *Dixie's Daughters: The United Daughters of the Confederacy and the Preservation of Confederate Culture* (University Press of Florida, 2019), 4, 96, 162.

19. James Randall, *Civil War and Reconstruction* (Heath, 1961), 146; Frank Owsley, "The Fundamental Cause of the Civil War: Egocentric Sectionalism," *Journal of Southern History* 7 no. 1 (1941): 3–18, https://doi.org/10.2307/2191262.

20. Early in his second term, Trump emphasized his administration's goal to end all US government programs emphasizing priorities of diversity, equity, and inclusion (DEI) in employment, contracting, and training programs. See, for example, Exec. Order No. 14151, 3 CFR 8339 (January 20, 2025).

21. Joshua Barajas, "In 3 Tweets, Trump Defends 'Beautiful' Confederate Monuments," PBS News, August 17, 2017, accessed April 29, 2025, https://www.pbs.org/newshour/politics/in-3-tweets-trump-defends-beautiful-confederate-monuments.

22. "President Trump Says It's 'Sad' to See U.S. Culture 'Ripped Apart' by Removing Confederate Statues," *Time*, August 17, 2017.

23. "Trump Says Admin 'Will Not Even Consider' Renaming Bases Named After Confederate Leaders, After Army Signals Openness," ABC News, last modified June 10, 2020, https://abcnews.go.com/Politics/reversal-army-now-open-conversation-renaming-bases-named/story?id=71151951. Over Trump's veto, in 2021 Congress established a commission to oversee replacing Confederate-named US military bases. During the 2024 campaign, Trump vowed to reverse the changes.

24. "Executive Order 13958 of November 2, 2020 on Establishing the President's Advisory 1776 Commission," Code of Federal Regulations, title 3 (2020), 70951–70954.

25. "The 1619 Project Curriculum," Pulitzer Center, accessed on April 29, 2025, https://pulitzercenter.org/lesson-plan-grouping/1619-project-curriculum.

26. Larry Arnn et al., *The 1776 Report*, January 2021, https://trumpwhitehouse.archives.gov/wp-content/uploads/2021/01/The-Presidents-Advisory-1776-Commission-Final-Report.pdf, 11, 29.

27. Arnn et al., *The 1776 Report*, 10, 15, 20, 30. The *Report* made no mention of US imperialism as such a threat: The only colonies that the report cited were Britain's rebellious North American ones in 1776. On the second Trump administration's apparent renewed interest in US territorial expansion, see Tim Roberts, "A Genealogy and Check-In on American 'Empire-Talk,'" *Ab Imperio* no. 1 (2025): 90–105.

28. Michael Goldberg, Scott Bauer, and Jill Colvin, "Trump Threatens to Jail Adversaries in Escalating Rhetoric Ahead of Pivotal Debate," APNews.com, last modified September 8, 2024, https://apnews.com/article/trump-harris-wisconsin-election-economy-a6923d6c5758dab b6d959417ea9d7d12; Amy Kaplan, *The Anarchy of Empire in the Making of U.S. Culture* (Harvard University Press, 2002), 34.

29. Melvyn Stokes, *D. W. Griffith's the Birth of a Nation: A History of the Most Controversial Motion Picture of All Time* (Oxford University Press, 2008), 171.

30. Exec. Order No. 14160, 3 CFR 8449 (January 20, 2025). The US Supreme Court considered the constitutionality of this Order in May 2025.

31. "Trump's Taste for Tyranny Finds a Target," *New York Times*, May 24, 2024; H. W. Brands, "From 1850 to 2025," *A User's Guide to History*, blog post, November 18, 2024, https://hwbrands.substack.com/p/from-1850-to-2025.

32. For discussion of this parallel, see Pease, "Preemptive Impunity."

33. Natalya Vince, *The Algerian War, the Algerian Revolution* (Palgrave, 2020), 113–14; Marlon Ettinger, "France's Xenophobes Are Claiming Charles de Gaulle for the Far Right," *Jacobin*, last modified April 6, 2022, https://jacobin.com/2022/04/france-election-zemmour-le-pen-de-gaulle; Scott McConnell, "De Gaulle's Ghost Is on the Ballot in France," *American Conservative*, last modified June 13, 2024, https://www.theamericanconservative.com/de-gaulles-ghost-is-on-the-ballot-in-france/.

34. Veugelers, *Empire's Legacy*, 151; Claire Eldridge, *From Empire to Exile: History and Memory Within the Pied-Noir and Harki Communities, 1962–2012* (Manchester University Press, 2016), 117.

35. Tamir Bar-On, "The French New Right: Neither Right, nor Left?" *Journal for the Study of Radicalism* 8, no. 1 (2014): 1–44, https://doi.org/10.14321/jstudradi.8.1.0001.

36. Amelia Lyons, "French or Foreign? The Algerian Migrants' Status at the End of Empire (1962–1968)," *Journal of Modern European History* 12, no. 1 (2014): 126–45. About four hundred thousand Muslim Algerians residents in France, mainly near Paris and Marseilles, also gained French citizenship from 1947 through the 1960s. These included nearly two hundred thousand Harkis ("movement"), individuals who fought for the French military in Algeria and fled the Algerian republic after 1962. Harkis, however, had to apply for naturalized citizenship.

37. Paul Aussaresses, *Battle of the Casbah: Terrorism and Counterterrorism in Algeria 1955–1957*, trans. Robert Miller (Enigma, 2004). Aussaresses declared that torture of prisoners had been and remained effective as a counterinsurgency technique.

38. Eldridge, *From Empire to Exile*, 61, 248.

39. Quoted in Benjamin Stora, "L'onde de choc des années algériennes en France: L'« Algérie française » et le Front national," *Esprit* 237, no. 11 (1997): 13–28, at 24.

40. Amy Hubbell, *Remembering French Algeria: Pieds-Noirs, Identity, and Exile* (University of Nebraska Press, 2015), 47.

41. David Blight, *Race and Reunion: The Civil War in American Memory* (Harvard University Press, 2009), 227–29, 284–89.

42. Karl Cohen, *Forbidden Animation: Censored Cartoons and Blacklisted Animators in America* (McFarland, 2013), 60.

43. Eldridge, *From Empire to Exile*, 109.

44. Quoted in William Cohen, *Europe's Invisible Migrants* (Amsterdam University Press, 2003), 132.

45. Frank Castigliola, *France and the United States: The Cold Alliance Since World War II* (Twayne, 1992), 112.

46. Naima, June 30, 2010, "Comment on [houwarid], "Zidane and the Complex Algerian-French Identity," Algerian Review (blog), last modified December 29, 2009, https://algerianreview.wordpress.com/2009/12/29/zidane-and-the-complex-algerian-french-identity. James Baldwin was an early critic of Harriet Beecher Stowe's portrayal of the enslaved man Uncle Tom as a sympathetic figure. His 1949 novel *Everybody's Protest Novel*, written in Paris, began the term's redefinition toward an effigy of servility. Linda Williams, *Playing the Race Card: Melodramas of Black and White from Uncle Tom to O. J. Simpson* (Princeton University Press, 2001), 62.

47. "France-Algeria: 50 Years After Independence, What Happened to the Harkis?" *International Business Times*, April 2, 2012; Cohen, *Europe's Invisible Immigrants*, 133. As observed by

the historian Benjamin Stora, perhaps the most analogous immigrant group in the United States to French pieds noirs and Harkis were Cubans who fled communist Cuba. Like pieds noirs, first-generation exiled Cubans were ambivalent about their situation, both loathing forces that drove them from their homeland and reminiscing about returning there. But over time those hopes and interest in returning from exile faded, and, like the *rapatriés* of France, many Cubans have become stalwart supporters of the nationalist (Republican) party. "Footprints of pieds-noirs reach deep into France," *New York Times*, March 5, 2009.

48. Hugh Roberts, *The Battlefield: Algeria, 1988–2002: Studies in a Broken Polity* (Verso, 2003), 116, 359. Ironically, Hugh Roberts argued that the FIS rebellion did not constitute a "proper" civil war because, unlike civil wars in the United States, France, and elsewhere, the conflict did not spawn Algerian political parties or remove military rule.

49. "What a President Needs to Know," *Time*, July 14, 2016; "Trump on the Civil War: 'Why Could That One Not Have Been Worked Out?'" *New York Times*, May 1, 2017; "Civil War Talk in Presidential Contest Reveals Fresh Divisions on Race," *Washington Post*, January 13, 2024.

50. CNBC Television, "Nikki Haley Declines to Name Slavery as a Cause of the U.S. Civil War in Town Hall," YouTube video, posted December 28, 2023, https://www.youtube.com/watch?v=cdY51_Tc5Vk; "Civil War Talk in Presidential Contest Reveals Fresh Divisions on Race."

51. "Texas Pushes to Obscure the State's History of Slavery and Racism," *New York Times*, May 20, 2021.

52. Kevin Roberts et al., *The 1836 Project: Telling the Texas Story*, Texas Education Agency, 2, 7, https://tea.texas.gov/academics/subject-areas/1836-document-telling-the-texas-story-final.pdf; TX Const. 1836, General Provisions § 9, 10, University of Texas Law Library, https://tarlton.law.utexas.edu/constitutions/republic-texas-1836/general-provisions.

53. Florida State Board of Education, "Florida's State Academic Standards—Social Studies, 2023," last modified July 19, 2023, https://www.fldoe.org/core/fileparse.php/20653/urlt/6-0.pdf, 4; Sven Beckert, *Empire of Cotton: A Global History* (Knopf Doubleday, 2015), xi, 109, 171; Alice Conklin, "The Civilizing Mission," in *The French Republic: History, Values, Debates*, ed. Edward Berenson, Vincent Duclert, Christophe Prochasson (Oxford University Press, 2011), 173–81, https://doi.org/10.7591/cornell/9780801449017.003.0020; Alice Conklin, *Mission to Civilize: The Republican Idea of Empire in France and West Africa 1895–1930* (Stanford University Press, 1998).

54. "Kemi Badenoch: Pupils 'Should Learn Benefits of Empire,'" *The Times*, March 21, 2022.

55. Katalin Madácsi-Laube, "A New Era of Greatness: Hungary's New Core Curriculum," Cultures of History Forum, June 28, 2020, accessed April 29, 2025, https://www.cultures-of-history.uni-jena.de/politics/a-new-era-of-greatness-hungarys-new-core-curriculum.

56. "Putin Adds Patriotism, War History to School Curriculum," *Moscow Times*, last modified May 22, 2020, https://www.themoscowtimes.com/2020/05/22/putin-adds-patriotism-war-history-to-school-curriculum-a70347; "Rewriting History—the Planned New School Textbook Accused of Whitewashing Russia's Imperial Past," BBC News Russian, September 1, 2023.

57. "Back to School in Russia—More Revision of History," European External Action Service, September 6, 2024, accessed April 29, 2025, https://euvsdisinfo.eu/back-to-school-in-russia-more-revision-of-history/.

58. Britain saw several thousand white refugees fleeing the end of settler rule in South Africa and Southern Rhodesia in the 1970s, aided by the 1971 Immigration Act that privileged them among other migrants, including those from so-called New Commonwealth countries. Kathleen Paul, *Whitewashing Britain: Race and Citizenship in the Postwar Era* (Cornell University Press, 1997), 181. The Brexit movement capitalized on nationalist British policies dating from the mid-nineteenth century, first in reaction against immigration of Irish famine refugees, which called for repatriation of British subjects of color to their countries of origin.

Daniel Renshaw, *Discourse of Repatriation in Britain, 1845–2016: A Political and Social History* (Routledge, 2021).

59. Veugelers, *Empire's Legacy*, 50–51, 159; Christopher Flood and Hugo Frey, "Defending the Empire in Retrospect: The Discourse of the Extreme Right," in *Promoting the Colonial Idea: Propaganda and Visions of Empire in France*, ed. Tony Chafer and Amanda Sackur (Palgrave, 2002): 195–210, esp. 198.

60. "Le Pen Upset Causes Major Shock," CNN, April 21, 2002.

61. Quoted in Claude Liauzu, "At War with France's Past," *Le Monde diplomatique*, June 2005; and from *France Horizon*, the monthly magazine of the Association nationale des Français d'Afrique du Nord, d'outre-mer et de leurs amis, in Eldridge, *From Empire to Exile*, 279.

62. French Republic, Law No. 2005–158 of February 23, 2005 On the Recognition of the Nation and the National Contribution in Favour of Repatriated French Nationals, https://www.legifrance.gouv.fr/loda/id/JORFTEXT000000444898; quoted in Liauzu, "At War with France's Past."

63. James Grossman, "A Paradox: History Without Historians," *Perspectives on History*, February 9, 2021.

64. "French Angry at Law to Teach Glory of Colonialism," *The Guardian*, April 15, 2005.

65. Laura Sims, "Rethinking France's 'Memory Wars': Harki and Pied-Noir Collective Memories in Fifth Republic France," PhD diss., University of North Carolina, 2015, 238. It is important to note that victimhood in national nostalgic ideology can be direct or by vicarious identification. Flood and Frey, "Defending the Empire in Retrospect," 207–08.

66. Liauzu, "At War with France's Past."

67. "Conservatives Are Changing K-12 Education, and One Christian College Is at the Center," NBC News, July 20, 2023, https://www.nbcnews.com/news/us-news/hillsdale-college-1776-curriculum-k12-education-conservative-rcna93397.

68. "CRT Forward Trends as of October 2024," CRT Forward, UCLA School of Law, October 31, 2024, https://crtforward.law.ucla.edu/crt-forward-trends-as-of-october-2024.

69. Nicholas Vinocur, "France Laid the Foundations for Campus 'Woke' Ideology. Now It's Leading a Global Backlash." Politico, last modified June 27, 2024, https://www.politico.eu/article/france-laid-the-foundations-for-campus-woke-ideology-now-its-leading-a-global-backlash. Bardella's condemnation of identity-based activism reflected a shift in the French right's call for education reform away from focus on salvaging the glory of French imperialism, the focus of Marine Le Pen in the 2010s. Le Pen termed critical history, especially of colonization, masochistic. Jennifer Sessions, "Why the French Presidential Candidates Are Arguing About Their Colonial History," The Conversation, last modified April 18, 2017, https://theconversation.com/why-the-french-presidential-candidates-are-arguing-about-their-colonial-history-75372.

70. "France's Far Right Turn," *New York Times Magazine*, March 31, 2022.

71. "Jean-Michel Blanquer : le wokisme est une «doctrine» à laquelle «la France et sa jeunesse doivent échapper»," *Le Figaro*, October 14, 2021.

72. Barnett Singer, *The Americanization of France: Searching for Happiness After the Algerian War* (Rowman & Littlefield, 2013), 175–99, esp. 199.

73. Madeline Bedecarre, "Unlearning *Francophonic*: Legacies of Colonialism in French Language Textbooks," in *Diversity and Decolonization in French Studies*, ed. Siham Bouamer and Louic Bourdeau (Palgrave, 2022), 33–50.

74. Akram Belkaid, "France and Algeria, a Long History of Distrust," *Le Monde diplomatique*, November 2021.

75. "Macron Says Won't Apologise to Algeria for Colonisation," France24, last modified January 12, 2023, https://www.france24.com/en/live-news/20230112-macron-says-won-t-apologise-to-algeria-for-colonisation.

76. "France Defends Colonial-Era Statues in the Face of Anti-Racism Protests," RFI, last modified June 16, 2020, https://www.rfi.fr/en/france/20200616-france-defends-colonial-era-statues-face-anti-racism-protests-macron-floyd.

77. Veugelers, *Empire's Legacy*, 106–108; Alice Conklin, Sarah Fishman, and Robert Zaretsky, *France and Its Empire Since 1870* (Oxford University Press, 2015), 177–86; Steve Ungar, "La France impériale exposée en 1931: une apothéose," in *Culture coloniale: La France conquise par son Empire 1871–1931*, ed. Pascal Blanchard and Sandrine Lemaire (Éditions Autrement, 2003): 201–12.

78. "Opinion Polling for the 2027 French Presidential Election," Wikipedia, accessed on April 29, 2025, https://en.wikipedia.org/wiki/Opinion_polling_for_the_2027_French_presidential_election.

79. EU Debates, "Jordan Bardella Debates on Trump POTUS US Election and the Future of American Power," YouTube video, posted December 3, 2024, https://www.youtube.com/watch?v=BvKFNyOvROE.

Index

A

Abbas, Ferhat, 128–34, 198n77

Abbott, Robert. *See Chicago Defender*

Abdelkader, Emir: Americans' image of, 5, 12, 15, 16, 18, 33, 44, 167n77; capture, 16; exile, 33, 163n22; memory of, 133; rule by, 16; tactics, 15, 17, 19, 38

African countries: Egypt, 12, 51, 119, 134, 162n4; Ethiopia, 120, 124, 196n39; Ghana, 137; Guinea, 137; Liberia, 59, 61, 62, 120, 124, 169n90; Libya, 120, 198n77; Morocco, 15, 106, 120, 121, 160n9; Senegal, 100, 122, 177n38; South Africa, 59, 94, 99, 137, 139, 204n58; Togo, 61, 62; Tunisia, 121, 130, 134

Algiers: as Barbary State, 3, 12, 13, 18, 24, 30, 82, 155; during July Monarchy, 14, 16, 74, 76; during French Second Republic, 11, 77, 168n78, 181n97; during French Third Republic, 61, 65, 66, 96, 126, 127; during French Fourth Republic, 135, 137; during French Fifth Republic, 137–40, 148

Algerian War of Independence (1954–62), 4, 9, 115, 125, 134, 150, 170n26

Alsace and Lorraine, 7, 84, 87, 90, 117

American Indians. *See* Indigenous Americans

Anglo-American imperialism: in Asia, 59, 73, 87, 99, 101; in North America, 14, 73–75, 81, 87; in South Africa, 59. *See also names of colonies*; British Empire

anti-colonialism: Abdelkader and, 15, 16, 18; as US civil rights issue, 135, 137; in France, 80, 125; opposition to US overseas territories, 98–101. *See also* Black Panther Party; Garvey, Marcus; Hadj, Messali

anti-imperialism. *See* anti-colonialism

asphyxiation, 18, 22, 31, 45

Atlantic Charter, 132

Australia: as part of settler revolution, 59, 73, 82, 188n82, 192n33; treatment of indigenous population in, 74, 80, 81, 89. *See also* British Empire; homestead policies

B

Baker, Josephine, 126, 128, 199n89
Baldwin, James, 135, 137, 203n46
Barbary States, 13–15, 22, 160n9
Bardella, Jordan. *See* National Rally (RN) (France)
Battle of Algiers, 138, 199n99
Bazaine, François Achille, 82
Bendjedid, Chadli, 139
Bigelow, John, 82, 84
Bigelow, Poultney, 70–71, 108
Black Panther Party, 115, 138–41, 200n109
Black soldiers, 9, 20, 61, 120–25
Bodichon, Eugène, 60, 61, 80, 185n39
Boumédiènne, Houari, 139, 140
Bouteflika, Abdelaziz, 140
British Empire: local government in, 59, 99, 104, 108, 193n56; memory of, 152, 204n58. *See also names of colonies;* slavery
Buffalo Bill (William Cody), 73, 81
Bureaux of Arab Affairs, 39, 82, 106

C

Caix, Robert de, 101–104, 191n22, 192n32
Calhoun, John, 22, 23, 146
California, 22, 24, 59, 86–87, 89, 193n56
Cambon, Jules, 106–8
Canada, 66, 73, 87, 99, 192n33, 193n56
Cather, Willa, 90
Catlin, George, 81, 186n44
Cavaignac, Louis-Eugène, 27–30, 77, 78
Chevalier, Michel, 77, 78, 85, 184fn19
Chicago Defender, 123, 132, 133
citizenship, among African Americans: in nineteenth century: 52–56, 60–65, 70–74; in twentieth century, 71, 128
citizenship, among Algerians: in nineteenth century, 52–54, 57, 64, 68, 74, 113, 188n80; in twentieth century, 51, 69–71, 103, 122, 129–32, 180n77, 203n36
citizenship: among European settlers in Algeria, 57, 66, 69, 74, 97, 183n7; among Indigenous Americans, 112; among *pieds noirs*, 149; birthright, 147, 183n7; in French colonies, 177n38; in the Republic of Algeria, 139; in US territories, 93, 97, 100, 101, 104–11
'civilizing influence', 30, 73, 97, 101, 113, 117

Clamageran, Jean-Jules, 85, 87
Cleaver, Eldridge. *See* Black Panther Party
Clemenceau, Georges, 52, 56, 59, 177n26
Cluseret, Gustave Paul, 55, 56
Confederate States of America: as insurgency, 5, 6, 40–45; during Reconstruction, 53, 56, 65–67, 179n73; Lost Cause, 144–46, 149–53, 202n23; Robert E. Lee, 44, 146
Cooper, James Fenimore, 36
Coudert, Frederic, Jr., 93, 104, 109–13, 193n56, 194n62
counterinsurgent warfare: in Algeria, 6, 37–39, 50, 199n99, 203n37; in the United States, 4–8, 38–42, 46–50, 98–100, 170n26, 173n73
Cremieux, Adolphe, 25, 26
Crimean War, 34, 41, 169n7, 172n43

D

Daumas, Eugène, 39
Davis, Jefferson, 6, 39, 45, 171n42
Degetau, Federico, 112, 113
Desjobert, Amédée, 80
diplomacy: Algerian, 4, 15, 132, 139; French, 21, 117; US, nineteenth century, 29, 49, 83; US, twentieth century, 107, 113, 134, 175n5, 190n10
Daeninckx, Didier, 199n88
Dred Scott v. Sandford, 111
Du Bois, W. E. B.: on Africa, 52, 120, 121, 127, 129, 198n60, 199n91; on African Americans, 51, 52, 61, 68, 118, 119; on France, 120, 134. *See also* Pan-Africanism
Duponchel, Adolphe, 89
Duval, Jules, 86, 87

E

Elkader (Iowa), 18
Embarek, Sidi, 17
Emerson, Ralph Waldo, 22, 23
Emperor Napoleon III (Louis Napoleon): 29–33, 55–58, 66, 71, 77, 79, 85, 86. *See also* French laws
exceptionalism: 142; Algerian, 141; American, 2, 7, 26, 94, 98, 166n52; French, 82, 166n51

extinction of indigenous peoples, 6, 59, 60, 75, 80, 81, 186n44

F
Fanon, Frantz, 8, 115, 116, 137, 139, 151, 200n102
Fauset, Jessie, 126–28, 135
Fly Whisk Incident, 24, 162n4
flying column, 40–42, 171n41
Fouillée, Augustine, 90
Franco-American Quasi-War (1798–1800), 15
Franco-Prussian War (1870–71), 7, 49, 54, 63–66, 75, 91, 117, 181n99
French laws: Code de l'indigénat (1881), 51–54, 67–71, 119, 123, 125, 132, 180n81, 181n85; Jonnart Law (1919), 122, 177n26; petit Sénatus Consulte (1887), 85; Sénatus Consulte of 1863, 66, 82, 85; Sénatus Consulte of 1865, 6, 74, 188n80; Warnier Law (1873)
Fuller, Hoyt, 137

G
Garvey, Marcus, 123–26, 129, 130, 138, 196n35, 196n39, 197n46. *See also* Pan-Africanism
Gasparin, Agénor de Gasparin, 55
Gaulle, Charles de, 132, 147, 148
General Orders No. 100. *See* Lieber Code
Germany: German Empire, 52, 61, 75, 110, 119–21, 182n3, 196n24; post-World War I, 120, 124, 130–35, 196n34, 198n61. *See also* Franco-Prussian War (1870–71)
Global War on Terror (2001–21), 4, 152, 199n99
Godillot, Alexis, 41, 42
González, Isabel, 8, 93, 98, 104, 109–12, 114. *See also* Insular Cases; Puerto Rico
Goumiers, 49
Governor-generals of Algeria: Bugeaud, Thomas, 16–18, 22, 38, 40–46, 52, 106, 164n27, 165n47, 173n68, 180n81; Cambon, Jules, 106–108; Cavaignac, Louis-Eugène, 27–30, 77–78; Clauzel, Bertrand, 14, 76; Lamoricière, Louis Juchault de, 29, 77–80, 167n69; Lutaud, Charles, 122; MacMahon, Patrice de, 187n68; Pélissier, Aimable-Jean-Jacques, 18, 22, 164n29; Randon, Jacques Louis, 79; Rovigo, René Savary, duc de, 127; Valée, comte Sylvain-Charles, 16

H
Hadj, Messali, 125, 132, 133
Harkis, 150, 153, 203n36, 204n47
Harlem Renaissance, 126, 128
Hay, John, 107, 108
Higley, Brewster, 90

I
India, 30, 99, 188n82, 195n20; like Algeria, 82, 94, 95, 103, 186n48. *See also* British Empire; slavery, in India
Indian Removal Act, 12, 18
Indigenous Americans: 49, 75, 76, 81, 83, 111, 153; like Algerians, 5, 6, 12, 19, 37, 39, 46, 74; described by American writers, 28, 38, 39, 44, 48, 70, 73; described by French writers, 31, 60, 69, 70, 79–81, 89, 165n47, 186n44. *See also* citizenship: among Indigenous Americans; populations: Indigenous Americans; Second Seminole War (1835–42)
Indochina, 8, 51, 106, 116, 134, 138, 147
Insular Cases, 8, 93–95, 99, 106, 109, 190n5. *See also* González, Isabel; Philippines; Puerto Rico
Islam: as law, 53, 57, 180n77; as racial category, 68; fundamentalism and, 144, 151, 154, 200n107; nationalism and, 125, 139, 197n58; nativism and, 3, 144; pan-Africanism and, 125, 137

J
Jackson, Andrew, 14, 20, 76, 82, 147, 151
Jomini, Antoine, 37, 40–45
July Monarchy, 21–25, 38, 44, 61, 79, 80, 86
Jusserand, Jules, 95

K
Kabylia, 84, 144, 177n37
Kennedy, John, 4, 134, 170n26
Khaled, Emir, 7, 51, 52, 68, 175n1, 175n2
King, Edward, 74

King, Martin Luther Jr., 138
Kipling, Rudyard, 101

L
Laboulaye, Édouard, 66, 71, 180n74
land policies: Arab kingdom, 57, 65, 79, 82, 84; *arch*, 79, 85; *beylick*, 82; *cantonnement*, 79; homestead laws, 74–79, 89, 91, 183n3, 183n12, 186n51, 189n93; laissez faire, 7, 91; *melk*, 85; *rapprochement*, 52; *terra nullius*, 81; US Homestead Act of 1862, 17, 74, 75, 79, 83–87, 90, 91, 188n81
Laugel, Auguste, 65
Lavigerie, Charles, 90
Le Pen, Jean-Marie. *See* National Front (FN) party (France)
Le Pen, Marine. *See* National Rally (RN) party (France)
Lebourgeois, Stanley, 89, 90, 184n19
Lee, Henry, 13
Leib, James, 15
Leroy-Beaulieu, Paul, 71, 85–89, 187n68, 192n33
Levasseur, Émile, 86, 87
Lhuys, Edouard Drouyn de, 84
Lieber Code, 6, 43–45, 105, 172n58, 172n60, 173n68
Lowell, A. Lawrence, 97, 98, 101
Lyautey, Louis Hubert, 106

M
Macron, Emmanuel, 154, 155
Maximilian I of Mexico, 36, 49, 57, 68, 82
McKinley, William, 101, 104–6
Mexican-American War (1846–48), 5, 12, 22–25, 171n41
military schools, 37, 38, 46, 105
Mishaqa, Mikhayil, 33
Mohammed, El Hadj Ahmed Ab d'el Kader ben el Hadj, 70
Morsly, Taïeb, 68
Mulzac, Hugh, 130–35
Murphy, Robert, 132

N
National Association for the Advancement of Colored People (NAACP), 121, 126–28, 137, 141, 150

National Front (FN) party (France), 144, 148–53
National Liberation Front (FLN), 134–39, 148, 149
National Rally (RN) party (France), 143, 144, 149, 154, 155, 205n69
National Reform Association, 76
Nostalgia: as melancholy, 90; as memory: 9, 119, 142–44, 147, 148, 155, 201n5
Nouvelle Droite (ND), 148, 149

O
Organisation armée secrète (OAS), 148, 153
Organisation for African Unity (OAU), 139
Orientalism, 3, 9, 13, 70, 117–19, 128
Ottoman Empire, 14, 15, 33, 84, 95, 162n4, 163n22, 166n49. *See also* Algiers: as Barbary State

P
Pan-Africanism: 121, 133, 196n39, 197n46, 198n60; Algeria within, 9, 116, 124–29, 137–39, 200n14; Algeria excluded from, 51, 61, 116, 120, 121, 127–30, 136, 137. *See also* Black Panther Party; Du Bois, W. E. B.; Garvey, Marcus
Paris Commune, 54, 55, 63–67, 182n104
Pélissier, Amable. *See* Governor-generals of Algeria; *see also* asphyxiation
Philippine-American War (1899–1902), 46, 117, 192n38
Philippines, 8, 94–101, 104, 108–13, 178n46, 183. *See also* Insular Cases
pieds noirs, 4, 10, 133, 148–55, 204n47
Plessy v. Ferguson, 69
Poinsett, Joel, 23
popular opinion: American, of Algeria, 3, 5, 12, 28, 83; American, of France, 25–29, 64, 98, 121; French, of the United States, 83, 120, 154
populations: Europeans in Algeria, 30, 74–76, 148, 188n72; Algerians in Algeria, 60, 74, 86, 187n68; Algerians in France, 134; Indigenous Americans, 74, 80
Porter, David, 14

Poussin, Guillaume, 78
Puerto Rico, 8, 94, 95, 100–113. *See also* González, Isabel; Insular Cases

R
railroads, as aid to territorial settlement, 7, 73, 83, 89, 181n91, 188n82
razzia. *See* counterinsurgent warfare
Reclus, Elisée, 58
Remington, Frederic, 70, 71
Remington Arms, 181n99
Republican Party (US): pre-Civil War, 31, 78; during Reconstruction, 53, 56, 59, 62–65; in twentieth century, 104, 203n47; in twenty-first century, 143, 151, 154. *See also* land policies: US Homestead Act of 1862
Réquin, Edouard, 122
Revolution of 1848: Algeria declared integral to France, 26, 57, 77; June Days, 27–29, 34, 77, 90
Roosevelt, Jr., Archibald, 132
Roosevelt, Theodore, 95–97, 103, 108–110, 190fn10
Randolph, Carman, 100, 110
Rush, Richard, 29, 30, 168n84
Russia, 95, 152, 172n43, 182n3

S
Sahara Desert: and agriculture, 89, 188n82; and slave trade, 21; as theater of war, 20, 76, 125, 171n42; in literature, 39, 70, 181n97
Saint-Amant, Pierre Charles Fournier de, 6, 59–62
Second Seminole War (1835–42), 18–20, 23
Sétif, 1, 133
Seward, William, 83
Singer Sewing Machine Company, 117
slavery: expansion of, in the United States, 21–23, 29, 31; in Africa, 13, 22, 30; in the Caribbean, 21, 25, 26, 30, 60, 77; in India, 22; memory of, 144–46, 149, 151–54. *See also* Confederate States of America
Smith, William Gardner, 135–37

socialism: Arab, 66, 139; Fourierism, 28, 168n78, 183n12; "red republicanism," 27, 64, 76, 77, 183n12; Saint-Simonianism, 28, 82, 168n78
Société Colonial de l'Etat d'Alger, 15
Spanish-American War (1898). *See* Philippines; Puerto Rico
Statue of Liberty, 7, 66, 71

T
Tell Atlas, 60, 76
Till, Emmett, 137
Tocqueville, Alexis de, 11, 23, 31, 44, 59, 76, 77, 80, 184n19
Treaty of Tafna, 16
Trump, Donald, 143–47, 151–55, 201n14, 201n20, 202n27
Twain, Mark, 99, 100
US military officers: Clinch, Duncan, 19; Crook, George, 47, 48, 105, 106; Custer, George, 47; Ellsworth, Elmer, 34–36; Grant, Ulysses S., 42, 47; Halleck, Henry, 37, 44; Jesup, Thomas, 19; Kearny, Philip, 38, 48; MacArthur, Arthur, 105, 106; Marcy, Randolph, 39, 48, 171n36; Meigs, Montgomery, 42; Otis, Elwell, 105; Sheridan, Philip, 6, 47–49, 50; Sherman, William, 6, 41–50, 173n69, 174n88; Trobriand, Philippe Régis de, 47–49; Wool, John, 38; Young, Samuel, 46, 105

U
United Kingdom. *See* British Empire
Universal Negro Improvement Association and African Communities League (UNIA). *See* Garvey, Marcus

V
Valée, Sylvain, 16
Vignon, Louis, 69

W
Wahl, Maurice, 85
Wallace, Hugh, 124
Wallace, Lew, 34, 35
Wharton, Edith, 106, 127, 181n97
Williams, George Washington, 68

Wilson, Woodrow, 6, 51, 52, 175n5
World War I (1914–18), 9, 131, 174n83, 177n26; racism during, 120–26
World War II (1939–45): anticolonial aspects of, 1, 133, 134; memory of, 143, 148; racism during, 9, 135
World's fairs: 1855 Paris Exposition, 79; 1889 Paris Exposition, 73; 1893 Chicago Columbian Exposition, 117; 1900 Paris Exposition, 9, 96, 118–21; 1904 St. Louis Exposition, 116–18
Wright, Richard, 135, 199n82

X

X, Malcolm, 138

Z

Zouaves, 34–36, 169n7. *See also* US military officers: Ellsworth, Elmer

www.ingramcontent.com/pod-product-compliance
Lightning Source LLC
Chambersburg PA
CBHW020815230426
43666CB00007B/1016